Gwyn Williams was born in 1904 at Port Talbot, Glamorgan. He was educated at University College of Wales, Aberystwyth and Jesus College, Oxford, and has spent most of his working life as a Lecturer and Professor of English Literature at the Universities of Cairo, Alexandria, Libya and Istanbul. Mr Williams, a Welsh speaker and a Welsh Nationalist, is a member of the Academi Gymreig.

Gwyn Williams

The Land Remembers

A View of Wales

Futura Publications Limited
A Futura Book

A Futura Book

First published in Great Britain by
Faber & Faber Limited in 1977

First Futura Publications edition 1978

Copyright © Gwyn Williams 1977

This book is sold subject to the condition
that it shall not, by way of trade or
otherwise, be lent, re-sold, hired out or
otherwise circulated without the publisher's
prior consent in any form of binding or
cover other than that in which it is
published and without a similar condition
including this condition being imposed on the
subsequent purchaser

ISBN 0 7088 1402 6
Printed by
William Collins Sons & Co Ltd
Glasgow

Futura Publications Limited
110 Warner Road, Camberwell
London SE5

To JOHN ORMOND
poet, imaginative film-maker and valued companion,
who asked me to contemplate
the television series which led to this book

CONTENTS

CONTENTS

MAPS

The necessary duplication of some long Welsh place names with English and occasionally Viking names overcrowds a small map of Wales and rendered almost impossible a map suited to this book. Reference to the following is suggested:

Wales and the Marches: Ordnance Survey quarter inch
Cymru, Ffyrdd, Trefi, Pentrefi (Parri, Penybont, Caerfyrddin) for Welsh place names
Wales and West Midlands: Dunlop Width of Road map
Southern Britain in the Iron Age: Ordnance Survey for the Celts, and other Ordnance Survey archaeological and historical maps

AUTHOR'S NOTE

I have dedicated this book to John Ormond, in friendship and in gratitude to him for asking me to plan, write and present a television series which bore the same general title as this book and which linked Welsh landscape, towns, villages and houses with important events and persons, up to the end of the eighteenth century, but this book might never have been written, or even thought of, but for Alan Pringle, of Faber and Faber, who first suggested it, encouraged me during its writing and patiently and generously admonished me when I took longer to finish it than had been planned. My thanks are also due to Alison Abel for her sympathetic care at later stages in the preparation of the book for publication and to Rosemary Goad for her helpful and efficient piloting of it through the press.

G.W.

INTRODUCTION

This book will present a view of Wales as seen from my home in central Ceredigion, from a house built by my grandfather on the thousand-foot contour, five miles, as the crow flies, from the sea, which appears to me to rise to its long horizon in the west. The house gives me a physical view of the whole of west Wales, from the Preseli mountains in the south, up the great sweep of Cardigan Bay to Snowdon and then out along the lovely profile of Llŷn to Enlli, Bardsey Island. I may appear to turn my back on anglicised Radnorshire and on the industrial areas of the north-east and south-east, but this is a tendency in myself which I hope to correct as the book proceeds. It is therefore a personal view, but I will do my best to take into account other attitudes than mine. The book was written five years after my return to this country from a working lifetime spent in universities of the Near East.

For the Welsh reader I hope to do something to clarify the present situation in Wales and I shall write about historical movements and events only when they appear to me to colour and condition the present. For the visitor to Wales I hope the book will present an attractive, varied country of great scenic beauty and cultural interest, a country different from his own but very friendly and welcoming so long as the visitor accepts the differences, respects the traditions and customs of Wales, and doesn't pretend either that they don't exist any more or that they have become museum pieces. The book will consider aspects of the history of the island of Britain from a Welsh point of view, since this is a book about Wales by a Welshman. Whilst not attempting to be a guide book it will suggest places and regular events to visit or be present at in order to get the fullest flavour of the country.

INTRODUCTION

The visitor should be aware that there are things in our past and recent history that rankle, things which may seem petty to him but which sometimes hold an agonising significance for many Welshmen today. I find that when I explain some of these things to English people they are quite suddenly sympathetic, never having thought or known of them before. Let me mention some of these grievances now, in the hope of being able to put them dispassionately into their contexts later in the book. There is Tryweryn and the drowning of Welsh valleys to provide water for England; the refusal of the Post Office to issue stamps to commemorate the Welsh Bible in 1970 and the fiftieth anniversary of *Urdd Gobaith Cymru,* the important Welsh League of Youth, in 1972; the tearing apart of Welsh skies by low-flying jets and by Concorde, planes which are costing Wales scores of millions of pounds and for which most Welsh people have no use; the continued use of Welsh soil and the increasing threat to our green acres for the upkeep of a war machine which costs Wales about £200 million a year and the need for which no government would dare put to a referendum in Wales. Then there are the pros and cons of the relationship between conservation and industry: the preservation of the beauty of the landscape (largely in the interest of visitors from outside) opposed to industrial development which would employ local labour. There is much unease over the buying up of cottages and small-holdings as second homes or holiday houses by well-to-do outsiders, for which no one can blame the nerve-racked conurbation-dweller but which causes artificial prices to rocket and speeds up depopulation. Lately too we have had the stigmatising of our young Welsh idealists as louts and hooligans by a High Court Judge, and as baboons by an ex-Lord Chancellor.

I mention these matters this early so that any visitor to Wales may realise that these are very spiky subjects, fresh in the national memory and to be approached with fair-minded sympathy rather than brushed aside as trivia. Differing opinions will be found in Wales on these matters, for ever since the Act of Union of 1536, and even before that, there have been Welshmen who have regarded complete union with England and the disappearance of the Welsh language as desirable.

Not all the grievances are recent and the visitor will quickly find that the Welsh have very long memories. 1282, 1847 and 1870 may not be dates of any great significance to him, nor to many Welsh people for that matter, since Welsh history is still little taught in English-language schools in Wales; but the death of Llywelyn ap Gruffydd, the Report of the Commission on Education in Wales (known to us as *Brad y Llyfrau Gleision*, the Treachery of the Blue Books) and the Education Act of 1870 are black events which seem almost contemporary to many of us and are certainly contemporary in their effects.

The coming decade or so will be a fateful time in our history. Are we heading for self-government or for a final merging with England? Are we faced with an open choice—the alternatives being movement forward to the free fulfilment of a considerable potential, or a dwindling into a British unity in which Welsh culture will fade away, only to be remembered in curious folk customs, literature in a dead language, the odd Welsh word or idiom in the English spoken in Wales, in haunting folk songs or hymns which will have English words and in the anglicised forms of the names of rivers, towns and villages? Is it possible for an Anglo-Welsh culture to take over enough of our traditions to maintain a difference from that of England? Should we be stressing our differences or sinking them in the sad uniformity of a western civilisation which is past its peak? Languages distinguish nations from each other more than any other human activity, certainly more than a racial mixture. Since prehistory Asia Minor has been a melting-pot of races and today I would say, even though many of my Turkish friends would not agree with me in this, that a Turk is a person who speaks Turkish, irrespective of what proportion of Asiatic blood runs in his veins. But is it possible for two nations to share a language? Hardly. Then what about America, you may be saying, what about Australia, New Zealand, Ireland, all of which use a kind of English? They have symbolised their difference from the root stock by modifying vocabulary, idiom and pronunciation into a language which is just about as different from English as its speakers are from the English. The slow, enforced penetration of Ireland by English speakers over the centuries may have pushed the Celtic language of Eire too far to the west for it ever to return, but the Irish have retaliated by moulding English into something which symbolises their difference from the English. It is too late for us to do this in Wales. The media of communication are today too powerful and too far-reaching. If Wales adopts English as its sole language it will be the language of television, with its fullness of Americanisms, or the language of trade union meetings, heavy with stale clichés and the avoidance of simple expressions. No, it is clear that language and nationhood are inseparable and that if one dies the other dies with it.

Why all this fuss about nationhood? Isn't it time we dropped such an old-fashioned concept and accepted the brotherhood of man, demolished frontiers and spoke one international language? There may be people who think so. I am not one of them. The way I look at it is this. Each living human being and, for that matter, each living animal or insect is for himself the centre of the universe, with lines radiating out from this unique centre, lines which are strong or weak, lines which reach to the limits of his sense perceptions or which fly beyond such limits to distances of which he may not be aware. These lines are his relationships with the world about him. The most important can be plotted. Mark yourself as the centre of the figure and draw lines out, away from yourself, to represent the human and social relationships of which you are conscious: your mother, father, brother, sister, other members of your family. These are involuntary bonds, into which you are born willy-nilly. Mark lines for your neighbours. Here there is an element of choice, for you can change your neighbours if you don't like them by moving to some other place. Now go on round the circle to record your chosen, voluntary relationships: your friends, your sexual mate, your children (to the degree to which they are wished and not accidental), your fellow workers, the people of the region in which you live and with whom you feel a kinship. You will come to your relationship to your nation, a rather more remote one than regional kinship or trade union membership or any social group to which you like to feel you belong. But it must not be too remote. The bigger the nation the further away and the less understood is the centre of control and the more likelihood there is of the people being forced along ways they don't understand or like into, for instance, the monstrous destructiveness of modern war. The enforced binding together of nations into one state has always resulted in the loss of individual liberty and the blunting and coarsening of values. Think of what we owe to city states. Just as a civilised community depends on free, integrated individuals who are committed to not doing serious harm to each other, so a world civilisation depends on free nations, able to fulfil themselves without being a nuisance to others. Some nations, the Romans, the English, the Germans, the French and, latterly, the Americans, among others, have gone beyond this reasonable requirement and made a great nuisance of themselves in the world. For it is necessary to distinguish between simple awareness of nationhood, which is an organic stage in the human system, and imperialism, which is a national urge for aggrandisement at the expense of other nations. The conquering nation may therefore be compared, according to your taste, either to the successful big business man or to the big crook.

Dr. Leopold Kohr in his book *The Breakdown of Nations* has set five million as the maximum population for an integrated nation capable of making the fullest use of its potentialities. Less than three million people live in Wales and this gives the country a sense of intimacy which would be lost with any merging into a much more numerous Britishness. It is possible in such a small nation for people who have the same interest or practise the same craft to know each other, for the fly fishermen, the bowling enthusiasts and the poets to have met. Everyone in Wales knows writers, county councillors and rugby players. Eisteddfodau, agricultural shows, sheepdog trials, clay-pigeon shooting competitions and the holiday camps of Urdd Gobaith Cymru bring young and old together from all parts of the country. Radio and television, though detrimental to Welsh culture in ways which will be discussed later, have in some ways proved unifying agents. They have familiarised the people of the north and the south with each other's accents and thereby increased the mutual understanding of these long-divided regions.

I have already asked a number of questions. It is useless to attempt to answer such questions and impossible to understand their significance, and that of any answers to them which may be offered, without some knowledge of what has happened to human society in Wales, from Paviland Man, eighteen thousand years ago, to the unities and divisions of our present day. During my years of work in Cyrenaica and in Turkey (I had felt no urge to do this in Egypt) I made as searching enquiries as I could into the prehistory and history of these countries and I found that this gave the observable situation in those countries a profounder contingency. What Herodotus and Strabo had to say about the Celts of Anatolia and the behaviour of those Celts of the first millennium B.C. in Asia Minor and in Libya told me a great deal about Wales and the Welsh. So, since my return to live in Wales, concerned with the doubts, hesitations and enthusiasms of the people I meet and read about in present-day Wales, I have made a similar enquiry into the past of the land, for the past is summed up in the present and conditions the future. This then will be my view of my own country, of a small nation uncertain about its future, still with its own language but in danger of losing it, beautiful in landscape and seascape but subject to pollution and desecration by industry and the war machine as well as to exploitation in various ways for the benefit of people who live outside its border, a hospitable, lively people who are happy about their difference from the English, but ready to live with them, on equal terms, in this island. Our poets no longer sing prophetically of sweeping the English back into the sea over which they came to us.

CHAPTER I

The Emergence of Wales as a Nation

Before History

There are features of the Welsh landscape, some observable from trunk roads and our rare motorways as soon as you get into Wales, others for which you have to follow paths high up into the hills, features which can't be understood or fully enjoyed unless you have some idea of how they came to be. You will soon learn to spot the winding concentric rings of fortification that mark a hilltop Celtic fort, much weathered though they may be after two thousand years of erosion by wind, rain and the feet of grazing animals. On a cross-country walk or pony-trek you may come upon a stone circle high on a moor and wonder what its purpose was. You may already have seen the Rollright Stones, or Avebury, or Stonehenge. They were put up by the same people. And you will learn to distinguish between these mysterious, lichened, weather-pitted standing stones, still far away from all habitation, and the recent stone circles erected in parks wherever a National Eisteddfod is held. For archaeologists of the future these latter may pose a greater problem. You will pass megaliths which are pathetically lonely and purposeless today and wonder at the engineering skill of the men who cut them and stood them up on end. You will visit some of our splendid *cromlechau*, the chambered tombs which fringe the coasts of Western Europe. You may visit caves in the Gower peninsula and ask how Palaeolithic Man ever came to live in our island and how the bones of hyenas, woolly rhinoceroses, mammoths and bears came to be buried in the low floor-levels of the same caves.

The first-known Welshman, though the epithet would have meant nothing to him, was buried in Paviland Cave on the southern coast of Gower some eighteen thousand years ago. He was first thought to be a girl and since his bones were covered with ochre he was for many years known as the Red Lady of Paviland. His head was not found with the bones, which now lie in the basement of a natural history museum at Oxford. What strange accident or unimaginable ritual separated the skull from the body? The heads of the dead have held a special significance all over the world and the red ochre suggests the ritual of some primitive religion. In early Welsh heroic poetry there is talk of the severing of the head of the leader killed in battle to rescue it from the insults of the enemy. Edward I took the head of Llywelyn ap Gruffydd to London to be mocked at. But Paviland Man lived millennia before such barbarous forms of warfare and pacification. He was a hunter of animals for food, not a killer of men. There could not have been enough people living in Wales then to split up into contentious tribes. But he had friends and relatives, or he would never have been given this special burial. Call him a cave-man if you wish, but don't think of him as the hairy, low-browed, ape-like figure with dangling arms who is so often presented by popular illustrators. The man buried at Paviland was a little over twenty-five years of age and about five feet six inches in height. He walked upright and had a brain as big as ours. He could make simple implements, setting microliths, flints about an inch long, into hafts of bone and wood. He made rough necklaces of animal teeth and he appreciated the beauty of ivory. He made harpoon barbs to spear fish, scoops to get limpets off rocks, scrapers to make skins fit for wearing. Over in central France, in the Dordogne region, his cousins were sculpting animals in stone and painting the splendid murals of Lascaux, but late Palaeolithic Man in South Wales had little time for art. He lived a tough life of hunting and food-gathering, on the fringe of a civilisation that stretched right across Europe to Asia Minor and beyond. The climate was cold and dry, tundra conditions with grazing for hoofed animals. If you visit Paviland, or the more accessible and architectural Bacon Hole not far away, remember that the sea did not then splash and erode the rock platforms before the caves as it does today. It was miles away to the south, with good hunting country in between. The great subsidence that followed the last Ice Age had not taken place, the Severn Channel was a narrow river, the English Channel did not exist and a land bridge to the Continent enabled the beasts of Africa and Asia to seek food in Wales, to be followed in turn by hunters with new techniques. (Diluvianism was the pre-Darwinian explanation of the presence of these exotic bones: they had been carried there by the flood that took Noah to Ararat.)

Thousands of years after Paviland Man a general submergence flooded the coastlands of Wales, widened the Severn Channel and created the English Channel. Places where men lived and hunted were lost under the sea. Flints have been found in dock excavations to prove this. At low tide the stumps of trees protrude from the sand north of Borth and at Aberdyfi you will be told that the bells of drowned churches, a pleasant anachronism, can be heard sometimes. The legend of Cantre'r Gwaelod, the Hundred of the Sea Bottom, refers to a time long before any form of administration we would recognise as such existed in Wales. With the climate getting warmer, about ten thousand years ago, trees flourished and forests covered much of the land. Today our woodlands are the steep slopes that can't be ploughed, but then there were trees everywhere. When I cut peat today, at over a thousand feet in a bog behind my house, I find bark of oak and hazel and birch in the dark, sweet-scented fuel. We were to wait several millennia for our characteristic and very human pattern of small fields and scattered dwellings. But perhaps five thousand years ago we began to clear patches of woodland on the lower slopes of hills, using the fine stone axes quarried from Penmaenmawr, to plant our first crops of grain. Not an original invention on our part but a notion which had taken another five thousand years to reach us, along devious routes through Europe from eastern Anatolia and the neighbouring hills of Syria, Palestine and western Persia. J. H. Breasted in his *The Conquest of Civilization* named this hill-country the Fertile Crescent and there, about ten thousand years ago, occurred one of the great steps forward man has taken, the Neolithic revolution, man becoming an agriculturist and ceasing to depend on hunting and food-gathering for sustenance. At about the same time the sheep, native to eastern Turkey and western Persia, was domesticated. Other useful animals, of wider habitat, followed. Once you clear a plot of land and cultivate it, you make it your base. The family stays there and if hunters go out on forays they come back there instead of venturing on to fresh hunting-grounds. So human societies

21

sprang up. All this took much longer in Wales than in more fertile lands and we have never been as good farmers as the Armenians, for example, became in Asia Minor. Many of us are still reluctant farmers and prefer stock-rearing on our good grass. In the valley you will see cows, often the sturdy Welsh Blacks, but you will see many more sheep on the green slopes and right up to the rocks where the Forestry Commission hasn't yet encroached.

Living where I do I'm much aware of my debt to Stone Age Man. I shoot and fish for pleasure as well as for food. There's something compulsive in my seasonal impulse to net prawns, to gather whinberries, cranberries, blackberries and at least eight kinds of fungus and to bring them home. I like my family to appreciate them and to share in them. I gather cockles all the year round, for in South Wales we love cockles, and the seaweed that makes laver bread. I don't like living very near other people and I hate to have powers outside my family and few friends interfere with the simplicities of my life. I am far from being alone in this in Wales and all this I take to be Palaeolithic with a touch of Neolithic. I love stone and putting stone on stone, and my father, grandfather and great-grandfather were master masons. In Wales we used stone to build houses for the dead thousands of years before we thought of doing this for the living.

Palaeolithic Man in Wales buried his dead in the debris of a cave floor. He lived in caves too. In central Anatolia Neolithic Man built houses at Catalhüyük, for instance, and buried his dead in the debris of the floor of the house. But caves are thin on the ground in Wales and there is no indication that stone houses were built before the Celts came. So chambered tombs were built, simulated caves, the first buildings we know of. These date from about 4000 to about 2000 B.C. and their construction was often a considerable feat of engineering. Great stones were quarried and made to stand firmly on end to outline a central chamber, and a capstone was placed over them to roof it. The Tinkinswood capstone, near Cardiff, weighs forty tons. Elaborations in the form of transepts and an entrance passage of varying length were sometimes added before the entrance was sealed and earth heaped over the whole structure. Barclodiad y Gawres, on a little headland between Aberffraw and Rhosneigr in Anglesey, was made cruciform thousands of years before Christianity came to Wales and has mysterious patterns cut on some of the upright stones. The covering earth has been carried or eroded away from some of these ancient structures and skeletons of our first mausolea stand bare and gaunt at Pentre Ifan in Pembrokeshire and St. Lythans near Cardiff.

Most of these *cromlechau*, or chambered tombs, are near the sea, on promontories or on slopes or raised places not far inland, suggesting that these architect ancestors of ours came to us and to Ireland over the sea. Some are in more secret places, erected as these early builders and newcomers probed the river valleys from welcoming estuaries and cleared patches of forest. These too are worth seeking out. There is such a one on the border of Carmarthenshire and Pembrokeshire. Go to Llanglydwen and follow the disused railway line for a little way westwards. The track has been torn up and the way flattened so that you can take a car along where the little trains once chugged and hooted down the lovely valleys from Cardigan to Whitland. Go along for half a mile or so and stop when you see a little bridge down on your right. Go up to a gate on your left and you will find the *cromlech* in a ring of noble trees. It's called *Gwal y Filast*, the Lair of the Greyhound Bitch. We are in Mabinogi land, the legendary land of Dyfed, and we wonder whether this was one of the greyhounds hunted by Arawn whilst their master, Pwyll, spent his strange year in the underworld.

Many of these *cromlechau* have been torn down by impatient cultivators and land-improvers. In Cardiganshire I know today of only one, the tiny, sad, uncared-for Bedd Taliesin, above Talybont, and the possible site of one on a ridge behind my house, but there are said to have been at least twelve at one time. Those that remain we treasure and visit with awe, for they are our first buildings and they are older than the pyramids.

Architecturally more modest but more conspicuous in the landscape are the cairns in which the people of the Bronze Age buried their notable, if not all their dead. These sometimes catch the eye like a low nipple on a reclining breast. The covering tumulus, or barrow, of earth and stone has in some cases been eroded away by weather or by pot-hunters to reveal a four-square grave lined with stone slabs and containing either bones or the ash of cremation burial. The urns often found in these graves indicate central Europe as the home of these peaceful invaders. Was it respect that made them bury their dead in these high places under the open sky? Shouldn't we respect these dead ancestors of ours and restore their resting places once the grave goods that art and science require have been put safely in museums? Quartzite seems to have been holy to them and is often associated with these cairns. The cairn near us is called *Garn Wen*, White Cairn, but most of the white stone has been taken away, I think by peat cutters and local farmers. A great lump of gleaming quartzite can help you spot the corner of a building or a gate or a tricky turn in a hedge at night. Look out for the words *carn, garn* and *carnedd* in names on the map. The cairn or tumulus may still be there.

Then there are the standing stones and stone circles of the megalith builders, so many of which still remain, though the lesser-known ones are in greater danger today than ever now that the farmer can call on the monstrous new machines to drop and bury these hindrances to easy ploughing. Only two summers ago some of the biggest standing stones in Wales were treated in this way in Pembrokeshire. These stones have been taken to be phallic salutes to the worshipped sun and the stone circles are inseparably associated in the popular view with the Druids and their mysterious practices, a view which is perpetuated by the National Eisteddfod today. But Professor Alexander Thom's careful study of these monuments from the Hebrides to Brittany has begun to open our eyes to their significance. He has shown these stone circles, with their outlying megaliths, to have been very exact scientific instruments erected to record and predict the appearance above the horizon of the sun, moon and some first magnitude stars, for ritualistic as well as more practical purposes. All this three thousand five hundred to four thousand years ago, when the stars rose sharply on clear nights, millennia before our skies were blurred and stained by the pollution of industry. (If the wind has blown from the east for a few days we in west Wales can smell industrial smog and see it fuzz our distances, blown perhaps from as far away as Rotterdam.) I quote Professor Thom in his book *Megalith Lunar Observations* published in 1971: 'It is remarkable that 1,000 years before the earliest mathematics of classical Greece, people in these islands not only had a practical knowledge of geometry and were capable of seting out elaborate geometrical designs but could also set ellipses based on Pythagorean triangles. We need not be surprised to find that their calendar was a highly developed arrangement involving an exact knowledge of the length of the year or that they had set up many stations for observing the eighteen-year cycle of the revolution of the lunar nodes.' Later he says: 'The clues which eventually led the author to the unravelling of the geometry of Avebury did not come from Stonehenge or Stanton Drew but from small unimpressive circles on the Scottish moors and the hills of Wales.' I had the pleasure of visiting with Professor Thom one of these clue-giving circles, the lovely little ring south-west of Corwen, Moel Ty Ucha, with its marvellous view and varied horizon. If we had mathematics so anciently in our blood is it surprising that village blacksmiths in Wales should have been masters of it, or that John Dee, of a Radnorshire family, should have been the leading mathematician and astronomer of the Elizabethan Age, or that Richard Price of Llangeinor in Glamorgan should have given insurance and actuarian practice its scientific basis?

These builders of stone circles probably brought with them from Europe the knowledge of how to make and use bronze. Excavation in Asia Minor is now pushing back the use of copper to thousands of years before the previously accepted Bronze and Chalcolithic Ages. Our bronze founders usually mingled one-tenth of Cornish tin with nine-tenths of the copper mined in many parts of Wales. They began by copying the shape of the polished stone axes of Penmaenmawr, cutting moulds in stone into which they poured the molten alloy. They showed much ingenuity in going on from that initial change. They beat out the cutting edge to make it thinner and sharper. They could now cope more rapidly with the clearing of woodland for agriculture. The simple metal axehead was fitted into a hole in the wooden handle and bound with thongs. Then came the palstave, an axehead with a wedge back fitting into the split-angled top of the wooden handle and bound there. But hard use eventually drove the axehead back through the handle and so they made socketed axes, the back of the axehead being cleverly cast hollow to receive the angled handle. Loops or wings were welded on to the side of the axehead so that it could be securely bound, once hafted. And then, quite unnecessarily from a practical point of view, the bronze axeheads were made more beautiful by the addition of raised parallel ribs. The result is a useful tool of lovely proportions. Halberds, axeheads with a spear point protruding from the top, are the first unhappy indication of warfare, unless this fearsome weapon was used to bring down a wild boar or a deer. Bronze Age Man certainly built no fortifications in Wales. But he was a hunter as well as a farmer and a pastoralist. The woods of Wales were full of tasty game and he experimented with new kinds of flint arrow-head. Flint is cheaper than bronze, one is apt to miss one's target, and an arrow isn't easy to find in undergrowth, so the Bronze Age hunter continued to use flint. He or his wife made good pots for use as cooking and eating utensils as well as for urn burial, and beakers, dishes and cups. There was time and material for luxuries now. He made razors and tweezers to improve his and her appearance and treasured ornaments of gold, bronze, amber and jet. A torque, made probably of Irish gold and found near Harlech Castle, suggests that these Bronze Age people may have been early waves of Central European Celts, since the torque, made of twisted gold as a decoration for the neck or arm, is typical Celtic Man's wear. An awareness of beauty was in everything they made and hardly anything made by man excels in purity and perfection the bronze shield found on Moel Siabod in North Wales and now in the British Museum.

So, long before the beginning of history, we had achieved the essential elements of civilisation. We exchanged goods and ideas within the British Isles and we received ideas from the Continent. Carnac in Brittany might well have been the centre of the mathematics of the megalith builders. We had agriculture and stock-breeding. We had commerce, for stone axeheads roughed out on Penmaenmawr were bought and then polished elsewhere. One has been found at Avebury. We had art on stone and in metal and we must have had some form of poetry, music and dancing, though these of course could not then be recorded. Whatever houses we had, though made of wood and wattles and clay and therefore impermanent, they might well have been snug. We had some form of religion and there is no evidence that we quarrelled with each other.

I'm not very superstitious but for over twenty years I've carried in my wallet a broken white flint knife or scraper, beautifully shaped, which I found in a lump of peat. It must have been dropped by a forebear of mine, just as I have dropped a knife in the bog and had trouble in finding it, or crushed an empty cartridge case into the ooze after missing or hitting a teal which has whistled past my head in the twilight of this sweeping upland hollow. And I cut peat there today, hardly ever seeing a living thing but the odd sheep or hare or fox, a teal, snipe or mallard, a crow or a kite. Nasty, brutish and short Bronze Age life might have seemed to renaissance man, but I sometimes wish we had stopped there, at that point, before the artistic and warlike Celt ever came to Wales.

The Celts

Of all the invaders of Wales the Celts left the most permanent and conspicuous signs of their settlement. Wherever you go in Wales, as soon as your eye has learnt to pick out the informing outlines, you will see hilltops where earthworks make a stepped silhouette and follow the contours of hills in concentric fortification. Wind, rain and the feet of grazing animals, mostly sheep, have rounded and blurred the original edge of these defensive walls. I say walls rather than earthworks since some of the carefully planned defences were faced with quarried stone. And you will learn to spot the entrances that snake their way-in a most un-Roman fashion into what the Romans called a Celtic *oppidum*, using the same word as they would for Pergamon or Antioch. These hill-forts are frequent in the south of England too and a map of south Britain in the Iron Age shows how the forts, varying in size from a fortified homestead for one family to a great tribal centre, follow the line of the two hill-ranges from the south-west in a north-easterly direction, and how they are linked by great ridgeways that mark the same lines. Such a map vividly suggests waves of progression from landing-places where the English Channel is narrowest. Once Wales was reached (of course it hadn't yet been given that name by the English) forts were built on the first rampart of hills, as though to resist further invasion, and a series of great fortifications roughly follows the line of the later Offa's Dyke. As you leave Oswestry on your way to North Wales a magnificent camp has a frontier look about it. These fortresses are all worth seeking out, for they are all different. Wherever they went and whatever the ground was like the Romans clamped down a rectangular fortification, either

27

for a one-night stand or to enclose a great town with its Hippodamian grid-system of streets which had come from Miletos in Asia Minor. The Celts accepted topography without attempting to dominate or modify the lie of the land, content to have their defences follow the contour and achieve a sinuosity such as we see in the decoration of their shields. I think we still feel this urge to deal locally with the problems that nature presents rather than to impose a general plan devised by some remote central administration.

The first Celts came to Wales about the year 600 B.C. The middle centuries of this first millennium B.C. saw a great movement outwards of the Celts from their mountainous homeland in Central Europe, westwards to the Rhineland, France, Britain, Spain and Portugal, southwards into Italy, along the Danube down into the Balkans and Greece and, early in the third century B.C., into Asia Minor, where they became known as Galatae or Galatians. But there was never a Celtic empire. They conquered in order to settle, as the Normans did later, never establishing an imperial capital to radiate out administration and to receive back loot, in the manner of the world's great empires. And yet for centuries they held a cultural and linguistic belt across Central Europe, from its most western shores to the Near East, a belt known to the ancient Greeks as Keltika, to indicate a homogeneous culture. The Celtic arms recorded on the great temple of Attalos of Pergamon, and the grave goods found in Galatian tombs near Ankara, are similar to those recovered in Britain.

At the foot of a frowning escarpment on the Rhigos Mountain, which separates the valleys of the Nedd and the upper Rhondda, lies a dark lake which is now a reservoir. About the year 600 B.C. a party of exploring Celts must have reached this wild spot. They may have been new arrivals in the country, just landed in Swansea Bay, or they may have been second-generation immigrants who had made their way along the invasion route of the South Wales coast from somewhere east of the Severn Estuary. To the Celts the gods were everywhere about them, but water, in springs, rivers and lakes, was especially holy and they must have recognised in this gloomy, remote headwater a fitting abode for gods it would be wise to propitiate. So they took things they could ill spare, two splendid riveted cauldrons of bronze, filled them with precious tools and weapons, well-made gouges, a looped razor, harness decorations and a fine iron sword of Hallstadt manufacture which they must have brought with them from the Continent. All these they carried down to the water's edge by the ring handles of the cauldrons and floated them out to slow sacrificial submergence in the dark lake. I was allowed to handle these things for a television programme, at the National Museum of Wales, Cardiff, and after the programme had appeared I got a letter from the foreman of the workmen who had found this treasure in 1912. Another man who had seen my programme approached me the other day at Aberystwyth. He came from Rhigos and his family still grazes the mountain. He was blue-eyed and so were all his family, he said. A Celtic fairness, still dominant after two and a half millennia.

Once settled, the Celts in Wales used stone to build houses and walls to protect them. The most interesting Celtic village I know (or would the Romans have called even this too an *oppidum*?) is perched on the summit of the lower of two peaks known as Yr Eifl, roughly between Caernarfon and Pwllheli. It's a pleasant walk up along a marked path, from the road that runs from Llanaelhaearn through Llithfaen to Nefyn, to this Celtic eyrie called Tre'r Ceiri, the Town, or Home, of Ramparts, an apt name. The walls of sharp bare stone are unmistakable, the entrance passages are distinct and could easily be restored. Outside there's an enclosure which must have been for penning cattle at night. Within the wall is a large turfed area with a look-out point of rock from which the view is staggering and a complex of buildings, houses and storerooms, with walls still several feet high. There are scores of these buildings and one of them is spacious enough to have been a chieftain's house or a tribal council chamber. Saddle querns which still lie about in the grass show how they ground the grain they grew on slopes lower down the mountain. Don't be deceived by the apparent grimness of the houses today. They once knew colourful splendour, with weapons and ornaments of iron, bronze and gold catching the firelight. There would be music and poetry, which we know the Celts loved well before the Christian era. Mead to drink, home-baked bread and meat, either hunted or stock-reared, would make a satisfying feast, but there wouldn't be hare on the menu. It was some kind of totem animal, used perhaps in divination but not eaten. There are still some of us who don't like killing a hare though we wouldn't think twice about bowling over a rabbit. It was at places like Tre'r Ceiri that Celtic life survived the Roman occupation to carry on its impulses into early Welsh poetry and the sculpture of the Celtic churches.

The Bronze Age people of Wales had shown an awareness of beauty happily allied to functional form, but the Celts brought a sensitive and all-pervading feeling for design such as has never been surpassed in human artifacts. A basic pattern in design (one might almost call it a basic life-pattern since so many human concepts and experiences are triple-faceted) was the triskele, three repeated curving forms swirling within a circle, sometimes of extreme simplicity, sometimes turning back and re-curving in a way that suggests animal movement or the swing of the constellations about the Northern Star. Forms like this sometimes follow each other in a scroll fashion along a collar, a scabbard, a shield boss, a mirror back, a flagon or a drinking-horn. Such scrollwork evolved in Christian times into the lovely interlacing which covers the Celtic stone crosses of Wales, put up before the advent of the Normans. All that is abstract, though not without meaning as comment on life, but the Celts also incorporated human and animal forms into their decoration, especially of those creatures—horse, wild boar, ox, bird and snake—which held some particular significance for them. Human heads are probably those of chieftains or gods, while grotesques may be there as protection for a chariot or a house. Something of ancient Celtic design has survived in the patterns of blanket-weaving and the carving of love-spoons, while the triskele has been pleasantly restored to contemporary decoration, though completely divorced from any meaning which I think it must once have carried for our forebears. A less happy return to a Celtic form is the rash of stone crosses in recent memorial sculpture.

The Celts brought us disunity, for they came in tribal groups that had already been established before they arrived here, not complete tribes but branches which broke away to forage in different directions. There were branches of the Tectosages in southern Gaul and in Asia Minor. This division into tribes made it easier for the Romans to subdue the country. The tribal divisions too survived the Roman domination and were the basis of the kingdoms of post-Roman and medieval Wales. The recent rearrangement of the Welsh counties into larger groups restores the old tribal boundaries with astonishing accuracy. Yes, it is to the Celts that we owe the feeling of difference that still exists between the people of the north and the south.

The most precious gift the Celts brought us was our language. Perhaps because of different waves of migration, continental Celts settled down in these islands into two main forms, the outer or western Goidelic and the inner Brythonic or Brittonic. Brittonic evolved slowly, through Early and Old Welsh, towards the Modern Welsh we know today, a stage which was achieved when books in Welsh began to be printed in the sixteenth century. But we should not forget that some lines in Aneirin's sixth-century heroic poem *Gododdin* are immediately comprehensible today. The poet speaks of the year's training and feasting which ended with death in battle and sums this up in the line:

> *a gwedy elwch tawelwch vu.*
> and after rejoicing there was silence.

We have no idea what language was spoken in Wales before the Celts came, though I've already hazarded the suggestion that the Bronze Age people were proto-Celts and therefore spoke a proto-Celtic tongue. And I wonder whether the collating of any sub-strata observable in the different Celtic languages might afford clues to the structure and vocabulary of earlier, possibly non-Indo-European languages once spoken in these regions. A twentieth-century Welsh poet, Waldo Williams, has written hauntingly of the forgotten achievements of our far-back ancestors, particularly of the lost languages. I translate a stanza of his poem, *Cofio*.

> The little words of vanished languages,
>   which once were lively in the mouths of men,
> sweet hearing in the talk of little children,
>   no tongue will ever call for them again.

The Romans

When Aneirin wrote, probably in what is today Edinburgh, the Romans had come and gone so far as Britain was concerned. What impact did their long stay have on this country which English-speakers call Wales? For the Romans Wales was one of the fringes of their empire, a north-west region to be pacified, fortified and policed rather than colonised. Forays and invasions from unconquered Ireland could disturb this ultimate edge of their *pax romana*.

As a base for their attack upon the Silures of South Wales the Romans built the great camp at Burrium, which is known as Brynbuga or Usk today, and here they assembled stores and supplies for the long marches into Wales, in the great storerooms, granaries and workshops which excavation is now revealing. Once they had tackled and pacified the Silures, Burrium was abandoned for Caerleon, which became their legionary base at the southern end of the Welsh border. Burrium was liable to flooding and the Usk was not properly navigable from the sea at this point. From Caerleon they built a road westwards to Maridunum, which is Caerfyrddin or Carmarthen today. Then the road struck north right up through west Wales to Segontium, outside present-day Caernarfon. This great fort has been tidied up and made comprehensible and, though hardly anything remains above ground level to compare with Caerleon or Caerwent, it's well worth a visit. One wonders what legionaries from Mediterranean countries thought of winter there, with the stubbornness of unconquered Tre'r Ceiri not far to the west. And a good example of how the Romans achieved flatness of ground and a rectangular shape for their forts can be seen at Castell Collen, near Llandrindod; while south of Llandrindod there is an area where the legionaries practised digging one-night stands for their campaigns in Wales. It sometimes occurs to me that present-day governments at Westminster would be just as happy as the Romans would have been to see the Welsh cleared from the hills.

From this north-western extremity of Segontium, with its eye on grain-bearing Anglesey across the straits, a connecting road ran to another great legionary centre at Chester, near the northern end of the Welsh border. The two border bases, Deva (Chester) and Isca (Caerleon), were in turn linked by a road that ran through the border country past Uriconium (Wroxeter, near Shrewsbury). Other roads, not today fully mapped, ran across country to link the major roads. When we were making a film of the Roman occupation of Wales, John Ormond, the producer, remarked on how our railway system, now rapidly disintegrating in Wales, followed the line of these roads. In either case the reason is of course topographical. In other more successfully colonised and more profitable lands the Romans were prepared to construct aqueducts and viaducts, and to dig cuttings and tunnels, for the easier movement of water, merchandise and soldiers, but in Wales coastal plain and valley were followed, with the occasional rise to a connecting pass. A favourite holiday route of Midlanders seeking the beaches of west Wales was pioneered by the Romans, for they must have had a road from Castell Collen (Llandrindod) to connect with the north-south Segontium-Maridunum road. The late Sir Thomas Parry-Williams indicated to me, across the valley to the left as one rises from Llangurig to the Steddfa Gurig pass on Plynlumon, a little fort which probably controlled this pass and the road down towards Llanbadarn. The Forestry Commission has left it unplanted and it is fairly easy to pick out where they levelled the hill-side to construct it. Roman forts are not today so easy to spot as Celtic hill-forts, and Roman roads have often disappeared under fields and modern roads, but, after a winding, wooded valley, when one is suddenly faced with a long straight stretch of road, south of Trawsfynydd for instance, one knows that the legionaries once marched here. These were no roads for dawdling and enjoying the scenery, for they were strategic, the quickest way of moving troops from one post to another. But they pass significantly near areas where mineral ores are to be found. In Gaul, and perhaps in Ostia itself, the port of Rome, the Romans would have heard (quite possibly exaggerated) accounts from Phoenician merchants of Britain's wealth of metals. This was one reason for their invasion of Britain. And they needed a pacified Wales in order to exploit these metals—gold, silver, copper, lead and iron. At Dolau Cothi in Carmarthenshire you may today see the remains of a huge mining and factory complex where they used slave labour to mine and process gold.

So the Silures were defeated and pacified and Suetonius Paulinus marched to the Menai Straits to deal with the Druids in the groves of their ancient centre, the Island of Môn or Anglesey. The Romans knew these Druids by repute not only as the teachers and philosophers of the Celts but as the inspirers of resistance to the Roman advance, even so far afield as in Gaul. Tacitus has a vivid description of how the Roman army, ready to board the flat-bottomed boats which had been prepared for the invasion of Anglesey, hesitated in consternation at the strange and frightening spectacle which faced them across the narrow water. The Celtic troops lined the opposite shore. Nearby stood the Druids, each with hand upraised, calling down high-pitched curses on their enemy, while women carrying torches ran through the ranks of the warriors. But the Romans crossed and carried out their slaughter.

Though the Romans did little in Wales but conquer, pacify and exploit, they made some attempt to turn the Celts of the country into a town-dwelling, taxable population. This they did notably at Caerwent, east of Caerleon, and to a lesser extent at Maridunum. After destroying a Silurian capital in the hill-fort of Llanmelin Wood they offered the Silures a new, Roman-style capital lower down and called it Venta Silurum, which is the modern Caerwent. A stone which was put up outside the Forum of the town and which is now inside the church porch states that it was erected by order of the *res publica civitas* (or *civitatis*) *Silurum*. This South Wales tribe had been given a senate, though one doubts whether it had then more authority than the Welsh Office has today in Cardiff. But the attractions and amenities offered by Venta Silurum seem to have tempted some South Walians to adopt the Roman way of life, for there were houses, shops, a forum, a market, baths, temples and an amphitheatre. It has the most impressive Roman town walls standing in Britain today, and this suggests that it needed protection against other Silures who resisted urbanisation and against Irish invaders. Founded about the year A.D. 75, it flourished for a while but declined in the third century. It changed its character, too, losing its civilian quality and becoming more military. Retired legionaries who married Celtic wives found it an agreeable place to live in. Many Welsh men and women are still reluctant town-dwellers.

It must have been through towns like Venta and Maridunum, and the few villas built in South Wales on the basis of the Roman pattern, that Latin words connected with building entered Welsh, for Wales had never before known domestic architecture of this quality. So we have *mur* for wall and *pared* for interior wall, *ffenestr* for window, *trawst* for beam and *sail* for foundation. Then words from road-building and the military life: *pont* for bridge, *ffos* for ditch, *castell* for fort and *llurig* for shield. A more luxurious standard of living brought words like *cegin*, kitchen, *torth*, loaf, *gwin* for wine and *maneg* for glove. More mysterious is the entry into Welsh of words for parts of the body, for the Celts must have had words for these: *corff* for the body itself, *coes* for leg and *boch* for cheek. There are counterparts to these borrowings in the other Celtic languages and the answer must be that the Celts had picked up these words in earlier contacts with the Romans, possibly in Italy itself. And we mustn't forget that the Romans themselves had adopted a number of very useful Celtic words before they ever came to Britain; the word *carrum*, for instance, from which an infinity of words has been derived in French and English: car, carry, cargo, chariot, charge, cart and so on. The Celts were experts at carrying things. They had put a seat in the chariot and the Romans took this idea over with its Celtic name, *eseda*. The Celts had evolved a four-wheeled chariot for heavier duty and this too the Romans adopted with its name, *petorritum*. The iron sword of the Celts had impressed them and their word for a sword, *gladius*, is of Celtic origin. The Celts were practised horsemen whereas the Romans fought on foot and, though there was a perfectly good Latin word, *equus*, for horse, the Roman soldier adopted the Celtic word *caballus*, a borrowing which eventually gave western Europe a host of important terms, *cheval*, *chevalier*, *caballero*, cavalry, cavalcade and chivalry.

The idea of chivalry is basically Celtic too, for it derives not only from the prowess of Arthur and his men on horseback but from an ancient Celtic attitude to woman and to love. There was no specific Celtic goddess of love, but sexuality was a constant aspect of the divine female. There were Celtic goddesses of motherhood, healing, war; there were consort goddesses, a horse goddess and innumerable nymphs of springs and rivers. I quote from Dr. Anne Ross: 'The basic Celtic goddess type was at once mother, warrior, hag, virgin, conveyor of fertility, of strong sexual appetite which led her to seek mates amongst mankind equally with the gods, giver of prosperity to the land, protectress of the flocks and herds. More static and more archaic than the gods, she remained tied to the land for which she was responsible and whose most striking natural features seemed to her worshippers to be manifestations of her power and personality.' (*Pagan Celtic Britain*, p. 297.)

Speaking of the medieval doctrine of Love, in its troubadour, Catharist and courtly forms, Denis de Rougemont says: 'The Brittonic background was so easily absorbed into the symbolism of courtly romance. . . . A Celtic background of religious beliefs— which, as it happens, were at a very remote period common to both the Iberian South and its *langue d'oc* and to the Irish and Brittanic North; semblances of Christian orthodoxy; a sometimes very compliant sexuality; and finally, the individual fancy of each of the poets —these, when all is said and done, are the materials thanks to which the heretical doctrine of Love . . . underwent its transmutations. In this way was the Tristan myth born.' (*Passion and Society*, pp. 129–30.) And de Rougemont quotes H. Hubert: 'It is through Tristan and Arthur that the most limpid and precious part of the Celtic genius was incorporated into the European spirit.' (*Les Celtes*, II, p. 336) Thus, though we live on this western fringe of Europe, is our culture intertwined with those of other nations by our contributions to them.

The vocabulary of religion is another aspect of this internationalism. Christianity came to Wales during the Roman occupation and with its slow penetration came a further flood of words which acclimatised themselves completely. Here are some of the many examples: *angel* (*angelus*), *disgybl* (*discipulus*), *eglwys* (*ecclesia*), *llyfr* (*liber*), *pererin* (*peregrinus*), *ysgol* (*schola*); but it must be stressed that the Romans had already departed when these words came into general use. When they left, Wales was still a pagan country. There is very little sign of Christianity at Caerwent and the names of the first Christian martyrs at Caerleon, Aaron and Julius, are significantly non-Celtic. Christianity was still a strange new foreign cult followed by a few Roman soldiers and officials and much less popular even amongst them than the cults of Isis and Mithras. Rome never sought to impose any of its religions on a conquered people but followed Alexander the Great's lead in seeking counterparts to the gods they themselves worshipped in a local religion. Such a dedication as that of a temple to Sulis-Minerva at Bath was intended to please both conqueror and conquered and probably helped towards Romanisation.

Rome had inherited from the Near East that perhaps greatest of human inventions, writing, so, with the many words already taken into Brittonic, the Romans left us their alphabet and the formal language of epigraphy. Latin had become the language of scholarship and administration in Wales. I have already mentioned the official stone, finely inscribed in Latin, at Caerwent. The Celtic kings and chieftains of Wales continued to use Latin for commemorative purposes after the Romans had gone. As a boy I used to walk over the Margam Mountain to a stone which recorded the burial on a mountain top, in a Bronze Age rather than a Christian manner, of one Bodvoc, son of Catotigirnus and grandson of Eteranis Vedomavus. In the Carmarthen Museum you will find the Votiporix Stone, the earliest remaining monument to any king in Britain and proudly though not elegantly inscribed *Memoria Voteporigis Protictoris*. Votiporix, Guortepir in Old Welsh and Gwrthefyr in Modern Welsh, ruled Dyfed until he died about the year 551 and a cross within a circle indicates that he was at least nominally a Christian. But according to Gildas, a learned cleric and writer of that age who knew Votiporix, he was far from living up to Christian ideals. Gildas, in his *De Excidio et Conquestu Britanniae*, calls Votiporix 'the crazy king of the Demetiae' and addresses him thus: 'You sit on your throne full of guile, from the sole of your foot to your head soiled with murder and adultery; you cast aside your lawful wife, who was killed through the cruel tricks of your shameless daughter.' Gildas is equally scathing in his attacks on Maclocunus, known in Welsh as Maelgwn Gwynedd and grandson of Cunedda, whom he finds 'sodden with wine pressed from the vine of Sodom'. This is a quotation from Deuteronomy 32:32, and Gildas had in him something of the ferocity of an Old Testament prophet. His avoidance of any mention of Arthur is taken by some to imply disapproval of that hero, even though he mentions the battle of Mount Badon, traditionally one of Arthur's victories. Could Arthur too have clung to paganism in spite of the cross he is said to have carried on his shield? But Gildas took an altogether poor view of his native Britain, to which he refers as 'the island stiff with frost and cold, in a far distant corner of the earth, remote from the sight of the sun'.

This massive memorial stone to Votiporix deserves still further consideration, for it has yet another interesting, though far from unique, feature. The Latin inscription is repeated in yet another alphabet, the Ogham script. This mysterious alphabet was invented in Ireland and is thought by some to derive from Etruscan, as the Latin alphabet itself does. It has five vowels, represented by one, two, three, four or five dots, for a, o, u, e, and i, and fifteen consonants, in the form of short, straight lines. The inscription always starts at the bottom left-hand side of the stone as you face it and then runs up the spine of the stone's edge and down the other side, if necessary. The dots are cut on the spine of the stone, five consonants approach the edge from one side, five from the other, and five are cut right across the edge. There are fifty-five known Ogham-inscribed stones in Wales, most of them in the south-west. Another bilingually inscribed stone of great interest is now in the church of Llandudoch or St. Dogmaels, near Cardigan. (So bilingual signs and notices, which we require in Wales today, are by no means new to our country.) Latin capitals running downwards along the face of the Llandudoch stone give us the name of Sagranus, son of Cunitanus. If you decipher the Ogham inscription you will find that the Latin *fili* has as its counterpart *maqi* in Ogham. This proves that the language represented is Goidelic, not Old Welsh or Brittonic.

During the centuries of Roman occupation there had been invasions of Wales by people from Ireland to settle in both the north and the south. Votiporix, king of Dyfed in the sixth century A.D., was himself descended from Eochaid Allmuir, who had led part of the Deisi tribe of southern Ireland into South Wales in the third century A.D. Similar settlements of Irish invaders had occurred in North Wales but these were dealt with by Cunedda, who moved there with his family and followers from North Britain about the year A.D. 400, quite probably at the suggestion of the departing Romans, worried about the vulnerability of this fringe of their already crumbling empire. Cunedda cut across the old tribal divisions of Wales by encouraging his sons and grandsons to grab little kingdoms for themselves. It was Ceredig who penetrated furthest south, to the Teifi estuary, to create the kingdom named after him, Ceredigion, afterwards Cardiganshire and today once more Ceredigion. By his actions Cunedda confirmed Brittonic as the language of Wales, at a time when we might have been drifting toward a Goidelic-speaking administration, but south of the line running roughly from the Teifi Estuary to present-day Breconshire the Irish element in our population and culture remained unimpaired. Well into the Norman era Welsh princes were proud to trace their descent partly to these Irish settlers.

Goidelic words remain in place and farm names, chiefly in South Wales where settlement was heaviest; words like *cnwc* or *cnwch* for a hillock (*clwch* in Anglesey) and *meidir* for a lane. Penyfeidir, Top of the Lane, occurs any number of times in Pembrokeshire today and when, at Cilgerran, I asked the way in Welsh to Gardd y Cnapan, I was told to follow *y feidir* round the back of the castle. We still associate Ireland with good butter and the Welsh for a slice of bread and butter is *brechdan*, an Irish word. The ending *-ach* in river and place names is of Irish origin and is equivalent to the Welsh *-og* or *-iog*, which make descriptive adjectives. The anglicised forms Brecon and Brecknock come from an Irish chieftain called Brychan, whose kingdom was called Brycheiniog, the Welsh name of the county, after him. If so much that was Irish remained and merged into our culture and genes may it not be this, rather than Celtic tribal division, that makes the South Welsh different from those of the North?

The most beautiful of our Celtic crosses in Wales are to be found in those parts where the Irish settled, in Anglesey, Pembrokeshire, Glamorgan and Breconshire, those parts where Ogham writing is to be found on stones, and they surely reflect, or are in the same tradition as, the lovely designs of the Irish *Book of Durrow* and *Book of Kells*.

The study of the separate development of Celtic mythology in Ireland and Wales, as reflected in the ancient tales and poetry of our two countries, has given us intriguing examples of conformity and divergence. This mythology has informed our landscape with fearful and lovely significances. Who would otherwise think of the gentle Aeron, the river which flows from Llyn Eiddwen near my home to charming Aberaeron, as a river of blood? And yet it is named after Aeron, Agrona, the Celtic goddess of slaughter. There's a story that the dread goddess was seen washing the dead at a ford; could it have been at Talsarn? Who can go to Harlech without listening for the magical birds of Rhiannon or straining his eyes to see the giant figure of Bendigeidfran wading over to Ireland with his revengeful ships? Or stopping at Arberth (Narberth in Pembrokeshire) to ask the way to Glyn Cuch, where Pwyll, lord of Dyfed, went hunting, met Arawn, king of the Underworld, and agreed to the strange and happy exchange of functions for the space of a year. Wales is full of lake and cave entrances to the Underworld and, once you have read *The Mabinogion*, places we still visit or live in will be haunted for you by the strange things that happened there. Not even London will be quite the same for you again.

Place names usually live longer than buildings, though we have no idea what our Stone Age ancestors called such buildings as the *cromlechau* of Barclodiad y Gawres and Tinkinswood. (Imagine the scorn with which our forefathers of those days would regard the triviality of the names given long after their day to these great monuments.) Some place names in Wales are clearly of the pre-Christian era. Both Cymbeline and Lear are remembered not far from where I am writing. Cynfelyn is the modern Welsh form of Cymbeline, from the old Celtic Cunobelinos, and there is a Llangynfelyn inland from Borth. Out to sea from near Aberdyfi a straight ridge of rock, popularly thought to be a submerged road to Cantre'r Gwaelod, the Bottom or Drowned Hundred, and visible only at low tide, is called Sarn Cynfelyn, Cynfelyn's Road. And there is a Llanllyr, Lear's enclosure, near Talsarn. This was once a nunnery. The sky, for us, has its memories too, for the Milky Way is called both Caer Arianrhod and Caer Gwydion, the Fort of Arianrhod or of her brother Gwydion. Gwydion and Arianrhod were the children of Dôn, whose home in Welsh is the constellation of Cassiopeia, Caer Dôn. And when my father, in astonishment, would invoke *Yr Andras Fawr* I suspect, in spite of the etymology given by *Geiriadur Prifysgol Cymru*, the half-completed *Welsh University Dictionary*, that he was calling on the dread goddess Andraste, as Boadicea did before she went into battle against the Romans. From Llyn Eiddwen, just over the hill from my house, a monster called *Yr Afanc* until not long ago used to come out of the water at night to devour cattle. Out of Llyn y Fan in north Carmarthenshire came a beautiful girl with a dowry of cattle to marry a young man who had seen her combing her hair on the surface of the water and had fallen in love with her, but after suffering the three forbidden causeless blows from her otherwise loving husband she went back into the lake with all her cattle and their progeny. Even the little black calf slaughtered for meat came to life, jumped off the hook and trotted after her back into the Underworld. But she left to her sons her book of cures and they and their descendants became famous doctors, *Meddygion Myddfai*, the Doctors of Myddfai. Their descendants are still said to possess extraordinary skill in treating animals and I know a very good doctor who claims descent from them. The Celtic and pre-Celtic worlds are still everywhere about us, striking pagan chords in our awareness.

The Celtic mother goddesses, known to the Romans as the *Matres* or *Matronae*, in Brittany as the Good Ladies or Good Mothers and in Jersey as the Dames, are remembered in the mountain called Moel Famau, in the Clwydian Range, which was probably sacred to them. (*Mamau* is the plural of the Welsh word *mam*, mother, and is here mutated.) These goddesses are usually depicted as three figures and are associated with ideas of fertility. Goddesses seem to go in threes: Paris had to choose one of three on Mount Ida and how popular the Three Graces became in classical and renaissance sculpture. With the decline of mythology into folk-tale and superstition the Mothers became the Fairies, and to placate these fearsome creatures, far removed from the tiny imps and elves of other countries, the Welsh called them *Bendith y Mamau*, the Blessing of the Mothers.

The pig was an important magical animal of the Celtic underworld and the journey of the magician Gwydion with the pigs he had got by a trick from Pryderi, pigs which were a present from Annwn, is said to be marked by pig place names, Nant-y-Moch, Mochnant and Mochdref, both the hamlet of Mochdref near Llandrillo in Denbighshire and the parish of Mochdref in Montgomeryshire. Llanrhaeadr-ym-Mochnant has an old township called Castellmoch; there is an old hamlet of Mochras on the sandy shore south of Harlech and one called Mochros in the parish of Llanarth, south of Aberaeron. Any or all of these may mark stopping places in the famous pig-drive from Pembrokeshire to North Wales. From north-east Wales they moved on to Snowdonia and a sty was built for the swine at Arllechwedd and called Creuwyrion. *Moch* means pigs in Welsh and *crau* or *creu* means sty and occurs in the Creuddyn place names of Wales. It must be remembered, however, that all these pig place names may be much older than the story and that the brilliant writer of *Math, son of Mathonwy*, the fourth of the Four Branches of *The Mabinogion*, simply used them to lend credibility to his strange tale. Either that or he used the story to try to explain the place names. Even so, to follow this trail with *The Mabinogion* and detailed maps in one's satchel or glove-tray would still be interesting, and locally one might pick up farm names and even field names that would link up.

Christian Wales

The Celtic gods survived the first introduction of Christianity into Wales and the Romans left a still largely pagan country. The old stone circles of the Bronze Age must still have held some religious or superstitious significance, for the first Celtic saints often set up their little cells within them, using the standing stones as vertebrae for their enclosure walls. This must have happened at Llangwyryfon, in which parish I live, for up to the middle of the last century the churchyard was still circular, with the old church in the middle. Some of the old stones are still standing in the churchyard wall of Yspyty Cynfyn, on the roadside between Pont-ar-Fynach (Devil's Bridge) and Ponterwyd. It's worth looking out for circular churchyards, particularly in old maps like that of the tithe maps of the 1840s. There are many of them in Wales, though some of them have been modified to extend the burial ground, or to build a church hall or a school, as happened at Llangwyryfon. These are likely to be the sites of old stone circles, where the new religion took over whatever holiness or superstitious awe attached to the old.

Even if Christianity had not yet been widely accepted, Celtic Britain had by the year 400 already produced a great heretic. This was Pelagius, possibly an Irishman from South Wales, a monk who never took holy orders but who had strong and highly reasonable views on doctrine. He rejected the notion of original sin, stressed the freedom of the human will and the responsibility of each one of us for his own actions and for the state of his soul. He went to Rome, where his teaching was taken up and publicised by an Irishman called Celestius, who became a monk too and followed Pelagius. The Celtic thinker was scandalised by the immorality and decadence he observed in Rome and was glad to get out of the city before its sack by the Goths in 410, during the anarchy of which forty thousand slaves took revenge on their cruel and dissolute masters. Pelagius travelled on, like other Celtic *peregrini* who got as far as Syria and the Holy Land, meeting St. Jerome in Jerusalem and arguing his views with the pillars of the Church, by whom he was condemned at the Councils of Carthage and of Ephesus. Gibbon says, 'the British clergy incessantly laboured to eradicate the Pelagian heresy, which they abhorred, as the peculiar disgrace of their native country.' Some of us still find ourselves Pelagian when we think of these matters.

It was on an anti-Pelagian preaching tour that Dewi Sant, St. David, performed the famous miracle at Llanddewi Brefi in Cardiganshire. He was preaching when someone at the back of the crowd, and they aren't slow to do this in Wales, complained that he couldn't see Dewi or hear him. The saint put a kerchief on the ground, stood on it and a hillock rose under his feet. You will find the very solid building of the church named after him on that hillock today, and you may think that that gives credibility to the story.

Not all the early Celtic saints were founders of churches or monasteries, or even preachers and proselytisers. Many of them were hermits, committed to a way of life that had been followed in the Near East since before the time of Christ, then notably by St. Antony in the Eastern Desert of Egypt round about A.D. 300. It was St. Pachomius who organised the first cenobitic or communal monasteries in Upper Egypt in the fourth century and it's interesting that, like Pelagius, neither Antony nor Pachomius was an ordained priest. From there the idea of retreat into communities spread to the Libyan Desert, to Sinai, to Anatolia, to Greece and eventually to the great French monastic orders which the Normans brought to Wales. The early Welsh hermits retired to wild, desolate places in the mountains, on the seashore or on the islands around the coast, there to meditate and mortify the flesh. They impressed people by the severe asceticism of their life rather than by missionary effort, and their influence was great. St. Justinian, a Breton about whom little is known except that he was a friend of St. David, retired to Ramsey Island (known today in Welsh as Ynys Dewi) and was probably murdered there. A chapel in his honour was built above the little cove called Porth Stinian, which is still the departure point for the island and precipitously accommodates the lifeboat station. The corbelled building is now roofless but is proportioned like a classical temple. (My wife pointed out the similarity of its proportions to those of a temple we had seen at Paestum in southern Italy.) For me this chapel is a neglected architectural masterpiece. Ramsey Island is now a bird sanctuary and the cliffs on its western side, facing the sea, are the breeding place and haunt of unusual seabirds.

Before settling down to the undisturbed life of worship these early hermits often wandered about the Celtic west, between Brittany, Cornwall, Wales and Ireland, and they are known as the *peregrini* of the early fifth century, the wandering pilgrim saints of what Professor E. G. Bowen has called the Western Seaways. They would stop at a likely place, set up a beehive cell or two, perhaps within a stone circle or on the outskirts of a bondsmen's village, preach the new faith and then move on. (In first-century Asia Minor Christianity had appealed strongly to slaves and bondsmen with its view of their equality with others before God.) These simple foundations of the early saints, which ultimately became parish churches, would bear their names. So the churches founded by or dedicated to Dewi (St. David) are called Llanddewi, followed by a distinguishing epithet such as Aberarth, Brefi or Sgyryd, quite often the name of the stream near which the foundation stood. There are dedications to Non, the mother of Dewi, who was noted for her piety. (Dewi is said to have been born and bred in the parish of Henfynyw, in which Aberaeron now stands.) It's curious that the Ceredigion Llannon should be in the equally old parish of Llansantffraid, a dedication to Ffraid, the Welsh form of the Irish Brigit, Celtic goddess of healing, learning, poetry and the crafts, whom early Christianity took over with the pagan sites. Suitably enough there are indications that Llansantffraid-Llannon, with its dedications to female saints, once had a Celtic nunnery, established by Non herself. And only five miles away is Llangwyryfon, the Church of the Virgins, and its associations with St. Ursula and the little academy for noble girls which she formed to stave off marriage to a pagan Anglo-Saxon prince. There is no other dedication to Ursula in Wales but there are at least seven more to

Ffraid. And think how much further this name Brigit travelled, of the lovely pin-ups of this century of ours, Brigitte Helm, Lollobrigida, Brigitte Bardot and all the other Britts, Brittas and Ulla-Britts of Scandinavia, perhaps not all springing from Ireland, for as Brigantia she was the particular goddess of the Brigantes of Yorkshire, her name was given to the rivers Braint in Wales and Brent in England and she is remembered in the place name Brigue in the Alps.

The word *llan* itself does not really mean either saint or church. It originally meant an enclosure, as in *perllan* (orchard) and *corlan* (sheep pen), but the practice of the early Celtic saints of fencing off a piece of ground which was then named after them or some other prominent Christian figure led to its being used for the church which was later built on the site.

So the early saints wandered about the Celtic west, St. Petroc crossing from South Wales to Cornwall and Brittany but leaving a Llanbedrog in North Wales as well, St. Samson of Dôl in Brittany visiting Cornwall, west Wales and Ireland. We are perhaps more familiar with the names of Illtud, Cadoc and Padarn, saints who founded monasteries which became great centres of learning, Llanilltud Fawr (ridiculously anglicised to Lantwit Major), Llancarfan (again in Glamorgan) and Llanbadarn Fawr, near present-day Aberystwyth. Llanbadarn was founded by the sixth-century Padarn or Paternus, a man of north Ceredigion who is unknown south of the River Aeron. The name occurs in Gwynedd, in Capel Padarn (Llanberis), Dôl Badarn, with its stout castle that fascinated Turner, Llyn Padarn and Nant Padarn, but there is no certainty that this was the same man as the founder of the great seat of learning in the Rheidol valley. Other early saints remembered in the place names of old Welsh centres are Cybi, in Llangybi and Caergybi (Holyhead), Garmon, Dyfrig, Cadog and Teilo. The heroic St. Michael, *Mihangel* in Welsh, became a popular dedication and I have noted forty-two occurrences of Llanfihangel, with its distinguishing additions. I haven't listed how many times Llanfair (St. Mary) occurs, but the dedications to Mary and Michael are all later than the first Celtic foundations.

In the Wales of the fifth and sixth centuries there were freemen and bondmen. The free aristocracy still lived in hill-forts or in some form of fortified isolation, whilst the bondmen, who farmed the land and did the menial work, lived together in hamlets or villages near to ground where the forest had been cleared for cultivation. (Until the beginning of our present century the typical inhabitants of a Welsh village or hamlet were the craftsmen, conveniently grouped together, the miller, the blacksmith, the carpenter and the wheelwright.) With the acquisition of a church such a village would become a place of general recourse and a marketing centre. It might even become a *maerdref*, or royal village, where the local king would occasionally hold court, collect his dues and settle the affairs of the district. Such an important village Trefilan, in Ceredigion, once was, though today it has only a school, a church, a vicarage, one farmhouse and one re-habilitated cottage. But the mound opposite the school suggests chieftainly associations and a very big old tithe barn shows how well the church once did out of the locality. The Norman Conquest was to strip many such villages of their importance.

I have mentioned the Celtic monasteries which were to fade away before the impact of Norman institutions. As you approach Aberyst-wyth from the east you cannot fail to notice the church which now stands on the spot where Padarn set up his *llan* and founded his monastery six hundred years before the seaside town began to rise within its Norman walls. The village was probably older still, per-haps a bondman centre linked with the Celtic *oppidum* of Pen Dinas, and this may have been Padarn's reason for his choice of site. In later centuries its distance from the sea failed to protect it from the raids of the Norsemen. Nothing remains of the early church, the monastery or the village of that day. They were all built of wood and have gone. But the stone crosses remain and are now kept in the south transept of the church, one squat and Neolithic in shape, like an early Anatolian mother-goddess, the other tall, phallic and with a pattern of tracery.

Each Celtic monastery had its own organised community, or *clas*, and every main church, like that of Llanbadarn Fawr, had its bishop or abbot. It was easier to become ordained into the Celtic church than into that of Rome and the Celtic priest was allowed to marry. There were even mixed monasteries. So the students of the University of Wales who recently asked for and got mixed Welsh-language hostels were following an ancient tradition. The Celtic priests cut their hair into a different tonsure (yet another precedent to follow?)

and they celebrated Easter on a different date. (There is a story of a curate who not so long ago announced, 'Wednesday should have been Ash Wednesday, but we forgot, so we'll have it next Thursday.') The acceptance of the Roman Easter, a feast that has since caused so much confusion, was, in the year 768, a step toward the gradual uniting of the churches, the surrender of the Celtic difference.

The New Invaders

The departure of the Roman legions from Britain in about the year 400 left open to attack those Britons who had been unfitted by three and a half centuries of Roman domination to resist these attacks. Desperate Romanised Britons of what is today southern England, after unsuccessful appeals to the Roman generals on the Continent, invited Hengist and Horsa, so the old story goes, to help deal with marauding Picts from Scotland. So began the Anglo-Saxon settlement in Britain, not as a planned invasion but as a gradual infiltration of foreigners who to some degree mixed with the Celtic inhabitants. There was no one Teutonic invasion, no general expulsion of Britons to the west. And the term Anglo-Saxon is here only a convenient simplification. Over the fifth and sixth centuries groups of Angles, Saxons, Jutes, Suevi, Franks and Friesians crossed over to south and east Britain. Slowly the newcomers took over control of the land in the south and east, sometimes by force of numbers, at other times by force of arms. Then there would be killing and burning, but we must take into account the likelihood of a decline in the Roman towns of south-east Britain similar to that which we observed at Caerwent. The steady penetration of the country by the gathering strength of these newcomers was halted by Arthur and his mounted men, perhaps from their base at Cadbury Hill, and west Britain was given decades of breathing space. Arthur never had to fight a battle in Wales, but St. Padarn, in an early biography, is said to have been in conflict with a certain king (*tyrannus*) called Arthur. Does this, coupled with the fact that Gildas, whilst mentioning the Battle of Badon, ignores his existence, suggest that Arthur, the bearer of the cross on his shield, who became in legend the ideal Christian gentleman and king, was really an unconverted Celtic pagan?

The people of Wales were not directly affected by these unhappy events but they would listen to the horror stories of refugees recounting the Anglo-Saxon burning of towns and villas and destruction of what signs of civilisation remained east of the Severn. To those Britons, now mostly Christianised and partly Romanised, the Teutonic invaders were illiterate, barbarous pagans. Some Britons from the south-west escaped over the sea to Brittany. (The Breton *Breiz* and the French *Bretagne* are forms of the word which has come down to us as the Welsh Prydain and the English Britain. The term Great Britain, which has been so jingoistically flaunted, comes to us from the French need to distinguish between Bretagne and Grande Bretagne, the bigger Britain over the sea.) These people, who were to become the Bretons, took with them stories of Arthur as well as their Brittonic tongue, which, in isolation, has evolved into modern Breton. They took with them their memories of mythology too, and place names associated with the ancient tales. I believe that the magical Brocéliande of Brittany remembers Bro Celidon, the region of Caledonia, the woodland where Tristan took Esyllt when he ran away with her.

Back in Wales the people were aware of what was happening and the early prophetic poets encouraged their hearers to prepare for the day when the Anglo-Saxon hordes would be driven back to the sea over which they had made their treacherous way to this island. History, story and verse record the centuries of unhappy relations between Wales and what was becoming England.

I remember enjoying, when I was young, a Welsh story about a boy who found the entrance to a cave high up in the Nedd valley, near Pont Nedd Fechan or Pont Neath Vaughan, and in the cave a group of warriors asleep about a round table. An iron bell hung near the opening to the cave, the boy pulled the rope and the bell clanged and echoed through the cave. The warriors rose to their feet, rubbing their eyes, and their leader called out, 'Has the hour come?' In terror the boy yelled, 'No, no' and ran out of the cave. Today this story exemplifies for me the Welsh tendency to dream rather than to act. But even so shrewd a character as Henry Tudor tried to cash in on this dream by calling his first son Arthur. Would it have been better for Wales if Arthur had lived to rule, instead of playboy Henry?

THE EMERGENCE OF WALES AS A NATION

I have said that I live in the parish of Llangwyryfon, the Church of the Virgins, which is dedicated to St. Ursula. This is the only dedication to her in Wales. There is one in London, where she can't possibly have lived, and one in Cologne, where she was martyred. Ursula was the daughter of a petty king and her beauty and intelligence were talked about outside the borders of the land still held by the Britons. An English king, still a pagan, asked for her hand in marriage for his son and sent envoys with an offer coupled with threats. Whilst her father hesitated, an angel visited Ursula and advised her to ask for three years' respite. During those years she should gather together well-born girls to study with her. At the end of the three years they all set off on a pilgrimage to Rome where, according to her *Life*, a Welshman called Kiric was then Pope. They are more likely to have sailed from Llanrhystyd in a simple ship of the Celtic waterways than in the splendidly rigged vessel of Claude's lovely picture, now in the National Gallery, London. They sailed up the Rhine to Cologne and then on to Basel, where they set out on foot for Rome. The Pope entertained them honourably until it was time for them to turn homewards. When they got back to Cologne the city was being sacked by a Teutonic pagan horde. Ursula's virgin companions were slaughtered but when the young pagan leader saw Ursula he offered her her life on condition that she married him. Ursula scornfully and piously declined the offer and received an arrow in her breast. The first version of the story is eighth century and it clearly belongs to a time before the conversion of the English. Her church at Llangwyryfon once stood within a circular churchyard, but it was pulled down during the last century, its rood screen broken up and the church was replaced by an undistinguished Victorian building. The church hall, however, is a beautifully masoned building put up in 1861 by my great-grandfather. The holy day, and holiday, of St. Ursula is something we lost at Llangwyryfon through the Reformation but her name, Wrsla in Welsh, occurs in more recent parish records.

During the seventh and eighth centuries, the old Celtic tribal divisions, which had simplified the Roman task of conquest in Wales, persisted in the four main kingdoms of Gwynedd, Powys, Deheubarth and Morgannwg. There was as yet no need for a common front between these kingdoms to face an invader. That was to come. An

49

English success at the Battle of Deorham in 577 enabled the new-comers to drive through Bath to Gloucester and the Bristol Channel. In the north the Welsh, allied with the pagan Penda, king of Mercia, had a series of successes against Northumbria. Then came defeats, culminating with Winwaed Field in 655. The Welsh had now been cut off from their Celtic cousins in North Britain and in Devon and Cornwall. There were to be no more excursions to the north, except in the imagination of our twelfth-century heroic poets; for as the Brittonic language and culture were swamped in North Britain the Welsh absorbed into their own culture the poetry and traditions of the north, the tales of Rheged and Gododdin, the prowess of Owain and Urien Rheged and the poetry of Aneirin and Taliesin. So to the English the people of this shrunken land of ours became known as Welsh, which means foreigners. Our name for ourselves, Cymry, which means people living together in a region, had been used for the North Britons too, there are traces of it in names like Cumberland, but now it stood only for the people of what we today call Cymru, Wales. Sir J. E. Lloyd, in his *History of Wales*, has said, 'Thus the year 655 forms an epoch of great importance in the history of the Welsh people; it closes the period of definition, during which they were gradually marked off from the other inhabitants of these islands and constituted a separate people; it brings upon the stage a nation, isolated and self-contained, dependent henceforth upon its own re-sources for its development.'

This isolation of the Welsh people was confirmed when Offa, King of Mercia, built the great dyke which bears his name between the years 757 and 796. Offa's Dyke established a frontier which remains very close to the present boundary of England and Wales. It ran from near Prestatyn in the north to where the River Wye reaches the Severn Estuary. Long stretches of it can still be followed and you can get a pamphlet to guide you if you care to walk it or pick it up at a con-venient point. It is well to remember that it was not a fortification but a demarcation line, to which the Welsh of Powys and Morgannwg must have agreed, physically establishing the limits of Mercia. Be-hind it the Welsh settled down to being a nation, not just a cut-off group of Celtic tribes.

The Struggle for Unity: Tribulations and Laws

Not that life behind Offa's Dyke became continuously peaceful. Before and after its construction there was bitter conflict, raid and counter-raid, the burning of homesteads. The old anti-Welsh rhyme must refer to this period:

> Taffy was a Welshman,
>   Taffy was a thief;
> Taffy came to my house
>   and stole a leg of beef.
> I went to Taffy's house,
>   Taffy was in bed;
> I picked up a chopper
>   and chopped off his head.

What we have here is the cattle-raid over the border and the driving off of cattle on the hoof. Hence the leg of beef. Then the retaliatory raid at night, the killing and the burning.

The most poignant reflection of those dark, troubled years comes to us in a series of poems associated with and attributed to the old chieftain Llywarch Hen and the princely girl Heledd, daughter of Cyndrwyn. These poems have been edited and annotated by Sir Ifor Williams in *Canu Llywarch Hen*. The events recounted took place in eastern Powys and western Mercia and Sir Ifor has shown that in the form we have them the poems are the ninth-century work of an unknown poet and that they may be the recorded verse high-spots of prose sagas which have been lost. Like Cunedda, Llywarch Hen, Llywarch the Old, began his life in north Britain but died in Powys after seeing his twenty-four sons killed in the relentless war against Mercia. In a tremendous 'Lament' he addresses his wooden crook, his only companion and support now that his sons are dead. He thinks back to his days of companionship, drinking, love and war, and bewails his miserable condition. He is plagued by the four things he most detests:

pas a heneint heint a hoed . . .
(coughing and old age, disease and longing)

He ends his complaint:

> The girls don't love me, no one frequents me,
>   I can't get about.
> O death, why don't you set me free?
>
> No sleep nor mirth comes to me now
>   that Llawr and Gwên are killed:
> I'm rotting carrion now, I'm old.
>
> A wretched fate was doomed for Llywarch
>   on his birth night;
> a long labour of grief that never grew light.

Heledd's laments are even more passionate, for she is young, her brothers have been killed and the life she knew is in pieces. The hall of her favourite brother, Cynddylan, at Pengwern, probably Shrewsbury today, has been burnt by the English and she mourns for its passing in agonised stanzas, fourteen of the fifteen stanzas beginning with the words *Stafell Gyndylan*. Again I translate some of these verses:

> Cynddylan's hall is dark tonight,
>   without fire, without music:
> my tears wear away each cheek.
>
> No lights hang in Cynddylan's hall
>   since the English killed
> Cynddylan and Elfyn of Powys land.
>
> Cynddylan's hall is dark tonight;
>   of Cyndrwynyn's breed
> Cynon and Gwiawn and Gwyn are dead.
>
> Cynddylan's hall stabs me each hour,
>   after the great bustle
> I've seen beneath its roof trestle.

In a more frightening poem she speaks of the eagle of Pengwern which will that night feast on Cynddylan's flesh, and the horror of it all is summed up in a poem on *Y Dref Wen*, the White Town, probably Whittington near Oswestry:

> White town between Trenn and Trodwyd,
>> more torn shields came from battle
> than homing cattle.

> White town between Trenn and Trafal,
>> there was more blood on your field's face
> than ploughshare's trace.

The gloom of a benighted warrior in these conditions is expressed in an astonishing three-stanza poem which was saved for us by being written into the margin of the ninth-century *Juvencus* manuscript. What understanding I have of this I owe to Sir Ifor Williams's interpretation, but I have attempted to translate it:

> I shall not argue even for an hour tonight,
>> my retinue is not over great;
> I and my Frank, about our cauldron.

> I shall not sing or laugh or kiss tonight
>> though we have drunk flowing mead,
> I and my Frank about our bowl.

> Let no one ask me for mirth tonight,
>> my retinue is poor.
> Two lords may boast together, one only speaks.

His companions are lost or dead and he has only the company of a foreign mercenary, a Frank, with whom he cannot converse on equal terms.

These were the agonies of a torn frontier region, but well back from Offa's Dyke all wasn't gloom and life could be normal and gay. A poem somehow copied into *Llyfr Aneirin* but clearly not a part of the *Gododdin* gives us a mother talking, or singing, to her little boy about his father's prowess as a hunter. It comes to us in a ninth-century form but one can only guess at its ultimate age, for a reference to a Derwent river points to a time when Brittonic was spoken in what is today England. We shall never know where or when little Dinogad and his mother lived but the poem must have been apt for singing or reciting in ninth-century Wales.

From the ninth century too there survives another happy poem, this time in the *Book of Taliesin*, in praise of Tenby. Far from Offa's Dyke, well away from Mercia and Wessex and before the arrival of the ravaging Norsemen, there existed security in which Celtic bards and warriors could feast, drink and enjoy poetry, heroic tales and music in the hall of a generous chieftain, all, however, with still a suggestion of the old Celtic internecine strife. Here's my version of one stanza:

> There's a fine fortress over the wide water,
>> an invincible stronghold with the sea circling it.
> Ask Britain who is master here;
>> chief of Erbin's line, may it be yours.
> There was a retinue and song in a wattled place,
>> an eagle above the sky and a path for the pale-cheeked
> before a brilliant lord, ready to set out,
>> of widespread fame, a leader who forms ranks.

Another stanza tells us of the bards over their cups of mead. These poems are lucky survivals which give us glimpses of a life which history tells us little about, but poetry annihilates time and while we retain our language we can make these immediate contacts with ways of thinking and acting of a millennium ago which still seem natural to us today.

Three great names are associated with the attempt to bind this new nation of Wales into a country with one leader, one government. They are Rhodri Mawr in the ninth century, Hywel Dda in the tenth and Gruffydd ap Llywelyn in the eleventh. In 844, Rhodri Mawr, the Great, came to the throne of a Gwynedd which had been made strong by his father Merfyn Frych, a descendant of that Llywarch Hen whose misfortunes we have been considering. Rhodri inherited Powys from his uncle and went on to annex the southern kingdom of Seisyllwg on the death of his brother-in-law, the King of Ceredigion. So he ruled from Anglesey to Gower but not the whole of Wales, for the kingdom of Dyfed, south of Cardigan and west of Carmarthen, and the south-eastern segment of Morgannwg, Gwent, Brycheiniog and Glywysing remained apart. He had six sons and when he died his domains were divided between them, once more into little kingdoms.

But the brothers stuck together in their attitude to Mercia and to the kings of South Wales. An unhappy result of this was that these South Wales kings, in order to protect themselves against Mercia and against Rhodri's heirs, allied themselves with Alfred the Great and did homage to him. Rhodri, however, had done much for Wales. He had shown that it was possible for the country to be united under a strong leader and he had kept the Vikings at bay. Their destructive raids, with the looting of monasteries and the carrying off of slaves for sale elsewhere, became far more frequent after his death. Great Orme's Head, near Llandudno, Pen y Gograth in Welsh, is probably named after the Norse leader Horm, whom Rhodri killed in battle.

There would not be so many Norse place names around the coasts of North and South Wales if the Vikings had only raided and ravaged, and had not settled there too. North Wales has Priestholm, the Skerries, Bardsey and Anglesey, named after one Ongul. These are the names of islands and suggest a purely maritime interest, almost Wales viewed from the sea. Even more frequent island and coastal names in south-west Wales suggest a similar point of view but here there were undoubtedly mercantile settlements. We have Norse island names, Caldey, Gateholm, Grassholm, Ramsey, Skokholm and Skomer; but Fishguard, Lydstep and Milford record settlements where the Norsemen found good harbours from which to carry on their trade. Along the South Wales coast there are more harbour, rock and island names, Swansea, Worms Head, Burry Holms, the Tusker Rocks, Flatholm; but eastwards from the Gower Peninsula inland names assert agricultural as well as mercantile settlement. There are Laleston and Lamby and there was once a Vallis Danorum near Stormy Down. In Cardiff there was Womanby and the city still has a Womanby Street. The Norsemen taught us the importance of sea power, widened our view of foreign trade and then peacefully merged into the population, Glamorgan probably getting the greatest contribution of their adventurous blood.

The tenth century saw an even more famous leader unite a large part of the country. The Welsh (for writing in English one must, I suppose, use the English word for the *Cymry*) were now a separate people and they had a separate language but as yet they had no code of law to which the whole country could refer. This was given them by Hywel Dda, Hywel the Good. His name is pronounced Howell, which is its anglicised form. The Celts had long had their tribal laws which may not have varied materially over the whole of Celtica. What Hywel did was not to invent laws but codify existing practice and issue this code to his people in organised form, as Justinian had done for Byzantium. Hywel would have learnt about Byzantine law during his visit to Rome in 928. But he had an example nearer home for such regularisation of law as well as for the visit to Rome, in the person of Alfred the Great, whom Hywel much admired. As a king of South Wales Hywel had inherited the condition of vassalage to the English crown and he seems to have accepted this situation without protest. When Idwal Foel, King of Gwynedd, rebelled against the English and was killed for his pains, Hywel attacked Idwal's sons and took the kingdom from them. Powys fell to him at the same time, as well as the kingdom of Rhwng Gwy a Hafren, roughly present-day Radnorshire. The kingdom of Dyfed already belonged to him, so Hywel came to rule over a domain much greater than that of Rhodri Mawr. Brycheiniog, Morgannwg and Gwent still stood out from this union.

Hywel Dda had a hunting lodge at Tŷ Gwyn (Whitland) in the heart of his kingdom of Dyfed, where two centuries later the Cistercian order built a great parent monastery. Here, according to a twelfth-century manuscript of the laws, Hywel called together representatives from every part of his domain to argue out and agree upon an acceptable text of the laws. The result covers the everyday life of the country in extraordinary detail. The position of every man and woman in society is defined and their rights specified. The compensation they must be paid for wrong done is laid down, with the damages they must pay for their own wrongdoing. For this purpose the value of almost anything a man or woman might possess was laid down. What an age it was, for the value of a thing to be so stable that it could be incorporated into the law of the land! The Celtic concept of a civil service was confirmed, so that the rights of the hall poet, the blacksmith, the falconer and the doctor could not be infringed. The value of all domesticated animals was set down in detail, with special attention given to horses, hunting dogs and bees. A heavy fine was to be imposed on anyone who robbed a hawk's nest.

A woman's financial rights in marriage and in divorce or separation were very carefully guarded and made almost too favourable in some situations. She did not lose her share of her husband's possessions if she left him for any of these three reasons: his contracting leprosy, the absence of sexual intercourse in the relationship, or his bad breath. Honest dealing was insisted upon, in marriage as in business, and a man who married a declared virgin and found her not to be so could strike her, but not kill her, turn her out of his house in a shaming manner, with her shirt cut short at her waist, and pay no damages for having had her. The provisions of the law swing from the primitive to the sophisticated but are still in many ways more just than the English Common Law under which we live today. A notable example is the common responsibility of a family for the criminal actions of one of its members and the insistence on specific compensation for insult or attack or robbery, a concept which English law is only recently getting round to, having long been satisfied with the apprehension and imprisonment of the thief, who may well have salted away whatever he has stolen, and bringing small consolation to the robbed.

Nothing is left of Hywel's hunting lodge and very little of Alba Landa, the Norman monastery, but it is still worth while searching out the few bits of masonry in their lovely green setting, and in that peace thinking of that first kind of Welsh parliament called there by a remarkable king who, in emulation of an English model, did more perhaps than any other man to stimulate the pride of the Welsh in their culture.

On the death of Hywel Dda the dispossessed sons of Idwal Foel struck to regain their lordship over Gwynedd and Powys. In the south, where the law of gavelkind, the splitting up of a man's property between his sons when he died, might have further dissipated the kingdom put together by Hywel by treating it as a private possession to be shared by the inheriting sons, the situation was saved by the early death of two of Hywel's three sons. So by 954, Owain ap Hywel Dda was sole master of Deheubarth, which he ruled for thirty-five years. Having failed, at a battle near Llanrwst, to recapture the North, Owain, with the help of his sons, worked off his frustrations on neighbouring, stand-offish Morgannwg in a number of pillaging raids. His son Maredudd (Meredith in English) reconquered Gwynedd and for the last thirteen years of the tenth century the kingdom of Hywel Dda was restored. It's interesting that to bolster up his claim to the kingship of Wales Owain ap Hywel took pride in his descent, on his mother's side, from Votiporix and Aircol Lawhir, the third-century Irish invader of South Wales. But not even the need for some sort of common front against the destructive raids of the Norsemen and the ever-present danger from England could hold Wales together for long.

The turn from the tenth to the eleventh century saw the fragmentation of Wales by men ambitious for regional control rather than with a vision of an united country. New men arose, from outside the royal line of Rhodri Mawr, the most notable being Llywelyn ap Seisyll, bearer of a name to become famous in England as Cecil. This Llywelyn married a great-granddaughter of Hywel Dda and so gave his son Gruffydd descent from Hywel and from Rhodri Mawr. And this Gruffydd ap Llywelyn did what his great ancestors Hywel and Rhodri had failed to do; he joined the whole of Wales, Gwynedd, Powys, Deheubarth, Morgannwg and Gwent into one kingdom, so that Wales for a few glorious years became united under one king. Gruffydd is said to have been a lazy, unpromising boy, but once he inherited the thrones of Gwynedd and Powys he took on strength and showed courage and ruthless determination. The story is a complex one of the elimination of Welsh rivals who, like Gruffydd himself, occasionally allied themselves with Saxons, Mercians and Norsemen. Gruffydd's first act when he came to the northern throne in 1039 was to fall upon the men of Mercia at Rhydygroes, on the fertile plain near where the Severn enters England, between Welshpool and Shrewsbury. The attack was unexpected, the Mercians were destroyed and Edwin, their leader, brother of Leofric and brother-in-law of Lady Godiva, was killed. Thirteen years later Gruffydd won another great victory at Leominister. He had shown not only that the English could be beaten but that they could be beaten on their own ground. The lesson was to ring in the heads of Welsh leaders right up to the Battle of Bosworth. And there were Normans in the English army routed at Leominster. Under Edward the Confessor the Normans were growing more influential in England. Gruffydd was aware of them as a potential danger to Wales and this was one reason for his attack.

It was not to last. In 1063 Earl Harold of Wessex took advantage of the temporary weakness of Mercia to march quickly through and attack the Welsh leader's stronghold at Rhuddlan. North Wales was ravaged while Gruffydd escaped by sea. There was to be no return to power, for Gruffydd died at the treacherous hand of one of his own followers. Three years later Harold was to die with an arrow through his eye at Hastings, on the day the Normans conquered England.

Gruffydd ap Llywelyn had shown that all Wales could be united under a strong king, he had made the border safe for the Welsh and had married the daughter of his friend and ally Aelfgar, Earl of Mercia. He turned back the slow tide of English penetration of Wales and recovered much territory east of Offa's Dyke. No future leader was to claim descent from him but more than one was to be inspired by his achievements.

Apart from their being increasingly conscious of their Welshness and of speaking a different language from their neighbours to the east, what kind of society did these leaders defend, what was it that would be slowly whittled away in the centuries of growing Norman and Anglo-Norman influence and domination? It is in the language rather than the landscape of Wales that we must look for records of changes that were to come to the way the Welsh lived, under the impact of the Normans, for changes in the meaning of words often reflect social change. Take the word *gwlad*, meaning country. For a Welshman today this means Wales when he says *fy ngwlad*, my country, though the word also has the same secondary meaning as in English, that is country as opposed to town. *Gwlad* originally meant the land ruled by one man and it was the attempts by different leaders to make all Wales their dominion that gave the word its modern meaning.

Another word that has changed its meaning is *cenedl*, which today means nation. Before the Welsh became one people, to whatever degree that unity has been reached, *cenedl*, never an exact term for long, variously stood for tribe, clan or sub-clan, or for the kinship of free men descended from a common ancestor of note, kinship usually reckoned to the ninth degree. Within these degrees of kinship there were established mutual responsibilities, those to the fourth degree, for instance, being greater than those to the ninth. All this was carefully laid down in the laws. It is no wonder that today we acknowledge family relationships over a much wider field than they do in England, or that in the quick familiarity one establishes with fellow Welsh people in train or bus or pub one often discovers a family relationship. Cousins, aunts and uncles proliferate happily in Wales, in town as well as country.

There was a fairly rigid class system. At the top were the royal families, most of whom claimed descent, as we have seen, from Cunedda or, in South Wales, from the third-century invading Irish chieftain Eochaid Allmuir. Most Welsh men and women belonged to the class of *boneddig* or free man, to which Welsh descent gave them the right. If they inherited or acquired land they became *uchelwyr*, or high men, but their status was not thereby raised above that of free men. They were simply wealthier.

Below the free man was the *aillt* or *taeog*, the villein or bond man. *Taeog* is today a term of contempt for a servile person. The bond man could have possessions and certain limited rights, he was the labourer, tied as a serf to his lord's land and, in principle, he was not allowed to hunt or fish, or to practise any of the highest crafts, such as those of the falconer, the blacksmith, the cleric or the professional poet. It was, however, possible for him to obtain, from the king or from his lord, the right to practise one of these crafts and in so doing become a free man. Bond men are thought to have been the descendants of the pre-Celtic inhabitants of the country, kept over the long centuries in this servile state.

Then there was a class of *alltud* or exile, a foreigner who was either a refugee from some other country, a hostage, or just a wanderer. He could have no claim on the use of land, which was all either private property or the common property of a *cenedl* of free men, but if he settled and became a villein he qualified for the rights of personal protection. Today a Welsh *alltud* is one who for some reason lives outside Wales. Lowest of all in the social scale were the slaves, or *caethion*, who enjoyed very few rights. They were always foreigners and often the captives of some war, but they are not thought to have been numerous at any time. Another type of foreigner, less frequently met with, was the *ffranc* or Frank, a foreign mercenary so-called presumably from his Frankish origin. We met him in the ninth-century *Juvencus* poem and his name occurs in Nant Ffrancon, or Franks' Brook.

CHAPTER II

Conquest and Resistance

The Normans

The Welsh were now to face a tougher and more determined enemy who, after his quick reduction of England, was to take over two centuries to subdue the Welsh, centuries which brought great changes to the landscape as well as to the social structure of Wales. Welsh tourist propaganda bristles with sunlit pictures of great Norman castles, most of them sustained today by the Ministry of Environment and much visited in the summer months. They are the most spectacular buildings in the country and they are splendidly sited in the landscape. They provide a setting for all kinds of trivial and important occasions, but many of us in Wales continue to regard them as the mailed fists which crushed the attempts of our leaders to unite the country in a demand for freedom. We have a deeper and warmer feeling for the tough-looking, less decorated and fanciful castles of the Welsh princes, Dolbadarn, Castell y Bere and Carreg Cennen. The most splendid castles are in the border country, the bases for Norman attack, and at strategic points along the coast, their far-flung fortresses, but it mustn't be thought that the Normans put up these magnificent fortifications immediately they got to Wales. They did not then know how to build them. Their first constructions of earthwork and wooden stockade were not much stronger than a Roman fort for a one-night stand and depended on the comparative weakness of a possible attacker. They were certainly not as strong as a Celtic hill-fort.

I have already suggested that the eleventh-century explosion of the Normans was in many ways like that of the Celts in the first millennium B.C. They had no grand imperialistic design, nor did they retain a centre from which their various drives could be co-ordinated, a centre such as Rome was for the Romans, who also had no grand plan for empire-building, but spread out piecemeal as the occasion demanded. The Normans were a military aristocracy who broke out in different directions. Since their settlement in Normandy in the year 911 they had given up their Viking habits and now, a century and a half later, they felt strong and ambitious enough to make further leaps of domination. So ruthless, adventurous men set out, in the ships they knew so well how to handle, to carve out new kingdoms for themselves with the sword wherever they found weakness, in France itself, in Britain, in southern Italy and Sicily, in the Crimea and in the Near East. 1096 saw their first involvement in crusades to liberate Jerusalem, which had been taken by Seljuk Turks, and on their campaigns and journeys the Normans became familiar with the military architecture of the Armenians along the southern coast of Anatolia. The Armenians had derived the castellated wall ultimately from the Hittites of the second millennium B.C., walls which were not unlike the fifth-century fortifications of Constantinople, but they had made skilful and effective elaborations which the Normans seized upon and further elaborated. Montgomery is a good place to observe the difference between the first and second types of Norman castle-building. In 1071, only five years after Hastings, Roger de Montgomery began his drive into mid-Wales along the obvious route of the Severn valley. His first castle, a little to the north-west of the present town of Trefaldwyn or Montgomery, was built to command an ancient and important ford across the Severn. It's still called *Yr Hen Domen*, the Old Mound, and the mound or motte of the castle is still there, though somewhat obscured by trees and undergrowth. You can walk along the earthwork which once surrounded the court-yard or bailey, remembering that this would have been stockaded with wood and that the baron's hall would have been of wood as well. The stone castle came many years later.

William the Conqueror's plan for dealing with the Welsh was to create three earldoms along the border, of Chester for the north, Shrewsbury for mid-Wales and Hereford for the south. These he bestowed on friends and relatives, giving them a free hand to invade and seize what they could of Wales in the hope that he could after-wards control them. Thus were established the Welsh Marches. Not that the Conqueror left Wales entirely to his border barons. In 1081 he marched right along the coast of South Wales to St. Davids, not to make the famous pilgrimage but to show his strength in this vulnerable part of the country. Castles were to spring up in his wake, again at first of earthwork and wooden stockade. One such was built at Pembroke and, before its replacement by the splendid castle which still stands, a romantic incident occurred there. At the beginning of the twelfth century Gerald de Windsor was custodian of the fortress of Pembroke and Henry I gave him as wife the dangerously beautiful Nêst, daughter of Rhys ap Tewdwr. She had already been seduced by the king, whilst under his care, and had borne him a son. She was to have many children, a famous son, Robert Fitzstephen by Stephen, Constable of Cardigan Castle, several sons to her husband and a daughter who was to be the mother of Gerald the Welshman. Owain ap Cadwgan, her second cousin and son of the Lord of Powys, fell in love with her, made a night attack on the fortress of Pembroke, burnt it to the ground and carried off its first lady.

Once a stone castle had been built the Normans put their usual plan into operation, a plan which had already worked in France itself, in the regions of the Dordogne and the Garonne. They encouraged the growth of a town in the shadow of the castle walls and then they walled that town to protect it against the Welsh, for these towns were completely foreign establishments. They gave the new towns stone churches, and you may notice how near these churches are to the castle in places like Pembroke or Aberystwyth. The creation of these new complexes of castle, church and walled town had a curious effect upon the landscape of Wales. As you drive through the country you may be puzzled by the situation of strangely isolated churches. When one sees a church one expects to see a village huddled about it, so one asks how this isolation came about. As the walled towns grew, markets were established outside their gates, as at Caernarfon, so that the Welsh country-folk, denied free entry into these towns, could sell their produce outside. Then Welsh craftsmen were accepted into the towns and eventually everyone was allowed to come and go and settle. So a Welsh settlement around an original *llan* would dwindle slowly to nothing, the wooden houses decayed and fell, or were not restored after a fire, the centre of commerce moved and the church was left high and dry in a setting of fields, with perhaps one farmhouse as neighbour. A conspicuous example is the church of Llywel, just off the A40 between Brecon and Llandovery. Bernard de Neufmarché, who grabbed and ruled Brycheiniog (Breconshire) till his death in 1125, built a castle at Trecastell, the site of which is indicated by a mound on the hill-top. The town which came into being at the castle's foot gradually drained away all life from the village of Llywel, though Trecastell still remains in the parish of Llywel. By today even the main road has abandoned Llywel Church to its peace. Thus, from a train or a trunk road, one observes these lonely church towers, monuments to centres of culture and commerce that have faded almost to nothing.

To replace the Celtic religious houses the Normans introduced cells, offshoots of great houses they had already established in England or of the original Dominican monasteries of Normandy. The earliest of these were in South Wales, since the Norman penetration ...ne more quickly there than in the north, under the protection of such castles as Chepstow, Cardiff, Cydweli, Carmarthen and Cardigan. One was established near Llanbadarn Castle, which pre-dates that of Aberystwyth, to replace the declining monastery of Padarn. These cells or priories were then endowed with Welsh lands and were highly unpopular outside Anglo-Norman society.

Other Welsh lands were appropriated for the introduction of the Norman manorial system, and these again were chiefly in the fertile lowlands of South Wales. The same system had been imposed on the English but here in Wales there had to be divergences from the usual Norman practice. Because of gavelkind, holdings had always been small in Wales and as a result the new manorial estates and the very fields were smaller than those of England and Normandy. Another difference was the division of manors into a Welshry and an Englishry, roughly *blaenau* and *bro* in Welsh, *blaenau* the heads of the valleys, *bro* the lower region, the better land being given to English tenants, the rougher, higher part left to the Welsh. Driving along the road from Cardiff to Swansea you will still see a sign to Welsh St Donats. In the Englishry the land holders paid rent and promised two or three days a week of work on the lord's land, known as week-work, and boon-work at certain times during the year, as at harvest time. In the upland Welshry men paid tribute to the lord of the manor but other-wise lived their own life very much in the old Celtic way. And it's in the narrow valleys and on the rounded hills of Glamorgan that some degree of Welshness has persisted to this day, in contrast with the anglicisation of the Vale of Glamorgan, *Bro Morgannwg*.

In spite of the Conqueror's triumphant progress through South Wales in 1081, little conquering of the country was done until the last years of the century. Rhys ap Tewdwr, father of Nêst, descendant of Hywel Dda and king of Deheubarth, must have come to terms with the Normans, for he appears to have conceded a kind of vassal-age. But he suffered little outside interference in the governing of his kingdom and Rhys had more trouble with Welsh rivals than with the foreign enemy. Only in Brycheiniog did the Normans achieve any considerable penetration before Rhys's death in 1093. But by 1099 they held most of South Wales.

The Norman drive into North Wales did not fare so well. A new leader, Gruffudd ap Cynan, appeared from Ireland and established a powerful Gwynedd which was to plague the Normans for two hundred years. Gruffudd's father, Cynan, had gone into exile in Ire-land after his father, Iago ab Idwal Foel, had died in internecine Welsh warfare. Cynan married the grand-daughter of a Norse king of Dublin and in Dublin his son Gruffudd was born and bred to be a Viking as well as a Welshman. Before the Normans had become a serious threat to Gwynedd, Gruffudd saw his opportunity to assert the claim his descent gave him to the kingdom. His first attempt in 1075 failed. To many Welshmen Gruffudd at first seemed to be just another Viking raider and his Norse mercenaries, whose payment depended on success, were unpopular. Two years later a second attempt failed. This time Gruffudd attempted to discipline his Norse followers, for whom loot was the natural and traditional fruit of victory, and when balked of this they forced him to return to Ireland. A victorious campaign thus went for nothing. Having twice failed after landing at Abermenai, he sailed in 1081 for a little harbour called Porth Clais, near St. Davids. Here he was blessed by the wise and learned Sulien of Llanbadarn, one of the last two independent bishops of Tyddewi, St. Davids. This time Gruffudd had a Welsh ally, another exile, Rhys ap Tewdwr, who was re-establishing himself in Deheubarth, and after a victory in Dyfed he pushed on northward to seize Gwynedd and begin his checkered but finally successful struggle against the Normans. When he died he had made possible the strength of his great son Owain Gwynedd.

So the struggle against the Norman kings of England and their barons of the Marches flickered, died down and flared up again through Wales from north to south. Effective opposition to Anglo-Norman power could only come from a strong leader with a considerable part of Wales in his possession. Gavelkind meant the break-up of estates, and kingdoms were, unfortunately, no exceptions to this, for once every generation the new leader could make himself strong only at the expense of brothers and cousins. Internal strife was often as destructive as the punitive expeditions from beyond the border and Ceredigion suffered terribly during these early years of the twelfth century. For some years this old kingdom formed part of the domain of the spineless Cadwgan of Powys. When Owain, son of Cadwgan and a much more spirited character, carried off Nêst, wife of Gerald of Windsor, in 1109, Henry I recruited two cousins and rivals of Owain and fell upon hapless Ceredigion in revenge for the insult to his underling. There was widespread destruction and burning, the wholesale killing and expulsion of the inhabitants from Llanbadarn Fawr down to Cardigan. Owain escaped with his father to Ireland. Cadwgan then made his peace with Henry and Owain slipped back into Ceredigion, where he gathered together a reckless band of adventurers. On a raid into Dyfed Owain killed an important Fleming called William of Brabant. Once more Henry stepped destructively in and Ceredigion became a marcher lordship. (What happened to Nêst during these violent years isn't known, but she lived for about thirty years after her abduction.) Gilbert de Clare immediately built castles at Aberteifi (Cardigan) and Aberystwyth, though well to the south of the present town and castle in the latter case. Other castles followed throughout the province to tighten the Norman hold on Ceredigion. It was the end of Llanbadarn as a Celtic Christian foundation: the abbey and its endowments went to the Benedictine Abbey of St. Peter's, Gloucester, and Benedictine monks set up a Norman priory at the old Welsh seat of learning. The wooden structures of the old Celtic *clas* disappeared and nothing remains to remind us of the great days of Llanbadarn but traditions and two impressive stone crosses. The present church dates from the thirteenth century. After all these changes and upheavals Owain ap Cadwgan himself came to terms with the king, went with him to Normandy and was there knighted by him. In 1116 he fought alongside Gerald of Windsor against Welsh rivals, but the fearful grudge still rankled and Gerald and his men seized an opportunity to murder Owain at Ystrad Rwnws, a few miles east of Carmarthen, near where the River Cothi joins the Tywi.

I have told this story in disproportionate, though perhaps insufficient, detail in order to exemplify the ordeals and incomprehensible changes suffered by the common people of Wales during these centuries of resistance to the Normans.

Deheubarth, that is South Wales, also produced its hero, another Gruffudd, this time ap Rhys, who, like Gruffudd ap Cynan, returned from exile in Ireland to harry the Normans at Swansea, Llandovery and Narberth and to settle down eventually at Caeo, near the gold mines of Pumsaint. There, to him and his wife Gwenllian, daughter of Gruffudd ap Cynan, was born the boy who was to become the Lord Rhys, ruler of Deheubarth.

So the Norman attempt to sweep aside Welsh resistance as they had done that of England was only partially successful. The Anglo-Norman kings and the powerful border barons found that they could not do without the collaboration of Welsh chieftains. From this followed the bitter and bloody internal conflicts and the tight-rope walking on the part of Welsh leaders between some degree of vassalage to the king and independent control of their lands.

A very old device of conquerors wishing to modify a recalcitrant population is to plant a settlement of foreigners amongst them and to give the settlement especial favour. I mentioned the important Fleming killed by Owain ap Cadwgan without explaining how a Fleming came to be in south-west Wales. I quote Humphrey Lhuyd's account, published in *The Historie of Cambria* in 1584. 'The yeare 1108, the rage of the sea did overflow and drowne a great part of the lowe countrie of Flanders, in such sort that the inhabitants were driven to seeke themselves other dwelling places, who came to King Henrie, and desired him to give them some void place to remaine in:

who being verie liberall of that which was not his owne, gave them the land of Ros in Dyvet or Westwales, where Pembroke, Tenby and Haverford are now built, and there they remaine to this daie, as may well be perceived by their speach and conditions, farre differing from the rest of the countrie.'

What was true in 1584 is still true today. English is now the language of these long-standing immigrants but as soon as you leave the southern slopes of Preseli you will notice Flemish names on shops. This part of Wales is popularly known, though not to the Welsh, as little England beyond Wales. I went into a shop in the main street of Haverfordwest during the week of the National Eisteddfod held there in 1972 and couldn't help hearing, so loud and confident was the voice, one woman say to another, 'I believe the Welsh have something on here this week.' Thus came into existence an Englishry and a Welshry on the most conspicuous scale of all, but still leaving the moorland and rough hill pasture to the natives.

So the Norman plan was put into operation and towns, which may seem typically Welsh to visitors today, sprang up, in South Wales first of all, towns like Tenby, Pembroke, Cydwely and Cardigan, to be followed later by Denbigh, Rhuddlan, Conwy, Caernarfon and Beaumaris, towns which for long years were purely foreign centres. The balance of Welsh religious life had been deeply disturbed by the new priories which, by taking the place of the old Celtic foundations, were an integral part of the long-term Norman plan for the weakening of the spirit of resistance, a plan not so ruthless perhaps but just as effective as the destruction of the Druids of Môn by Suetonius Paulinus, or, some would say, comparable to the effect of television in English on Wales today.

But resistance was not crushed. From 1153 on, the century is dominated by two great figures, Owain Gwynedd in the north and the Lord Rhys in the south. When Gruffudd ap Cynan died in 1137 he left his son Owain a solid foundation for a strong kingdom in North Wales. Owain was known as Owain Gwynedd to distinguish him from another Owain ap Gruffudd of this age, who became known as Owain Cyfeiliog. Owain inherited from his father a tradition of patronage of poetry. There is an old tradition that Gruffudd brought poets and musicians with him from Ireland; we know that he had an official harpist and he is credited with bringing order to the craft of verse. The poets certainly flourished in the security and in the atmosphere of a new heroic age which came to Wales with these great leaders of the twelfth and thirteenth centuries. Meilyr, the first great poet of this heroic revival, lamented Gruffudd's death and remembered his coming from Ireland:

> After green waves topped with foam
> prancing stallions carry the armour. . .,

and the feasts for which he was famous:

> Before Cynan's son went below the gravel
> there was mead and spiced ale to be had in his hall.

Meilir's son Gwalchmai inherited not only his father's land but his position as court poet to Owain Gwynedd, a practice associated more with Ireland than with Wales. Gwalchmai and Hywel ab Owain Gwynedd and Cynddelw wrote not only of war but also about ˗˗˗˗ape and the beauty and charm of women. One wonders how much of these new elements in bardic verse is traceable to an Irish influence too, remembering that Hywel was Owain Gwynedd's son by an Irish girl called Pyfog.

There was plenty of warfare to write about and this was done in awareness of the earlier heroic age of confrontation with Anglo-Saxon invaders and with echoes of Aneirin and Taliesin. This poetry makes difficult reading for us today and the very leaders praised probably understood only enough of it to know that they were being lauded in the grand manner. Hywel ab Owain, as a king's son, was free to write as he pleased and he is the most comprehensible of the poets. It is he who blends these elements of love, nature and campaigning into the finest poetry:

> I love its household and its strong buildings
> and at its lord's wish to go to war.
> I love its strand and its mountains
> its castle near the woods and its fine lands,
> its water meadows and its valleys,
> its white gulls and its lovely women.

That was the mid-twelfth-century North Wales of Hywel ab Owain.

Go to Aberffraw in south-west Anglesey (its people today call it Bérffro) and you may find it hard to believe that it was for centuries the capital of Gwynedd, and of a large part of Wales. But the essentials were there, a fortifiable headland overlooking a westward-facing creek where boats could be brought up and not far from Abermenai, the mouth of the Menai Straits. Behind it were great stretches of fertile land and beyond Abermenai the mountains of Snowdonia rose in a defensive wall, the harsh, rocky passes a deterrent to the enemy. The island was a refuge when campaigns went wrong and its security fostered the spirit of resistance. It was from this base that Owain Gwynedd extended his control over North Wales, without ever wishing to take over South Wales as well. He defeated the Normans and was defeated by them but rather than waste himself and his country in continuing struggle, and seeing a chance of accommodation with the line of Anjou which had come to the English throne, he accepted the title of prince instead of king and with it the Norman feudal link. But he retained an unusual degree of autonomy, claiming the right, for instance, to appoint the bishop at Bangor. He died in 1170 and was buried in Bangor Cathedral, where his simple, arched tomb may be seen in the south wall. He was a great ruler and he was adequately praised by the poets of his court. Gwalchmai began a poem:

> I praise the generous one of the stock of Aeneas;
> I praise the bold lion, the lightning flash of honour;
> I praise the most splendid of Britain's princes
> and the fine kingdom of golden Owain.

Owain had not only extended and strengthened the land of Gwynedd but made possible the careers of his famous descendants, Llywelyn the Great and Llywelyn the Last.

The trick of building stone castles, which the Normans had learnt in the Near East, was quickly passed on to the Welsh chieftains. Owain Gwynedd is thought to have built the fortress of Dolwyddelan, which flanks the road between Blaenau Ffestiniog and Betws-y-Coed. The great square tower, with its unprotected stone staircase, looks grim enough today, but if this was a home of golden Owain it must once have been warm and happy with feasting, poetry, song and other splendours. The ancient track, which still finds its way over the high moorland and along mountain streams from the Lledr valley to the Gwynant, between the Arddu and Cribau mountains, would have been a useful escape route to Anglesey if things went wrong, but would hardly seem attractive to an invading force.

In the south too stone castles were being built by Welsh princes, notably by the Lord Rhys, Rhys ap Gruffudd of Deheubarth. He built Dinefwr, Dynevor Castle in English, to be his main fortress and the centre of his administration of a large part of South Wales, which he dominated for the second half of the twelfth century. The site had been used by his forefathers and the great round tower with its surrounding bailey wall still looks down from the wooded cliff-top on to the winding Tywi and the fertile plain. England had been weakened by the revolt against Stephen but the ruthlessness of the Angevin Henry II was demonstrated by his cruel mutilation of twenty-two hostages after the failure of his campaign in North Wales in 1164. So the Lord Rhys played a cautious game of advance and retreat with the English king, doing submission when it suited him and making war and driving the Normans from their castles as far east as Gower and Aberafan, when Henry's attention was distracted by other problems. Such an occasion occurred when Henry II brought about the murder of Becket in 1166. Rhys had already taken the whole of Ceredigion from Owain Gwynedd's poet-warrior son Hywel. Henry II realised the hopelessness of any further attempt to crush the two Welsh leaders of the north and south and was glad to make an ally of Rhys. Henry was worried enough about the growing power of the Norman barons in Ireland without having to wage continual war against the Welsh who lay across his routes. He made Rhys Justiciar of South Wales, to act as his deputy there, and he released Rhys's son Hywel from a long imprisonment. This Hywel went with a detachment of Welsh troops which helped Henry in England and Normandy.

In matters of culture too the Lord Rhys trod a well-judged path. Though staunchly opposed to the Norman domination of Wales, he could see good in some of the ideas and institutions the invaders had brought with them. Dinefwr became a feudal centre of administration rather in the Norman style. He adopted Norman styles in dress, household management, law and, of course, castle design. He saw some good too in the French monastic orders introduced as part of the plan to Normanise Wales, in the beautiful architecture and many-sided activities of the foreign-style abbeys which had replaced the declining Celtic monasteries. To counterbalance this seeming submission to a foreign culture, Rhys called what we would name an eisteddfod during the Christmas holiday of 1176, in the castle he had built at Aberteifi, Cardigan. This eisteddfod was proclaimed, as is still done today, twelve months in advance, and was open to competitors from Ireland, Scotland and England as well as from Wales. Two chairs were offered and won, for poetry and music. A remarkable man, this Rhys ap Gruffudd, and worth thinking long about as you look down from his tower a mile or so west of Llandeilo Fawr in Carmarthenshire. But steer clear of the long-horned white oxen in the park as you walk over to the old castle.

During his last years Rhys was much troubled by the turbulent behaviour of his wild sons. When he died most of what he had achieved fell to pieces and his great domain was broken up in the fashion sadly traditional to Wales. Gavelkind, an excellent implement of social justice, was disastrous in its application to kingship and the Welsh princes were beginning to see the advantages of feudalism.

Just as Dolwyddelan typifies the determination of rugged Gwynedd to resist the Norman penetration, these castles of Deheubarth show the will to dominate the gentler landscapes of South Wales. To sense this, go to Carreg Cennen, again built by Rhys or a member of his family, splendid on its rock overlooking the quiet Cennen river, a few miles south-east of Llandeilo. Another of these Welsh castles is much battered Dryslwyn, which overlooks the Tywi some six miles west of Llandeilo. A road from Dryslwyn to Llangathen, and thence to Llandeilo, skirts the hill-fort of Grongaer, the Round Fort. Grongaer is the Grongar Hill of John Dyer, the early eighteenth-century poet who lived at Plas Aberglasney, at the foot of Grongaer. The blackthorn under which he is said to have sat to observe the landscape he describes in his poem was still being pointed out in 1875:

Old Castles on the Cliffs arise,
Proudly tow'ring to the Skies!
Rushing from the Woods, the Spires
Seem from hence ascending Fires!
Half his beams Apollo sheds
On the yellow Mountain-Heads!
Gilds the Fleeces of the Flocks;
And glitters on the broken Rocks!

This poem, first published in 1726, indicates one of the places where romanticism was born:

Ever charming, ever new,
When will the Landskip tire the View!
The Fountain's Fall, the River's Flow,
The woody Vallies, warm and low:
The windy Summit, wild and high,
Roughly rushing on the Sky!
The pleasant Seat, the ruin'd Tow'r,
The naked Rock, the shady Bow'r;
The Town and Village, Dome and Farm,
Each give each a double Charm,
As Pearls upon an Aethiop's Arm.

The Lord Rhys was generous to the abbeys of Ystrad Fflur (Strata Florida) and Talyllychau on their foundation and it's difficult to imagine how staggering these buildings must have been in a landscape and to people unfamiliar with such architectural refinement. Imagine a boy coming down from the hills of north Carmarthenshire, on his first visit perhaps, to Llandeilo Fawr and seeing on his way the shining new abbey of Talyllychau (or Talley, as it is monstrously anglicised) with its immense and tall church, the high, pointed east and west windows rich with unimaginable glass. Interesting how quickly the Welsh princes took to these new establishments, founded and fostered them, went to them to die and be buried, as Owain Cyfeiliog did at Ystrad Marchell. The monasteries thus became centres of Welsh culture and the copying-place and repository of priceless manuscrips. Reference will be made later to the high regard in which these abbeys came to be held, as well as to criticism of the way of life of some abbots and to their decline and dissolution in the sixteenth century.

Churches have survived far better than monasteries, since they were not stripped and dismembered by the ruthless Tudor monarch but sometimes benefited from the looting. So we go to churches to look for modifications of the Norman style by the still-living Celtic traditions of carving in wood and stone. Go to the little church of Llanegryn, perched on its ancient Celtic site above the Dysynni valley north of Tywyn, and pick out the Celtic motifs from the medieval and renaissance in the lovely wood-carving of its rood loft. Or cross the Border to see what was happening beyond Offa's Dyke, at Kilpeck, just inside Herefordshire. It was once called Cil Pedec, the retreat of an obscure holy man called Pedec, and a Welsh church was founded here about the year 650, under the mother church of Llandaf. The present church is Norman in date and style, twelfth-century Romanesque. It lay in the Welsh commote of Erging, a part of England today which I like to call Cambria Irredenta, and it remained Welsh in character long after the Norman take-over. The curate in charge in 1587 was called Thomas ap Gwilym. A strong Celtic element runs through the decoration of the church, stone-carving of such beauty and humour and bawdry that you shouldn't miss it if you're anywhere near. It's strange that one can think of this little church on the fringe of Wales as a melting-pot of international ideas, but that is what the stone-work records. The nearest I've seen to the external carvings are on the ninth-century church on Aghtamar Island in Lake Van in eastern Turkey. And there's stone-carving at the shrine of St. James at Compostella in Spain which seems to have inspired some of the work at Kilpeck. Viking, Saxon, Scythian, I imagine one could trace other echoes. In the twelfth century the pilgrimage and the crusade were the two great journeys which brought home new ideas. Is that what the two trousered Welshmen, and trousers were a Celtic garment, were doing on the main doorway at Kilpeck, one setting out for Compostella, the other for Jerusalem? Up at Leominster, similar Norman-Celtic stonework shows another trousered Welshman reaping with his sickle and looking over his shoulder in case the enemy should attack. But the crusader on the doorway of Kilpeck, if that's what he is and not just a Welsh warrior going out to meet the foe, is well prepared and well armed. Stone makes for confidence and a long memory.

The break-up that happened in Deheubarth after the Lord Rhys's death had happened in Gwynedd too. After Owain Gwynedd's death his five sons fought each other for power and it was left to Owain's grandson, Llywelyn ap Iorwerth, to pull North Wales together again. He too was at first involved in this fearful internecine warfare and extended his domain piecemeal at the expense of relatives. By 1203 he was master of all his grandfather's lands and came to be known as Llywelyn Fawr, the Great. After some hesitation King John decided to be friendly and gave Llywelyn Joan, his daughter by an unknown mother, as wife. Joan kept her husband and her father on good terms for five years until John, who knew of the possibility of getting other Welsh chieftains to help him, attacked with some success. But Llywelyn retaliated, regained his lost lands and added new parts of mid-Wales to them. This intermittent skirmishing with the English crown went on during the reign of Henry III until Llywelyn's death; castles were taken, burnt and rebuilt but Llywelyn remained unshaken in his authority over North Wales. He cleverly arranged dynastic marriages for his children with his powerful Norman neighbours, de Lacy, Ranulf of Chester and William de Breos, lord of a great domain in South Wales. De Breos had been Llywelyn's prisoner in 1228 but had been released on payment of a ransom and agreeing to the marriage of his daughter Isabel and Llywelyn's son Dafydd. In 1230 he was back on a visit to Llywelyn and an adulterous affair between him and Joan came to light. Llywelyn had de Breos hanged in public. Nothing more clearly demonstrates his power than that he could do this to a great Norman baron.

When Llywelyn married Joan, had he perhaps taken her to Dolwyddelan, his grim fortress in Snowdonia where he may well have been born, a castle which would hardly have seemed as golden to her as it did to the poets? Did she pine for the French songs and music for dancing, for the fashions of courtly love, for the elegance of the Anglo-Norman court in contrast to the more primitive splendour into which she had been cast, and were these memories given flesh by this splendid baron from South Wales? Llywelyn forgave her and must have loved her. A dramatist of our own day, Mr. Saunders Lewis, has written a great tragedy, *Siwan*, to analyse the interesting situation from all three sides of the triangle. (Siwan is a Welsh form of Joan and is pronounced Shóo-an.)

In 1230, the year he hanged de Breos, Llywelyn proclaimed himself Prince of Aberffraw and Lord of Eryri (Snowdonia). He was buried at the Abbey of Aberconwy, whose chief patron he had been. His empty sarcophagus now rests in the Gwydir chapel at Llanrwst church. The elegant chapel, gaunt Dolwyddelan, unremembering Aberffraw, these are places not to be passed without thinking of Llywelyn the Great.

Breaking with the old disruptive tradition of inheritance, Llywelyn had named Dafydd, his son by Joan, as heir to his position and most of his domains, and this was accepted both by Henry III and the Pope. Llywelyn had an older son, Gruffydd, whose illegitimacy did not bar him—by Welsh custom—from a full share in the inheritance, and Henry found it useful to play the two half-brothers against each other. But Gruffydd broke his neck escaping from the Tower of London and Dafydd himself only reigned for seven years before his death. Gruffydd ap Llywelyn's son, another Llywelyn, had been a favourite of his Uncle Dafydd, and had been regarded as his heir, but he in turn had to deal with his brothers, whom he defeated in battle, before taking the crown of Gwynedd in 1255.

After a tour of Wales (when he was twenty-three years of age), on which he made a series of sketches of castles in landscapes, J. M. W. Turner exhibited a picture of Dolbadarn Castle, near Llanberis, in the Royal Academy exhibition of 1800. In the catalogue for this exhibition, as a comment on the castle, he included the following lines of his own composition:

> How aweful is the silence of the waste,
> Where nature lifts her mountains to the sky.
> Majestic solitude, behold the tower
> Where hopeless Owen, long imprison'd, pin'd,
> And wrung his hands for liberty, in vain.

This Owen was probably Owain Goch, who was imprisoned for more

77

than twenty years by his brother, Llywelyn ap Gruffydd. It must have been in these early visits to Wales that Turner began to see in castle towers a desperate attempt by man to emulate the strength of rock and the height of mountains, but the tower-like rock which frowns over Dolbadarn Castle in the picture shows how vain this ambition is on the part of mankind. From this very experience in North Wales quite probably sprang Turner's view of the puniness of man in the vast, swirling or towering universe, however noble may be man's effort to achieve height and grandeur in castle, spire, campanile and the masts of sailing ships. These latter come nearest of all man's works featured in Turner's pictures to reaching the top of the canvas, perhaps because they make use of a force of nature. This was a view of man and his works that was to inform all Turner's pictures from now on. Notice the smallness of the dying Nelson at the foot of a mast; Hannibal and his army, elephants and all, crawling like ants under an alpine mountain and a fearful storm. There's a good deal to think about as one looks at the round keep of this Welsh castle on its rock at the northern end of Llyn Peris.

Once established Llywelyn ap Gruffydd extended his lands to Chester and moved southwards to take Dinefwr and Carreg Cennen. He destroyed castles as far as Norman-held Glamorgan. England was weak and the Border barons disunited. The Welsh lords did homage to Llywelyn ap Gruffydd and he proclaimed himself Prince of Wales. He built a castle at Dolforwyn, to the west of Montgomery, as an answer to that Norman stronghold and to protect the town he planned to build at Abermiwl, to give the Welsh the commercial advantages of Montgomery town. Like his famous grandfather he arranged a marriage for himself with the daughter of an ally across the Border, Eleanor, daughter of Simon de Montfort, then thirteen years old. But Simon de Montfort was killed at the Battle of Evesham, Edward I took Eleanor into custody at Windsor and it was not until thirteen years later, in 1278, that the marriage took place in Edward I's presence, at Worcester Cathedral. Eleanor died giving birth to her first child, a daughter who was to become a nun.

The final revolt against Edward I came after a few years of uneasy peace. The Welsh had grievances and these were now tried under

English law, which was one of the grievances. Maddened by all this, Llywelyn's spirited younger brother, Dafydd, rebelled and was joined by lords from all over Wales. Llywelyn seems to have been reluctant to take part in the war. The end came soon. Llywelyn was separated from his men in a skirmish near a bridge over the Irfon, west of Builth. He was struck down by the spear of one Stephen de Frankton, who had no idea of his identity, and was taken prisoner in this dying state. When it was realised who he was his head was cut off and taken to London, where it was carried on a pike in triumph through the streets. His body was rescued by the monks of Cwm Hir Abbey, north-east of Rhaeadr and a place he had loved. In our own day an impressive monolith has been raised to his memory near the road-side, and near where he died, at Cilmeri. An inscription at the foot of the monument refers to him in the traditional way, but with more attention to the rules of Welsh prosody than to fact, as Llywelyn ein Llyw Olaf, Llywelyn our Last Leader. History books now more often call him Llywelyn II or the Last.

What had gone wrong with Llywelyn ap Gruffydd's attempt to unite Wales under one monarch? Had he failed to realise that England had become united under the vigorous Edward I? Had he forgotten the importance of sea power, which even his thinned-down Viking inheritance might have kept in the forefront of his mind? In 1276 the English fleet took Anglesey and cut Llywelyn off from that traditional granary. Or had he made too many enemies amongst the Welsh on his way to power, enemies who would raise their heads whenever Edward I attacked? His grandfather had understood the virtue of feudalism in holding a country together but the Welsh lords didn't take kindly to the idea of doing homage to one whom they regarded as an equal. It was the old spectre of gavelkind which forced him to imprison his brothers and which once more killed the fight for independence. And his successes and the praise of the poets may have partially blinded him to the dangers which surrounded him. But it was the poets who recorded the feeling of tragedy and of national disaster which swept through Wales at the news of his death. Gruffudd ab yr Ynad Coch's lament on the death of Llywelyn is one of the most splendid in the literature of the world. It is passionate and personal and it moves forward from the collapse of the poet's own

world, through the general deprivation and suffering of the people of
Wales, to the involvement of the whole of nature and the very order
of the universe. Shakespeare did something similar in *King Lear*. The
climax of this long poem comes in a passage which I translate thus:

> The heart is chilled under a breast of fear,
> lust shrivels like dry branches.
> Don't you see the way of the wind and the rain?
> Don't you see the oaks beat together?
> Don't you see the sea stinging the land?
> Don't you see truth equipping?
> Don't you see the sun sailing the sky?
> Don't you see the stars have fallen?
> Don't you believe God, demented men,
> don't you see that the world is in danger?
> A sigh to you, God, that the sea may come over the land!
> Why are we left to linger?
> There's no retreat from the prison of fear,
> there's nowhere to dwell, alas for the dwelling!
> There is no counsel, no lock, no opening,
> no way of delivery from terror's sad counsel.

Llywelyn's brother Dafydd, who had provoked the last revolt, did
not long survive him, though he continued for a while to rule as
Prince of Wales from his fortress of Dolbadarn. Welsh resistance had
faded with the death of Llywelyn and Dafydd was betrayed by a
fellow Welshman. He was taken to Shrewsbury, tried as a traitor, and
hanged, drawn and quartered there. Dafydd had married Elizabeth
Ferrars. The king took their five children, put the three daughters
into nunneries and imprisoned the two sons in Bristol Castle. The
young Llywelyn died there and Owain was last heard of there in
1305. Edward I had ruthlessly put a stop to a line of succession from
Rhodri Mawr.

Wales had changed a good deal during the two centuries of Norman onslaught and settlement. The land bristled with castles, native
and foreign held, though the most visited and famous castles were
yet to be built, or were under construction when this fearful change
in Welsh affairs took place. New towns had been built, new centres

of commerce, though the Welsh had as yet little or no access to these. The new monasteries had brought marvels of architecture to astonish remote corners of Wales and, though utterly foreign to begin with, had quickly become sympathetic to Welsh culture and even to Welsh political aspirations. Poetry had flourished under the great leaders of the twelfth and thirteenth centuries, whilst the ancient tales of *The Mabinogion* had been brilliantly retold in the atmosphere of a new heroic age and, for the first time to our knowledge, recorded. The laws of Hywel Dda still governed relationships in a civilised way within Welsh society and were acknowledged even by the Border barons when it suited them.

An awareness of nationhood had grown even more intense in Wales under the hammer of the Normans. No one expressed this better than did Giraldus Cambrensis, Gerald of Wales, or the Welsh-man, Gerallt Gymro to the Welsh. Gerald's mother was the daughter of Nêst and Gerald de Windsor and she had married William, son of Odo de Barry. So he was three-quarters Norman and only a quarter Welsh in blood, but his feeling for Wales and the Welsh was second only to his admiration of the Normans. He had a very low opinion of the English, he felt more Welsh as he grew older and he fought, as a cleric, for the independence of St. Davids from Canterbury. He claimed that Manorbier in Pembrokeshire, where he was born, was the most beautiful place on earth. In 1188 Gerald accompanied Archbishop Baldwin on a tour of Wales to gather soldiers for the Third Crusade, preaching sermons which were little understood, since they were not in Welsh, and which roused little enthusiasm amongst the few who understood them or who listened carefully to the in-terpreter. A war in the Near East must have seemed remote to the Welsh, who had problems of their own. But the journey led to Gerald's writing two books which are of the greatest interest to us today, *Itinerarium Kambriae* and *Descriptio Kambriae*, books which not only offer a well-observed view of Wales at that time but are full of good stories. In translation they are known as *The Itinerary* and *The Description of Wales*. The Description ends with the story of the old man of Pencader who was asked by Henry II, then riding through west Wales on a punitive campaign, how it would all end. Henry II would have heard of the legends of Arthur, probably from

Geoffrey of Monmouth's great work, and this Norman king would have greater respect for Welsh and Breton traditions than later English monarchs had. The old man's answer was that though Wales could be overrun and weakened, it could never be subdued. 'Nor do I think', he said, 'that any other nation than this of Wales or any other language shall in the Day of Judgement answer for this corner of the earth.'

The New Order (1283–1485)

Though ruthless enough in some ways, Edward I had a clear notion of political possibilities and he went slowly about the so-called settlement of Wales. The Marcher lordships remained and indeed were extended to cover a large part of Wales from the territory east of the River Conwy through mid-Wales down to the Bristol Channel in the south and to Cardigan Bay south of the Teifi Estuary in the west. The lands of the defeated Llywelyn and David now became the personal property of the king and he divided them, for administrative purposes, into the counties of Anglesey, Caernarfon, Merioneth, Cardigan and Carmarthen. Pembroke and Glamorgan were counties palatine, that is with royal privileges but run by Norman lords. The traditional old boundaries were kept, but the *cwmwd*, or commote, replaced the *cantref*, or hundred, and became the unit of administration. (*Cantref* means a hundred homes and this was an area which contained roughly one hundred important homesteads.) The *cantref* of Penweddig, for instance, was bounded by the Dyfi Estuary to the north and the River Ystwyth to the south, whilst the sea provided the western limit and the Pumlumon (Plynlimon) range the eastern. The rivers Clarach and Rheidol divided this *cantref* into three commotes, Geneu'r Glyn, Perfedd and Creuddyn, names which are still in use today. The only Cantref I know as a place name today is the parish of Cantref, once Cantref Cynnedd, on the northern slopes of the Brecon Beacons. And of course there is Cantre'r Gwaelod, the Bottom Hundred, the submerged land off Aberdyfi.

Edward I had been victorious in 1282 and 1283 and Welsh resistance was for the moment crushed, but he realised that he could not compel the Welsh too far against their ancient customs. He announced in the Statute of Wales, or Statute of Rhuddlan, in 1284, that he permitted the continued recourse to old Welsh law in minor civil matters, cases which were tried in the commote courts. But in matters of greater importance English law was now to prevail in the newly established county courts and the first sheriffs, the estate agents of the king, were all English. With English criminal law came the coroner, one of whose functions was to secure for the king any possessions of a convicted felon, or anything which had caused an accidental death—a horse, a cart or even a knife. A system of heavy fines was also profitable for the king. Edward I did not abolish gavelkind, but he made it illegal, contrary to old Welsh custom, for an illegitimate child to share in an inheritance.

Old Welsh law had been based on an elaborate system of responsibilities and fines, and the purpose of the fines had been to bring peace between the families of the offender and the sufferer. The three chief crimes were killing, burning and stealing. A life could be taken for a life only if full retribution had not been made for a killing. As we have seen in the case of the girl who falsely claimed to be a virgin when she married, shaming played an important part in punishment, and the shaming was sometimes symbolical. A bad-tempered wife's apron was pelted with rotten eggs whilst her husband's trousers were held aloft in respect. But the scold's bridle, the ducking-stool, the stocks, pillory and whipping-post were all to come and were all foreign to Wales. Norman justice could be harsh and cruel. With trial by jury came the torture of the accused to extract a confession or information about others, the *peine forte et dure* which now became a feature of trials and which is not unknown today. Horrors like the hanging, drawing and quartering of David II at Shrewsbury in 1283 were to proliferate from this time to the seventeenth century. The new county courts applied a law which most Welsh people did not understand and in a language they did not understand, English, not Norman-French or Welsh.

To enforce this new régime Edward I set about building castles which he hoped would stand up to any Welsh protest. Flint and Rhuddlan were the first, both begun in 1277. Look at Rhuddlan Castle, blunt, untrammelled and functional on its hill overlooking the River Clwyd. No frills here but an expression in stone of the determination of its creator. He chose the site carefully, moving away from the original Norman motte and bailey to a spot at which the river was navigable from the sea and where a bridge could be built which would facilitate and control movement along an important route into North Wales. As chief master mason Edward I employed Jacques de St. Georges, who had learnt his craft from his father in Savoie, in eastern France and western Switzerland. Thousands upon thousands of workmen were brought in from England, about two thousand to dig ditches and the moat, and the cost of wages, materials and carriage would run into millions in our present-day money. The advance in style was not complete, for the town wall of Rhuddlan was still an earthwork with a wooden palisade. The wooden bridge would have a drawbridge or swingbridge section to permit ships to move up to the square tower, known as Gillot's Tower, at the south-western corner of the wall, where at high tide ships could turn into the moat for unloading. From there the entrance to the river was protected by a dock gate. Once the stone bridge was built, in the middle of the fourteenth century, the river bank north of the bridge became the town harbour and it continued to be so up to the nineteenth century.

It is unlikely that Jacques de St. Georges did more than expertly carry out the king's wishes. Edward I had been on the last crusade, which had been led by friends and relatives of his in France, and he had seen and studied the Armenian castles of Asia Minor and the splendid constructions they had inspired earlier crusaders to build, castles like those of Anamur and Korykos, Acre and Crac des Chevaliers. So Edward went on to put his observations into practice, at Aberconwy, Caernarfon, Harlech and Beaumaris, choosing the site as a man experienced in these matters, and fitting the castle to the site, each one a completely original solution to the immediate problems, with no Roman forcing of a pre-determined form on to varied topography. The Cistercian abbey of Aberconwy stood in a situation which could control the coastal route to Caernarfon and Anglesey. Edward I demolished it and used the stone to build the magnificent castle of Conwy, with its completely walled town, the best remaining example of such a town in Britain. He compensated the monks by giving them land higher up the Conwy valley at Maenan, and helping them to build a new monastery there. The sarcophagus of Llywelyn the Great was removed to Maenan and, at the Dissolution of the monasteries, found its way, without body or lid, to the Gwydir chapel alongside Llanrwst church. The castle-building went on. Caernarfon Castle was sited on the shore downhill from Roman Segontium, whose stones were used for the building, and between the river Seiont and a lesser brook and the sea, to ensure a good harbour and an easily dug moat. Here the king permitted himself an element of fantasy, for the tall turrets are surely more than strictly functional. And here Edward I played his famous trick on the Welsh, bringing Queen Eleanor there to give birth to his son in 1284 and then offering the Welsh a prince who could speak no English! Such was the king's haste to carry out this piece of open duplicity that the queen must have been accommodated in a temporary wooden structure, since the Eagle Tower was hardly more than started when Edward II was born.

Beaumaris is another splendidly designed seashore castle, with a salt water moat and a harbour protected by an outer wall, whilst Harlech was perched on a great rock which

> serves it in the office of a wall,
> or as a moat defensive to a house.

In those days an arm of the sea came up to the foot of the rock and the castle had a water gate. These castles were meant to be impregnable but they did not prove to be so. In 1294 Caernarfon Castle was taken and the town burnt by Madog, thought by some to have been the illegitimate son of the last Llywelyn. Conwy Castle was taken by Owain Glyndŵr's men in 1401, whilst the garrison was in church, and Owain took Harlech in 1404. Only Beaumaris was never attacked, though it saw many bitter quarrels between the natives of Anglesey and the entrenched newcomers. Perhaps it is its situation at sea level, the way it seems to float on water and its unscathed appearance that give it today a peaceful, unthreatening, almost dreamlike look.

It took many long, contentious years for these new castle and walled town dwellers to come to civilised terms with the Welsh of the countryside outside the walls and it is difficult not to take the row of latrines perched high in the town wall of Conwy as the symbol of an attitude as well as a measure of hygiene. Six of them were incorporated neatly into the building of the wall and they can be seen from the car park on the land side of the town and castle. Another view is from inside, on the wall walk.

So from his base at Rhuddlan, with these massive outrider fortresses, Edward I prepared to impose his will on Wales. The country relapsed into an apathetic despondency, a kind of dispirited acceptance. War, so often written about by Welsh poets, now tended to drop out of poetry and the poets sang of the beauty of girls and of the solitude and safety of woodlands, which still covered much of the country. Cattle raiding was no longer a popular sport and the object of an illicit raid was likely to be a girl rather than a drove of heifers. Gruffudd ab Adda, writing toward the middle of the fourteenth century, put it thus:

> I am a thief, a wound binds me,
> thief of a fair girl, not a black stallion;
> for tonight no thief of a ram,
> thief of a maiden this happy time;
> no thief of a cattle enclosure,
> thief of her, wave-coloured, in the fair wood . . .

Some Welshmen still hankered after war, and to these the English cleverly offered service abroad in their armies. These Welsh mercenaries were no mere hand-to-hand fighters; they took with them their skill with the longbow, which in their hands was a deadly weapon. The Welsh arrows brought down the horses and then the heavily armoured knights would be as helpless as stranded turtles on the ground. Five thousand Welsh bowmen won the Battle of Crécy for the English. Fifteen thousand Frenchmen were killed.

Those who stayed at home saw more of their women and children. They did more work in the fields. There wasn't really much good farming land in Wales but the great land-grabbing enclosures hadn't yet taken place. The Welsh were still largely a pastoral people and had little time for gardening. They are still not such devoted gardeners as the English are. Their food came mostly from animals, that is milk, butter and cheese. And meat, of course, at its best fresh or salted to keep over the winter. How many of us can remember salting the pig or eating salted mutton, a very different flavour from the lamb which is so highly thought of today? Herbs and spices were important to enable people to stomach meat that had gone off and in the fifteenth century Guto'r Glyn was to write in praise of

> *Sinamon, clows a chwmin,*
> *siwgr, mas i wresogi'r min.*

> Cinnamon, cloves and cumin,
> siwgr, mace to warm the lip.

Here it's fairly obvious that the spices were used to mull wine or ale, but the foreign words indicate the newness of these additions to food in the Wales of the Middle Ages, as well as the fact that it was via England that they came from Turkey and ultimately the Far East. Wheat and barley can be harvested in Anglesey and on the strips of lowland near the sea in the west and south; oats grow best in the hills, but the weather makes this a chancy harvest; rye could be grown in poor, sandy soil where no other grain would survive and in less favourable weather. So grain was precious and oatcakes were eaten and different forms of porridge and gruel. Fruit has never been grown on a large scale in Wales except in Gwent. The potato had not yet arrived to fill out the daily *cawl*, or broth, and how hard it is to imagine the rural Welsh diet without the potato and a cup of tea. The leek, not only our national emblem but also an important ingredient of *cawl*, was grown in fields, like peas and beans, as they still are today. There are few references and no poems to gardens in Welsh.

It was wild nature that appealed to the fourteenth-century Welsh poet, and there was plenty of it. What more fitting memorial could there be for Dafydd ap Gwilym than the yew-tree under which he is said to have been buried in the graveyard ringed with harsh mountains at Ystrad Fflur (Strata Florida). Dafydd used the terms of his religion, the lovely words of the Catholic faith in Welsh, to describe the landscape he loved, the woods into which, when May came and Lent was over, he tried to entice the many girls he loved, even the Abbess of the nunnery of Llanllugan. (It's no use going to look for this Cistercian nunnery on the bank of the River Rhiw, four miles

south-west of Llanfair Careinion in Meirionnydd. It got short shrift
in the Dissolution and has disappeared without trace.)

> Then the slim eloquent nightingale
> from the corner of a grove nearby,
> poetess of the valley, sings to the many
> the Sanctus bell in lively whistling.
> The sacrifice is raised
> up to the sky above the bush,
> devotion to God the father,
> the chalice of ecstasy and love.
> The psalmody contents me;
> it was bred of a birch-grove in the sweet woods.

The freedom and beauty of the woods for Dafydd implied scorn for
the new order and for the new towns where no self-respecting Welshman would live. Gruffudd ab Adda sums up this attitude in his lovely
poem to a birch tree cut down to provide a maypole for the Anglo-
Norman town of Llanidloes, a *cywydd* (a characteristic verse form)
full of contempt for town-dwellers and their petty commerce, and of
love for the free hills and woodlands. He asks the tree what it would
prefer to do, in the certain knowledge what its answer would have
been:

> To seek your lovely woodland home
> or shrivel down there in the town?

The birch and the oak are native and traditionally admired Welsh
trees. This was not a time for much political poetry and the poets'
standpoint is often only to be sensed from the way they use the word
Sais (Englishman).

The Cistercian monks had brought large-scale sheep farming to
Wales as they had done to Yorkshire and there are parts of Wales
that have not changed much since they did this, where sheep dot
steep mountain sides and broken moorland, and stone walls of astonishing length crawl up bare, treeless slopes from minute fields and
little homesteads. The wool trade enriched the monasteries and the
king too, for he taxed the export of wool and woollen materials. And
it benefited the country in general. Fulling-mills sprang up everywhere to wash and clean the wool, and the word *pandy* occurs in

place names. Tonypandy means Fulling-mill Hill. There was work for weavers in every part of Wales. In the 1350s Carmarthen was made the centre for taxation and export but farmers and monks in North Wales found Shrewsbury a more convenient place. Through Shrewsbury and Bristol, Welsh woollen materials were exported to Ireland, France and Spain.

Other industries flourished too in the fourteenth century. There was much lead-mining in Ceredigion and the mining of iron-ore in Glamorgan. The iron-ore was often delivered raw to castles, monasteries and churches throughout the country to be processed and beaten into the needed tools, weapons and utensils. Cymer Abbey, near Dolgellau, had its own furnace near Trawsfynydd and the countryside would be familiar with columns of smoke and the ringing of hammer on metal. Wood was the fuel used, for there was still plenty of timber. Coal was mined in Glamorgan and in Flint, but peat, where obtainable, was preferred as domestic fuel, since coal was considered dirty and dangerous.

New little towns came into existence, this time Welsh in origin and atmosphere, towns like Bala and Tregaron, with no castle or protective wall, and they became places of assembly for drovers and their cattle and centres of local commerce and culture. Most Welsh people still didn't live in towns, but they had to live somewhere. What were their houses like? They were still of wood, and the considerable quarrying that went on was for castles and churches, or for the famous mill-stones of Anglesey. The possibilities of slate were being discovered and houses in Chester were already being roofed with Welsh slate. Giraldus had said in the twelfth century that the Welsh 'do not live together in town or village or fort but stay in the woods, like hermits. And on the edge of the woods it is not their custom to put up fine, costly, stone or brick buildings but wattled huts to last a year or so.' Now, in the more stable conditions of the fourteenth century, better houses were being built, at least for the gentry. The style is interesting and is said to be an old Celtic house design. The roof was supported by two parallel lines of columns consisting of hewn tree-trunks. On each trunk a strong branch was left to curve inwards and these were joined or coupled at the top in what is known as a 'cruck truss'. The roof-tree, the spine of the roof, was a straight piece of timber running along the top of the crucks. A wooden frame was then built on to this basic support and the walls and roof were wattled and thatched. A further and lower line of posts, parallel to and outside the main columns, resulted in a three-aisled structure, the outer aisles giving sleeping accommodation on low platforms. Cruck structures may be seen at the Folk Museum at St. Fagans.

Another type of house common in Wales in the Middle Ages, and still to be seen in modified form, has been given the general name of 'long house' by Dr. Iorwerth Peate. This was a long, straight, rectangular, low-roofed farmhouse which took in outhouses under its continuous roof. Cows and horses were kept indoors in winter and a connecting door or an opening in the wattled partition, or simply a drop in floor level with no partition at all, enabled the cattle to be milked and all the animals to be fed without anyone leaving the house when the weather was bad. There would be open-ended lofts at wall-plate height for storage of fodder and for servants' quarters. The living section would be stone-paved but the other part would have a trodden earth floor. This arrangement wasn't new in the fourteenth century. A story called *The Dream of Rhonabwy*, usually included in *The Mabinogion* and though recorded in the fourteenth century probably written in the twelfth, describes a chieftain's hall, but one which had fallen into sad decline. Rhonabwy and his two companions sought a night's lodging at the hall of one Heilyn Goch and this is what they found: 'They saw an old hall, very black and with a straight gable end, with thick smoke coming out of it. Inside, the floor was all holes and bumps and so slippery with cattle dung and urine that they could hardly keep their feet on it. Some of the puddles were ankle deep. On the floor there were branches of holly that had been nibbled by the cattle. When they came to the main part of the house they saw dismal, dusty platforms and on one of them an old hag tending a fire. Whenever she felt cold she threw a lapful of husks on to the fire and the smoke was almost unbearable. . . . The old woman gave them barley bread, cheese and watered milk for supper. . . . That night they were much bothered by fleas and by the discomfort of the platform they lay on.' Of course there were better-kept houses than that in rural Wales of the fourteenth century, but the old plan is there, the lower part of one great room for the animals, the upper part, with low platforms on either side, for human habitation. This type of house went the way of most wooden structures, but stone-built, slate-roofed long houses are still to be seen in Wales and are known as *tai hirion*. Look out for them as you take the mountain road, for instance, from Abergwesyn to Tregaron. When new farmhouses were built in the nineteenth century the old long house became their outhouses. So look out for a long, straight, low unit of outhouses with a newer, more square and taller house standing a few yards away.

I have already referred to the small Welsh towns which grew organically out of the needs of the countryside and whose inhabitants had no feeling of difference or antagonism toward country-dwellers, a feeling which persists in places like Flint, Aberystwyth and Tenby. They had no need of walls behind which only escaped Welsh serfs had been acceptable. But in this uneasy peace of the fourteenth century there was horror in store for townsmen and countrymen alike, horrors worse than war. A series of fearful pestilences, flooding across Europe from the Far East, some brought by ship to places like Bristol, now came to Wales. Of these the most terrible was the Black Death of 1348–50. Half the town-dwellers of Wales were carried off by this plague, many dying of despair when they saw the dreaded black spots on their skin. It hit the countryside too, for even there people gathered together in church, tavern and mart. So many bondsmen died that the great landowners found themselves too short-handed to till their estates and they were forced to let out farms to free men on better terms than had ever obtained before. Townsmen who had grown rich now for the first time invested money in land. The social pattern of Wales was changing; tribe and family meant less, money and possessions more. Money payment replaced payment by labour.

So the fourteenth century saw the emergence of the typical Welsh countryman, the small farmer, who is still today the backbone of rural Wales. With this development the landscape changed, to look much more like it does today. In those parts of the country, that is in the south and the east, where the manorial system had been established, many of the great manorial fields, which had been hacked by bondsmen from waste land and forest for their Norman lords, were now broken up into smallholdings. And on these scattered holdings lived most of the population of under a quarter of a million. With the new shortage of labour and the higher value set on their work the peasantry of the whole of Britain began to demand freedom from serfdom and better living conditions. The English peasants revolted in 1381 and took London by storm, but Welsh peasant discontent had to wait twenty years more to be canalised by Owain Glyndŵr's rebellion.

Before considering Glyndŵr's great bid to set Wales free we must not forget that such an attempt was almost made by Owain Lawgoch. Welsh archers had fought for the English king at Crécy, and they were to do so again at Agincourt, but there were hundreds of dissident and adventurous Welshmen in the army of the French king, too, in this second half of the fourteenth century. The leader of one of these bands, a great soldier who won victories for the French in Italy, Switzerland and Brittany, was Owain ap Thomas ap Rhodri, known to his admirers in Wales as Owain Lawgoch, or Redhand. The French called him Yvain de Galles and knew him as one of the *Compagnons Gallois*, and he is highly praised by his contemporary Jean Froissart, in his *Chronicles*. In Wales he was recognised as the last lineal descendant of Rhodri Mawr, through the two Llywelyns. His name, Owain, was highly evocative, for this had often been the name of the foretold leader in prophetic verse, and many now saw in Owain Lawgoch the promised deliverer. Between campaigns Owain made his plans in the French court and in 1372 he issued an impressive proclamation justifying his claim to rule Wales. Gruffudd ap Maredudd of Anglesey wrote a resounding *awdl* (poem) calling on Owain to take up arms against England and to return to Wales to take up his rightful inheritance:

> *A gwedy delych gwaed hyd deulin* . . .
> And once you have come blood up to the knees . . .

(The poem is in the *Red Book of Hergest*, folios 1313–4.)

The English were alerted and took measures to resist an invasion. Owain set sail and got as far as Guernsey, where his name entered legend and folk poetry, but he was recalled to perform a further service for the French king. English reaction did not end there. The London government hired one John Lambe to cross over to France, ingratiate himself with Owain and murder him. This he performed and was rewarded with a fee of one hundred francs. A spirited miniature painting records the death of Owain whilst he was besieging the castle of Mortagne-sur-Mer near Bordeaux, a fortress then held by the English. The story goes that Lambe plunged a dagger into Owain while preparing to shave him and ran into the castle. There he received his reward from the English commander, who expressed his detestation of this murder. In the miniature, one of a group of crossbowmen is seen reloading and looking toward Owain, who has a great dart in his breast.

Owain was buried at the church of St. Leger, four miles from the scene of his death. After his death his company was led by Ieuan Wyn, another *Compagnon Gallois* at the French court, a soldier and a famous lover who became known as *le Poursuivant d'Amour*. There are no monuments in Wales to these adventurous Welshmen, but the life they led in France is vividly portrayed in the chronicles and collections of miniatures at the National Library of Wales at Aberystwyth and in such works as *The Flowering of the Middle Ages*, edited by Joan Evans, and *The Age of Plantagenet and Valois*, by K. Fowler. The gaiety as well as the violence of their exile springs to colourful life in contemporary hunting scenes and hunting picnics, views of Paris and Vincennes with courtiers and elegant ladies, scenes of battle on sea and land, the grim reality of the looting of a house. Conway Castle is depicted with ships approaching and it is hard not to speculate about what might have happened if Owain Lawgoch had lived to carry out his invasion plan. He might well have been more successful than Owain Glyndŵr, since he had powerful support, much more support from abroad than Henry Tudor was to have for his successful invasion. Unlike Henry Tudor, Owain Lawgoch put forward no claim to the English throne. He would have been satisfied with Wales. The imaginable effect on the history of Wales and of England is both complex and sweeping.

In spite of the Black Death and unrest and discontent in Wales, lightened occasionally by the flaring up of hopes of liberation, there were still great Welsh landowners who carried on the old traditions and who entertained in the old style, though not without innovations. Poets usually appreciate good food and drink, often because they can't afford them in their own homes, and Sypyn Cyfeiliog and Iolo Goch paid with verse for their splendid entertainment at the houses of their patrons. This was how Iolo was received at Llanelwy by the Bishop of St. Asaph:

> A grand sweet splendid mass
> we get, and that in song,
> tenor and quatrible, lively prolonging,
> with a steady undersong of fair tone.
> After mass we go together
> to the well-timbered hall.
> I am caused to be placed
> correctly in this hall,

(Iolo is delighted to be honoured in the ancient Welsh way, as a poet of the highest order, by his position at table)

> to sit, when silence is proclaimed:
> fine custom, at high table . . .
> Drink for drink comes to me
> from his vineyard, from his fair hand;
> and poetry, eloquent of longing,
> and music. We get glory.
> A sweet fair quiet concert,
> then pipes and dancing every day.

Welsh life was not without its fun, even in that rather grim age. Again Iolo Goch describes the accommodation for the professional poets at Sycharth, where he was received by Owain Glyndŵr with equal honour:

> Couplings secure the rooftree,
> each rafter safely coupled in . . .
> Four sweet lofts joined together,
> where travelling poets sleep . . .
> Spirits and finest bragget,
> all liquors, white bread and wine,

with meat and fire in the kitchen . . .
There'll be no lack of gifts,
no fault, no famine, no shame,
no thirst ever in Sycharth.

(Translation here fails to convey the play upon the word *sych* in the last line of this *cywydd*, for *sych* means dry and *syched* thirst,—

na syched fyth yn Sycharth.)

Iolo Goch died before Owain Glyndŵr, at the age of forty-six, revolted against English rule, and this happy state of affairs at Sycharth was not to last long. Sycharth is where Glyndŵr was born, about the year 1354. It lies about four and a half miles south-west of Oswestry, just inside the present Welsh border, and though it is little visited by Welsh people, who are neglectful of these significant places in their history, it is well worth a visit. The wooden structure Iolo describes has gone, but the mound still stands, with its surrounding moat and earthwork, splendidly placed on a hill, with trees about it and overlooking a fertile valley. The southward-facing slope to the north-west of the mound must have been Owain's vineyard and at the bottom of the valley, between the vineyard and the mound, you can still make out the shape of the fish-pond which supplied his table.

Owain ap Gruffudd took his distinguishing name Glyndŵr from Glyndyfrdwy, a favourite part of his domains, and he lived in the Dee valley, at Carrog, half-way between Glyndyfrdwy and Corwen. His home is said to have been Carrog Uchaf, a fine medieval stone house, today a farmhouse, which looks down on the A5 a little to the east of the turning down to Carrog. Nearby is a mound known as Yr Hen Domen, the Old Mound, which is thought to have been the site of one of his halls and in the village of Carrog there were until recently remains of other establishments of his, including a prison-house. Owain was able to trace his descent back to royal lines in North and South Wales, and he was given the best education there was, including seven years studying law at the Inns of Court in London. You remember Glendower's proud response to Hotspur in Shakespeare's *Henry IV Part I:*

I can speak English, lord, as well as you;
For I was train'd up in the English court;
Where, being but young, I framed to the harp
Many an English ditty, lovely well,
And gave the tongue a helpful ornament.

It's a pity these English verses of Owain's, if he ever wrote them, haven't survived. Was he the first Anglo-Welsh poet and would he have liked the description? In the same scene the courtship of Owain's monoglot Welsh daughter by Mortimer is a triumph of love over language-difference.

Owain practised soldiering too in England, campaigning in Scotland for Richard II and probably for Henry Bolingbroke, later to be Henry IV. So, with his essentially Welsh background and his foreign experience, he was well equipped to rule Wales. On 16th September 1400, he was proclaimed Prince of Wales at Glyndyfrdwy by a gathering of Welsh noblemen. The rebellion slowly grew, bringing to Glyndŵr's home at Glyndyfrdwy not only many friends and relatives but government officials, who were by now Welsh at the lower levels, peasants and craftsmen, and clergy too. Workmen and students flocked back from England to join Glyndŵr's colours. At Oxford, Welsh students met at the house of one Alice Walsh to plan their return. They were said officially 'to have plotted against our Lord the King and the Realm for the destruction of the Kingdom and the English language'. Over-reaction you may think, but Westminster was alarmed; Glyndŵr was not so accessible as Owain Lawgoch had proved, and if the Tripartite Indenture of 1405 between Percy, Mortimer and Glyndŵr, an arrangement dramatically conveyed by Shakespeare, had stood, the fears of the southern English would have been justified and government from London reduced to about one third of the area of England and Wales. What in the north of England was a drive for regional autonomy was in Wales a national movement for liberation. Castles and towns, the hated symbols of foreign domination, were taken and destroyed.

Henry IV struck back, marched to Anglesey and destroyed the monastery of Llanfaes. In the following year, 1401, a great victory was won on the banks of the Hyddgen on Plynlimon, over an English army which had marched up from Pembrokeshire. One wonders what the English were doing on the northern side of Plynlimon, unless they were taking a short cut or an evasive route to Shrewsbury. In the autumn of the same year Henry IV marched from Hereford through Brecon and Llandovery to Carmarthen. He struck northward and stationed his troops in Strata Florida Abbey, after ejecting the monks, who favoured Owain's cause, and drove on to Llanbadarn.

In a quick sweep in May 1403 by an English army led by Prince Henry, Shakespeare's Prince Hal, later to become Henry V, Glyndŵr's halls at Sycharth and Glyndyfrdwy were burnt to the ground in his absence. He made a home for himself and his family in Harlech Castle. By the end of this year he controlled the whole of Wales except Pembrokeshire and by 1405 that was his too. In 1404 Glyndŵr had called together a parliament at Machynlleth. The building in which they met still stands, though no one knows how much it has been modified since that time. Owen sent ambassadors to France and signed a treaty with the French, who recognised him as *Owynus dei gratia princeps Wallie*, an independent ruler. A copy of the seal attached to this document (the original is in Paris) is to be seen in the National Museum of Wales, Cardiff. A martingale which must have belonged to Owain and which was found at Harlech is also in the museum. Another parliament was called at Harlech in 1405. This was government by consent, consent from every corner of the country.

Yet another parliament was called in 1406 at Pennal, a little place well situated on the northern side of the Dyfi estuary, with the bastion of North Wales behind it and the opening landscape of South Wales before. Pennal had once been an important Roman station but had no Anglo-Norman associations. It was here that Glyndŵr outlined his plan for Wales. There were to be two universities, one for the North and one for the South. Welsh bishops were to be appointed to the sees of Wales and the Church was to be freed from Canterbury, acknowledging only the authority of the Pope at Avignon (not Rome, in deference to Glyndŵr's French friends).

But French opposition to England weakened and the murder of Louis of Orleans robbed Owain of a good friend. Another friend, and enemy of Henry IV, the Earl of Northumberland, was killed in battle

near Tadcaster in 1408. The English were gathering strength and beginning to concentrate their power against Wales. Aberystwyth and
then Harlech fell to Henry, and Owain's authority was slowly whittled
away, though his friends and supporters stood by him to the end. We
don't know when or where or how the end came but there is a strong
tradition that Glyndŵr died at Monnington Straddel, a few miles west
of Hereford and on the edge of the Golden Valley, facing the Black
Mountains. The manor farm is now called Monnington Court and
the present tenant, Mr. Stokes, courteously and helpfully showed me
the places associated with Glyndŵr, the mound in which he is said to
be buried, the Bloody Meadow where he is said to have fought his
last battle, and the little half-timbered building which was a chapel in
Glyndŵr's day. This was one of the estates of Sir John Scudamore,
who had married Glyndŵr's daughter Alice and who had been custodian of Carreg Cennen Castle for the king. Another member
of this Border family, Philip Scudamore, had died fighting for
Glyndŵr.

The poets refused to believe Glyndŵr was dead and there are no
elegies to him. The historian Sir J. E. Lloyd has said of him: "Throughout
Wales his name is the symbol for the vigorous resistance of the Welsh
spirit to tyranny and alien rule, and the assertion of a national character which finds its fitting expression in the Welsh language.' We have
no other memorial to him, but September 16th has recently become
a day of remembrance for him.

This time it wasn't at all like 1282. There'd been defeat, certainly, a
Welsh bid for freedom crushed. The leader seemed to have vanished
into thin air, as Shakespeare's Owen Glendower might have done, but
instead of the consternation and despair that followed the death of
Llywelyn the Last, this time the newly roused national pride barely
went underground. It was to surface again soon, to be canalised into
support for Henry Tudor and to sweep him to the English throne.
But what happened in the meantime? Owain Glyndŵr's men, unable
to stomach English rule, took to the woods which still covered so
much of Wales. They were known as *gwerin Owain*, Owain's folk. One
of them was Dafydd ap Siencyn of the Conwy valley, about whom
Tudur Penllyn wrote:

Your castle is now the woodland
and the oaks of the meadow your towers.

Some of the poets became outlaws too. A very good poet, Llywelyn ap y Moel, had his lair at Coed y Graig Lwyd, probably near the Claerwen valley in mid-Wales, a valley now drowned to provide the English Midlands with water. Writing of his companions in banditry he said:

Far better than wandering minstrelsy
for a man who covets goods
is to take and unharness an Englishman
under your branches, o sweet spot.

His poems of love and nature have images of war, as have those of another soldier-poet, his contemporary, Guto'r Glyn, who wrote a fine poem to lament Llywelyn ap y Moel's death. Waiting for a girl in a birch grove Llywelyn sees the branches as straight as arrows and the trees themselves standing in order like the spears of Owain's best men. He could laugh at himself, as Dafydd ap Gwilym could, and there is an amusing poem in which he describes how he and his friends were routed, at a place called Waun Gaseg, by a body of Englishmen they had hoped to rob.

Chaos, then, in Wales, with the liveliest spirits refusing to toe the line. Henry IV had to do something about it. Laws were passed to protect the merchants of the Border region and the people of the English boroughs in Wales against this sort of attack. If goods stolen from an English merchant were not returned within a week, the townspeople concerned could retaliate on any Welshman they could lay hands on. This was collective responsibility with a vengeance. Welshmen were not allowed to carry arms or fortify their houses. An Englishman marrying a Welshwoman lost all his rights. No Englishman could be convicted in Wales by a Welsh jury. The Welsh were forbidden to assemble for any purpose whatsoever. These are the first English laws against the Welsh, who couldn't now be anything but countrymen. The rift between town and country was racial as well as instinctive.

The great Border lordships were in a sense buffer states between the

Welsh and England. Originally part of the Norman feudal system, the Marcher lords had become petty kings in their way and difficult to control from London. Beyond the Welsh Marches, Henry IV held Flint and a belt of west Wales from Anglesey down to Carmarthen, all this by right of conquest. And in these parts, outside the developing towns, there was much poverty. There were plenty of sheep on the hills, certainly, but life in the cottages of the land was grim and hard. The poet Guto'r Glyn at the same time observed a degeneration in the way of life of the Welsh gentry. He remarks:

> Suppliants are all our chieftains
> and they do nothing but beg.
> Brawling, wandering poets are they;
> those of the past never sang for money.
> They beg each ploughing ox,
> they beg horses, they beg gold.

A self-respecting landowner would commission a professional poet to write a poem of asking, and would not do it himself. Society was falling apart. Like Guto, many Welshmen were glad to get away by joining the king's army. Their great weapon was still the longbow and they helped Henry V win the Battle of Agincourt as their forefathers had done for Edward III at Crécy.

There were more disastrous wars at home, the Wars of the Roses, which divided both England and Wales from 1455 to 1485 and were as destructive and meaningless to the common people as the Black Death had been in the previous century. Roughly speaking the royal lands in Wales, the Principality, that is, were Lancastrian, together with Pembrokeshire and Breconshire and odd pockets down along the border. Along the border too there were Yorkist strongholds and Denbigh, Powys and Glamorgan were solidly for York. Parts of what is today Gwent were Lancastrian in sympathy and Henry IV's son, who was to become Henry V, was born at Monmouth. Shakespeare shows that this enabled Henry V to claim to be a Welshman when it suited him to do so, as in his conversation with Captain Fluellen. The white rose in this symbolical opposition stood for York but there is no record to my knowledge of the red rose ever having been carried by the Lancastrians in battle. Henry VII may have invented this, when he cleverly married a Yorkist of royal blood and created the double Tudor rose as an emblem of the merging of the two great rival families and the ending of the fearful civil war by his victory at Bosworth.

The Yorkist cause, being largely that of the powerful Border barons, was strong in Wales until 1469, when Sir William Herbert of Rhaglan, who became Earl of Pembroke shortly before his death, was captured at the Battle of Banbury and beheaded afterwards. His defeat and death were a disaster for Wales and were lamented as such by the poets, for many Welsh gentlemen fell at this battle or were executed afterwards. Guto'r Glyn mourns:

> Yesterday he went under the black planet
> through the hills yonder to fight;
> trust in a feeble fate
> tricked him into leaving Gwent.
> Woe is me, over my poor wretch,
> that he didn't stay in his own land.

The Welsh gentry, partly through ambition for power at the court of Westminster, had become involved and had involved their unfortunate followers in a quarrel which had nothing to do with Wales, was an upper-class sport and only a matter of personal fidelity to most Welsh people. Trevelyan's view was that the Wars of the Roses were a squabble between rival Welsh lords, whose Celtic tribalism thus brought disorder to England and its government. But in 1471 young Henry Tudor became the Lancastrian claimant to the throne of England and the Welsh swung to his side. Here there was hope for the future, something more important for Wales than English politics could ever be. These wars gave Henry Tudor his chance and England a Welsh king.

We must go back a little in time. Owain Tudur had become a member of the household of Henry V, introduced perhaps by his great friend Maredudd, son of Owain Glyndŵr, who had already become a courtier there. These are the early days of the appeal of London to ambitious Welshmen, an appeal which continues to deflect them from the affairs of their own country and which may now fade before the higher status of Brussels. When Henry V died, Owain Tudur married his widow, Queen Catherine, Catherine of Valois in France, the lively princess whom Henry courted in Shakespeare's play, where she is made to utter some charming bawdry. Owain Tudur came from the important old family of Penmynydd in Anglesey and it was there that he proudly took his wife to introduce her to his friends and relatives. They spoke no French or English and though welcoming they must have remained silent during the meeting, for she is said to have re-marked that they were 'the goodliest dumb creatures that she ever knew'. Penmynydd is between Llangefni and Porthaethwy (Menai Bridge) and the fourteenth-century church has effigies of some of Henry VII's ancestors, partly chipped away because the alabaster was thought to have some healing virtue.

Owain and Catherine, living quietly and happily out of the public eye, had five children. Two of the sons, Edmund and Jasper, were be-friended by their elder half-brother, Henry VI, and made Earls of Richmond and Pembroke respectively. That's how Henry Tudor got his English title of Richmond, for he was Edmund Tudor's son. Henry was born in Pembroke Castle in 1457, very soon after his father's death. His mother was Margaret Beaufort, daughter of the Earl of Somerset. She was fourteen years of age at the time, left him in the care of his uncle and remarried. But it was through her that he got his Lancastrian claim to the English crown. So Henry was brought up in Wales, had a Welsh nurse and would naturally have spoken Welsh. His adviser and the main architect of his triumph was his uncle Jasper, Siaspar Tudur to the Welsh.

In 1471, after the Lancastrian failure at Tewkesbury, Jasper Tudor and his nephew escaped to Brittany and there they planned and pre-pared for the landing that was to be the first step on their way to London.

They made for Pembrokeshire, which, though outside the Princi-pality, was Lancastrian in sympathy. They landed on the north shore near the entrance to Milford Haven on Sunday, 7th August 1485. The Battle of Bosworth, in Leicestershire, was fought and won on 22nd August—only a fortnight's march and a march on which they had to pick up forces. Not everyone, not even the doughty Rhys ap Thomas, came over to their side at once, but their landing was unopposed and the drive up the west side of Wales began. English records of this march are naturally scrappy and inadequate but Welsh tradition is full of good stories about it. Local tradition places the landing at Mill Bay, a mile and a half south of Dale. If you go through Dale and on to St. Ann's Head you will get a magnificent view of the sea from the lighthouse. Then, if you take the path down past some houses in the direction of the haven, you will see the bay where the landing took place. It's said that on landing Henry Tudor said, 'This place is brunt,' and that that was how Brunt Farm, which you see uphill from the beach, got its name. The name has baffled historians, commentators and etymologists. But take it that he spoke Welsh to a companion and described the place as *brwnt*, foul, a foul place to land. The remark could have been passed on from soldier to soldier: '*Be wedodd e*? What did he say?' '*Mai brwnt yw'r lle*. That the place is foul (*brwnt*).' So the place got its name, and a rough, rocky beach it is for a landing, with a steep climb to reach a road. Thus Henry Tudor and his two thousand men landed from his handful of ships. A small beginning, but as Hall says in his *Chronicle*, 'presently after breathing of his native country's air began his forces to increase.' From here the Tudor army marched on Dale, a surprise attack, if an attack was necessary, and then on northward. Again tradition tells us that at Mullock Bridge, less than two miles north of Dale, Rhys ap Thomas joined him, thus breaking his oath to the English king but salving his conscience by stooping under the arch of the bridge for Henry and his army to march over him. He had sworn to King Richard that only over his body would such an invasion take place. There is a stone bridge there today but I am not sure that this is the very arch under which the patriotic deception took place.

Henry and Jasper Tudor marched on, gathering strength as they went, though there was as yet no certainty that Rhys ap Thomas and Sir Walter Herbert would bring their forces to join them. The news of their landing spread fast, barely giving the poets time to compose odes of welcome which prophesied victory. Cardigan, Llanbadarn, Machynlleth, the progress swept rapidly on, flying the red dragon banner of the ancient hero Cadwaladr. (The motto on the present Welsh flag, *Y ddraig goch ddyry cychwyn* [The red dragon made the start], comes from a poem of greeting presented to Henry by Deio ap Ieuan Ddu.) Houses along the route claim to have entertained Henry on his way. One such is Wern, a lovely house, still lived in, on the road-side between Llanarth and Ceinewydd (New Quay) in Ceredigion. A plaque on the wall of the modernised bathroom states that it was once the bedroom Henry Tudor slept in. At Mathafarn, east of Machynlleth, he is said to have stayed at the home of the notable gentleman poet Dafydd Llwyd. (The present elegant house has replaced Dafydd Llwyd's, higher up the hill, which was destroyed by fire.) The story goes that Dafydd did not feel sufficiently confident to prophesy the success of the campaign, so he consulted his wife. Her answer was categoric. 'Don't be a fool! If he wins you'll be rewarded. If he loses he'll never come back this way.' Dafydd not only produced the poem but accompanied Henry to Bosworth and was made esquire by him at the end of the day.

At the Long Mountain, east of Welshpool and on the border between Wales and England, Henry was at last joined by Rhys ap Thomas, who had come up through mid-Wales, and the Herberts of south-east Wales, all bringing men, as well as by chieftains from North Wales who brought cattle to feed the swelling army. But they were still much fewer in number than the army of King Richard, who met them in a planned position on the low rise of Bosworth Field. Richard had treated the invasion too lightly and in a speech to his men before the action began he poured scorn on Henry Tudor, calling him 'a Welsh milksop, a man of small courage and of less experience in martial acts . . . brought up . . . like a captive in a close cage in the court of Francis duke of Brittany'. But Henry had courage and his uncle had the experience. The battle was joined and the issue remained uncertain until Sir William Stanley, who had hesitated till the end, came in with soldiers from north-east Wales. Hall tells us that 'the whole conflict endured little above two hours'. The victory was complete, though not well documented. King Richard was killed in the battle and Welsh tradition has it that Rhys ap Thomas placed the crown of England on Henry's head at the end of the day, and that he was knighted for his pains.

For the Welsh people this appeared to be a triumph for their cause and others outside Wales agreed with them. The Venetian ambassador in London wrote back to his government, 'The Welsh may now be said to have recovered their former independence, for the most wise and fortunate Henry VII is a Welshman.' And later, Francis Bacon said, in his *History of Henry VII*, 'To the Welsh people his victory was theirs; they had thereby regained their liberty.' Henry himself insisted that it was the military victory rather than a successful argument over rights that gave him the throne and he delayed his marriage with Elizabeth of York until this was established.

The royal palaces were taken over by this new and cautious king, the Tower for its ancient and grim purposes, Old Whitehall for the holding of trials, Westminster Hall for legal business and entertainments, and residences at Richmond, Greenwich, Windsor and Woodstock for living in. He hunted deer in Windsor Great Park and in January 1504 he was there for thirteen days, going out every day with the Prince of Wales, later to be Henry VIII, 'into the park and the forest to hunt deer and other game'. Perhaps because he put the English economy on its feet, and left the royal treasury very much fuller than he found it, Henry VII has acquired a reputation for frugality, even meanness, but in fact he was no skinflint. He already had the Tudor love of colour and pageantry. Again it is the Venetian ambassador who gives an account of how the king received him 'at the small palace of Woodstock . . . in a small hall, hung with very handsome tapestry, leaning against a tall gilt chair, covered with cloth of gold. His Majesty wore a violet-coloured gown, lined with cloth of gold, and a collar of many jewels, and on his cap was a large diamond and a most beautiful pearl. . . .' The queen was also in cloth of gold. Cloth of gold! A golden age had begun for England. Queen Elizabeth may have commissioned Shakespeare to write a dazzling play for the Twelfth Night of Christmas in 1601 but her grandfather in 1494 had the Great Hall at Westminster, where Shakespeare's play probably received its first performance, 'hung with arras and staged round with timber, that the people might easily behold' the show he put on for the Twelfth Night of that year. Henry VII was an all-round patron of the arts. In 1494 he commissioned Vérard of Paris to print a *Lancelot* on vellum, with woodcuts and miniature paintings of Arthur and the Round Table, with Galahad and the Holy Grail, and a Lancelot with the head of his grandfather, Owain Tudur.

Henry married Elizabeth of York, daughter of Edward IV, on 18th January 1486. Their first son was born in September and christened

Arthur, 'of which name,' says Francis Bacon, 'Englishmen no more rejoiced than outward nations and foreign princes trembled and quaked'. The thirteenth-century English poet Layamon had told his countrymen that every Briton still looked forward to the day when Arthur would return, and it was from this hope that Henry Tudor intended to profit. It was Cadwaladr, whose standard he had carried to Bosworth, that Henry regarded as the last king to rule south Britain, including Wales, but by this time the story of Arthur had acquired tremendous prestige and in this new prince it appeared to have come full circle. Beginning with scanty and puzzling references to the British hero in the earliest Welsh poetry the story had been carried into Brittany, France, England, Germany—into every country in Europe, in fact. It had flowered into an astonishing body of romance, in which the leader of a resolute band of Celtic horsemen had become a great king. In the fifteenth century this great body of story was brought together in English by Sir Thomas Malory, in the book we know as *Le Morte D'Arthur*, and this book was printed and published by William Caxton in London in 1485, the very year of Bosworth. As well as a way with men and money, Henry VII had a strong sense of history and a thoroughly Welsh concern with lineage and relationships, and he employed the best Welsh genealogists to establish the ancestry of his grandfather Owain Tudor.

Henry Tudor's Welshness has been played down by many English historians, who find the whole business of Bosworth Field embarrassing, but the evidence for it is in the records. Twelve years after his accession to the throne he paid thirteen shillings and fourpence (multiply perhaps by fifty to get today's equivalent) to a Welsh poet for a poem. I think the clerk who recorded this payment must have been an Englishman who thought it a waste of money, for the account book says: 'To a Walshe rymer in rewarde 13s 4d.' On St. David's Day 1492 the king gave the Welshmen at his court £2 (call it £100) to celebrate their national holiday, a cheerful *noson lawen* (a traditional evening's entertainment of poetry, song and dance) in a very great house. The court was full of Welshmen, many of whom settled in England and got themselves estates and good jobs. David Seisyllt, of Alltyrynys in Ewyas, had gone into exile with Henry Tudor in Brittany. He received his reward and founded one of the great English families. It is difficult to think of the glory of the Elizabethan age without remembering its main architect, William Cecil, Lord Burleigh. Descendants in our own time have been Lord David Cecil and the Marquess of Salisbury. No one has yet adequately summed up the contribution of Welshmen and men of Welsh extraction to the great age of Elizabeth and James I, of men like the Herberts and John Donne in poetry, Inigo Jones in architecture and theatre design, John Williams in jewellery, Dr. John Dee in mathematics, Sir Roger Williams in the art of war, Morris Kyffin in army administration, Hugh Holland, traveller extraordinary and poet, and Sir Hugh Myddelton as Lord Mayor of London.

Naturally, there were people who didn't care for this Welsh influx. Amongst the *One Hundred Merry Tales* collected by the court poet John Skelton there is one which describes how even in heaven people were complaining that too many Welshmen were getting in. They took their complaint to St. Peter, but to no avail until an Englishman from the Border country, who knew something of the habits of the Welsh, suggested a solution to the problem. Teach a man the Welsh for toasted cheese, he said to St. Peter, and get him to carry a tray on his head outside the walls of heaven, shouting *Caws pobi, caws pobi*, and then open wide the gates. This was done. All the Welshmen in heaven, the imagined aroma of their loved delicacy in their nostrils, rushed out. The gates were clapped to and heaven was for the moment rid of the Welsh.

The fact is that Welshmen did better in England under Henry VII than they did in Wales itself. But many Welshmen did stay at home and prosper too, and one of Henry's first acts as king was to grant a pension to his old Welsh nurse. He may well have been too busy at first consolidating his position in England and putting the administration of the country to rights to bother much about Wales or to do all the things that were expected of him. Welshmen he favoured were given letters of denizenship to release them from the disabilities imposed on the country by Henry IV. New charters enfranchised North Wales, that part of the country ruled directly by the king. Not everyone liked this either, for it meant a comparative loss of privileges for the Anglo-Norman towns, and the burgesses of Conwy, Caernarfon and Beaumaris protested. Welsh sheriffs were appointed and Welshmen as bishops to Welsh sees. Gavelkind, the splitting up of an estate on the owner's death, was abolished at last.

The Border barons had torn each other to pieces during the Wars of the Roses and their power had been undermined. Henry VII hated feudalism and under him power became more concentrated in the king and London. He established the Court of the Star Chamber and the Court of the Council of Wales, the latter dealing with the affairs of the Principality of Wales and the Marches. Both these courts became popular as correctives to feudal tyranny and as places of appeal against unjust judgements, and they continued to be so until they were misused by the Stuarts. Effectively, Wales was now governed from Ludlow and Ludlow Castle became a centre of culture and power, in sad contrast to the fading out of Dynefor and its family in the west. Today both castles are equally empty and derelict, but they are also equally full of memories. The Lord Rhys had organised an eisteddfod at Dynevor; Milton's *Comus* was to be given its first performance within the walls of Ludlow.

The Tudor peace brought security for Wales, as it did for England, and with this a change in domestic architecture. The Welsh gentleman lived in a fortified manor house rather than a castle or a wattled hall. There was more light from windows, more elegance and comfort within. Right up the Welsh border, and this is essentially a Welsh border style, the late fifteenth century saw the evolution of the half-timbered house, a building with visible timber frames filled in with fired brick. From Llanidloes to Stratford upon Avon, and north and south of this line, through the still-preserved old hearts of towns and lovely villages, this style continues to delight the eye. Timber-framing was an old Celtic building device but this new style was surely more attractive than the cruder clay and wattle filling of the old chieftain's halls. It could only have come into being in a secure time and in a belt of country where oaks grew well on a clayey soil. Tretower Court, with its older castle, is an example of how architecture responded to the changed conditions. Here, near Crickhowell in Breconshire, a Welshman who had inherited a thirteenth-century castle in the middle of the fifteenth century tried to make it a pleasanter place to live in. Two hundred yards from the grim, towering, round keep (not too far to run to in case of need) he built a new kind of house with splendid in-

terior woodwork, a wide covered balcony looking down on the central
courtyard, expensive glass in the windows but still with castellation
on the outer wall. That's what Sir Roger Fychan, or Vaughan in English
rendering, and his son Thomas did from about 1450 onward. These
Vaughans of Tretower played their part in the Wars of the Roses,
were much involved in the English administration of Wales under
Edward IV and Richard III, and got their rewards for their services
to the English kings. They are frequently named and praised in the
Welsh poetry of their day but they had to wait two centuries for a
poet of their own family, Henry Vaughan, the Silurist. Was the fact
that he wrote in English already foreshadowed in the leanings toward
England of his fifteenth-century ancestors?

Even before Henry Tudor's march to Westminster and the end of
the ravaging wars, the arts of writing and of building had flourished
in Wales. Once the shock of Owain Glyndŵr's failure and of Henry
IV's vengeance had been absorbed, Wales was seen to take a full
share in the culture of Europe. Any number of manuscripts remain
from this century with treatises in Welsh on the serious subjects of the
moment and translations from Greek, Latin, French and Italian. It
was the greatest century of poetry in Welsh, with names like Sion
Cent, Dafydd Nanmor, Lewys Glyn Cothi, Guto'r Glyn, Dafydd ab
Edmwnd and a host of others. Sir John Wynn of Gwydir later wrote
of 'Edward the First who caused our bards all to be hanged by martial
law as stirrers of the people to sedition, whose example, being followed by the governors of Wales until Henry the IV's time, was the
utter destruction of that sort of men'. The general hanging of poets
does much to discourage poetry, but the slackening of control during
the Wars of the Roses brought its benefits to the culture of Wales. The
poetry of the fifteenth century is full of delight in the beauty of this
world and the value of personal relationships. There is no more poignant poem than Lewys Glyn Cothi's lament on the death of his little
son.

There was great church architecture too. Consider the fifteenth-
century tower of St. John's, Cardiff, how the delicate tracery of pin-
nacle and finial grows out of the strength and solidity of the tower.
The fine churches of Wrexham and Gresford are of this period too.
Lovely woodwork was cut for the interiors, durable roofs with fluid

interplay of rafters, collar beams, arched braces and carved wall-plates. The carved rood screens that have survived from the fifteenth century are things of intricate beauty. At the simple church of Partrishow, in the Grwyne Fawr valley north-east of Crickhowell, there is a lovely screen and rood loft. The most perfect of all is in Llananno Church, on the east bank of the River Ithon, on road A483, some four miles south of Llanbadarn Fynydd, between Newtown and Crossgates and Llandrindod. In the borders of this screen the fine work of a school of Montgomeryshire craftsmen remembers the interlacing of ancient Celtic design. At Llanegryn, north of Harlech, in a church which to me clearly stands in an ancient stone circle site, another screen has varied stylised panels which I prefer to the saints —or are they the prophets?—of Llananno, and once more much use is made of the grape vine in the borders. Supreme amongst the ceilings of this period is the oak ceiling of St. Davids cathedral. Abergavenny (Y Fenni) church has interesting wood carving too and a wooden figure of Jesse which had a special meaning for Welshmen of the Tudor period. The Tree of Jesse, Christ's family tree, seemed to make more respectable their own efforts to establish an impressive ancestry.

Organs were now installed in some of the wealthier Welsh churches for music that must have been as splendid and intricate as the wood carving of the age. All this amounted to a flowering of culture, a blending of native and foreign impulses, on which the Tudor monarchs were to turn their backs and eventually try to kill.

Henry VII died at Richmond in 1509. Did his conscience prick him at the end that he hadn't done enough for Wales, the country that had brought him to the throne of England? A hundred years after his death George Owen, in his *Description of Pembrokeshire*, recorded a tradition that the dying king had charged his son, who was to become Henry VIII, 'that he should have a special care for the benefit of his own nation and countrymen, the Welshmen'. He could hardly have foreseen how his son would interpret this wish.

It is remarkable that Henry Tudor, with hardly any legal title to the throne, should have ruled for twenty-four years and died in bed, after bringing England prosperity, internal peace and a new regard for law. His achievements, and the width and variety of his interests and pleasures, show him as the most complete man to have sat on the throne of England. He was especially fond of music and, like that earlier Celtic king Luerius of pre-Roman Gaul, he always took musicians with him when he travelled. The records reveal payments by him for organs, flutes, lutes and for the tuning of his clavichords. He rewarded string minstrels and singers to the recorders, the fiddle and the Welsh harp, as well as bagpipe players and trumpeters. From this civilised environment, and the growing confidence in his authority, Henry Tudor was outward-looking too. His years at the court of Brittany probably gave him a realisation of the value of cultural as well as political contact with Europe, particularly with France and Italy, and of awareness of the opening world beyond Europe. He rewarded John Cabot for his discovery of Newfoundland in 1487. He established the post of Latin Secretary (today we call him Foreign Secretary) and appointed an Italian, Carmeliano, to fill it. He appointed a French scholar as his Poet Laureate and enjoyed his Latin poems of praise, even though the Latin was criticised by Erasmus. He commissioned the Italian, Polydore Vergil, to write his *Anglica Historica*, with the intention of justifying the Tudor monarchy in Europe. Through Hall's use of it this book coloured Shakespeare's view of English history, and ours as well. A link with the Celtic past was Polydore Vergil's edition of *Gildas*.

Apart from the places connected with his march to Bosworth there are few things to be seen in Wales today which bring Henry Tudor to mind. His monument is in London. To Westminster Abbey he added the chapel which bears his name. Under the fantastically intricate fan-vaulting, with its ribbed pendants and delicate drop tracery, he commissioned the Italian sculptor Torrigiano to design a huge grilled and gated tomb, and there he lies alongside his queen, not in alabaster or old-fashioned painted marble but in renaissance bronze, renaissance which is already anticipating baroque in the cupids (or are they little angels?) at the corners of the monument. They lie there calm and cold amidst the beauty he created; but for truer, more natural portraits of them go to the Abbey Museum in the Norman undercroft at the far end of the cloisters. For centuries it was the custom to carry a life-sized wooden or plaster effigy of the dead king or queen, dressed in their actual clothes, in the funeral procession. These effigies and clothes were found not long ago bundled into chests and they were brought out to form the nucleus of this fascinating little museum. The heads of Henry and Elizabeth are there, looking uncannily alive. He has the typical North-Walian high and prominent cheekbones, wise, tolerant, rather sceptical eyes and the mouth of a careful man. She has been given a blonde wig and a headscarf which qualify, with her bland face, for the thirties of this present century, if not for our own decade. The shores of Milford Haven, where he was born and where he landed from Brittany, and Westminster, not only for his chapel but for the administration he created there, these are the places where one best ponders this man's life and work. But the rather dull landscape of Bosworth Field becomes interesting too as one works out the movements of the two armies on that fateful day. When I did this I stayed at the Three Tuns in Atherstone and found that the hotel had, framed on its walls, maps and studies of the battle made by local military men, together with much anti-Tudor propaganda.

CHAPTER III

Union with England

Under Henry VIII

A beautiful new bridge now spans the Severn Estuary to link England with Wales, a bridge which is paying for itself at the rate of £1 million a year in tolls, tolls which are collected only on the English side so that for many of us the bridge has become the symbol of the nature of the more general link between the two countries. Before the bridge was built a car ferry plied, according to the state of the tide (and this is the tide that brings the famous Severn bore and the swarms of elvers seething up the river), from Aust to Beachley and back. On the Welsh side, at least, the ramp used by cars to board and leave the ferry is still there, lurking, wind-swept and slimy, almost under the rising sweep of the bridge. Even before the motor car came, animals, men and goods were ferried across this stretch of water, right back at least to Tudor times. The Romans may have crossed it regularly, somewhere opposite Caerwent, to link that town with Aquae Sulis (Bath). Their main road ran through Glevum (Gloucester). But up to the sixteenth century, crossings by South Walians were not always lawful occasions. It wasn't unknown for raiding parties to slip over from Gwent and ferry back rustled cattle under cover of darkness.

Henry VIII could do little to cope with this kind of disorder from his palace at Westminster, but in 1534 he was to send Bishop Rowland Lee, a stern believer in law and civil peace, to be President of the Court of Wales and the Marches. The border country ran northwards from this point where the Wye joins the Severn and the sea, the Marches which were still largely governed by the descendants of those Normans who had grabbed great estates here, and of Welsh gentry with whom they had intermarried. They were a law unto themselves and were usually ready to turn a blind eye on crime if

113

there was any profit in it for themselves, even to the granting of sanctuary to felons on the run from other domains. Bishop Lee soon put an end to the uncontrolled use of ferries over the Severn at night, and the lowing of stolen cattle no longer echoed through the darkness of this troubled border country. But though considerable parts of the Marches had by this time passed into the control of the crown, there were still men whom the king distrusted and feared in South Wales.

Of these the richest and the most dangerous was Edward Stafford, Duke of Buckingham, who was born in Brecon Castle in 1478. (The castle suffered badly in the Civil War of the seventeenth century but it's a pleasant exercise to try to trace what remains of it, including parts of a hotel, and of the old town wall. There's a good view of it from the road bridge in the middle of the town.) Buckingham owned large estates which straddled the border, with important lordships running from Newport up through Brecknock, as it was then known —the English attempt to pronounce Brycheiniog, though the Welsh name of the town is Aberhonddu, whilst Brycheiniog was the old kingdom. From Brecon the lordships extended through Hay into Gloucestershire. Buckingham had been a ward of Henry VII and when he came of age he set about trying to recover and exploit the estates his father forfeited when he was executed by Richard III for helping Henry Tudor toward the throne. The executed duke is an important character in Shakespeare's *Richard III*. The young Buckingham had dreams of restoring for himself the feudal power of the first Norman barons. He claimed the right to keep a private army of two or three hundred men, necessary, he claimed, to protect him when he rode through lawless South Wales. He raised great sums of money, and he was not alone in this, by encouraging his tenants to buy themselves out of the time-wasting duty of attendance at the Great Sessions, and justice suffered as a result. His vast enclosures of land were naturally unpopular and when he built himself a castle at Thornbury in Gloucestershire he turned a thousand acres into a park where he could ride and hunt. Unloved in his domains, he was equally disliked by the powerful Cardinal Wolsey, whom he in turn despised. There is a story that Buckingham was holding a bowl for Henry VIII to wash his hands when Wolsey tried to make similar use of the water. Buckingham poured the bowlful into the Cardinal's shoes. For the king the most worrying aspect of Buckingham was that he had a claim to the throne and might well have hoped for the succession if Henry VIII died childless. A charge of treason was trumped up against him and he was executed in 1521.

Over in the west another descendant of a man who had helped the Tudors to the English throne was executed in 1531. This was Rhys ap Gruffudd, grandson of Sir Rhys ap Thomas of Mullock Bridge fame, a proud man who was angry at not being granted his grandfather's office of Chamberlain for the king in South Wales and more angry still at its granting to Walter Devereux, Lord Ferrers. The stranglehold was being applied from Ludlow now, for Ferrers was an important and ambitious member of the Council set up there for Princess Mary when her father sent her down to inspect Wales and the Marches and to attempt to bring order there in 1525. No one in west Wales was to be allowed an embarrassing degree of power any longer. Quarrels broke out between Rhys and Ferrers. A squabble occurred over the lodging of retainers at Carmarthen, Rhys was jailed at the castle there, there was a riot possibly started by his wife, the government was alarmed and he was tried by the Court of the Star Chamber. Released, with a warning to the two nobles to keep the peace, Rhys was in and out of the Tower of London in 1529 and 1530. Anne Boleyn hated him (she was to be made Marchioness of Pembroke in 1533), Rhys was a staunch Catholic and was certain to oppose Henry VIII's divorce, marriage to Anne Boleyn and break with Rome. His leadership in south-west Wales could interfere with the king's plans. He was tried by the King's Bench, found guilty, on flimsy evidence, of plotting to escape to Scotland to conspire with the Scottish king against Henry VIII, and was executed. The house of Dinefwr, which had worried the ruthless Normans, was not to be allowed to plague the more ruthless Tudor monarch.

Another cause of worry for the government in this corner of Wales was an influx of Anglo-Norman-Irish refugees from the rebellion of the Earl of Desmond. The earlier Irish immigrants had merged into the population, the Flemings had remained apart and were not likely to give trouble, but these newcomers showed scant respect for officers of the crown. Tenby was said to be full of them. The Tudors had reason to know what could happen to a movement which started in south-west Wales, the campaigns of Gruffudd ap Cynan from Porth Clais and of Henry Tudor from Dale were cases in point, and order had somehow to be restored. The king was moving toward greater control over Wales and toward its eventual union with England. Potentially dangerous men had to be removed and Rhys ap Gruffudd became a sacrifice to Henry's fears and plans.

To bring order to those parts of Wales not controlled by the government at Westminster, Henry VIII held a meeting with the Border barons at Shrewsbury in 1534 and then established Rowland Lee as Lord President of the Marches. Under him all those who had committed crimes in Wales were tried in the nearest English county and he was given the power to put down crime by capital punishment. He was one of Thomas Cromwell's men and in a letter to his master he said, 'If we should do nothing but as the common law will, these things so far out of order will never be redressed.' In another letter he describes how an outlaw was 'brought in in a sack, trussed on a horse, and hanged on a gallows for a sign on market day in the presence of three hundred people.' Of any outlaw he grimly jokes, 'If he be taken he playeth his pageant'. Good fun for the English counties of the borderland, where they were not short of this kind of entertainment in Bishop Lee's day. Ludlow was his official base but he had another near Shrewsbury where he had a manor. And of course he held courts up and down the Border. He disliked the granting to Wales of Justices of the Peace and said of this in 1536, 'If one thief shall try another all we have here begun is foredone.' He showed little sympathy with traditional Welsh ways and it is said that it was he who first compelled Welshmen to shorten their names and use only the last element as a surname. But the Welsh continued to call themselves *ap* this and *ap* that up to the end of the century. In a play called *Sir John Oldcastle* (*c.* 1600) by Drayton and others, Davey, who has been involved in a Welsh clan quarrel at Hereford, offers as his surety for bail 'her coozin ap Ries, ap Evan, ap Morrice, ap Morgan, ap Lluellyn, ap Madoc, ap Meredith, ap Griffin, ap Davy, ap Owen, ap Shinken Shones'. All one person, of course, but the judge, whether unfamiliar with the Welsh way of naming people or fancying himself as something of a wit, as judges are apt to do, abruptly says, 'Two of the most sufficient are enow.' (He meant the most well-off.) But I

blame Henry VIII, not his servant Rowland Lee, for my present surname, which one of my daughters has lately renounced.

These considerations have taken us beyond the border and, just as
one has to go to Westminster, Richmond and Woodstock to sense
the evolution of a great Welsh king of England, so one goes to Ludlow to get a feeling of the isolation of the place in relation to Wales
and things Welsh. To impose the new régime there had to be a convenient centre, convenient for London if not for Wales, a stronghold
with a direct and not-too-distant link with London and roughly the
same distance from the four corners of the country to be governed.
Ludlow Castle was to provide this and for a century and more Wales
was to be administered from here. I get a strong sensation of unreality
at Ludlow Castle. It seems to turn its back on the town and yet not
look towards Wales, from which it is screened by green hills and
woods. Hereford and Shrewsbury face Wales more frankly, if cruelly
in the case of Shrewsbury and its history. But Ludlow seems to prefer
to pretend that the country isn't there. There's a remoteness about the
castle which was to make it the ideal setting for John Milton's poetic
double-talk, the courtly entertainment which sprang from the conflict of puritanism and hedonism in the poet. Milton displays an
urban fear of the wild woods:

> ... the perplex't paths of this drear wood,
> The nodding horror of whose shady brows
> Threats the forlorn and wandring passinger.

Not thus would Dafydd ap Gwilym have thought of this woodland.
Yet, having come so far from Cambridge, Milton was aware of being
near to contact with

> An old, and haughty Nation proud in arms.

To this fortress, then, came the orders from London and from here
control radiated out to every part of Wales.

For these control lines to function the Border country had to be
directly subservient to the king, and Henry VIII had yet another
reason for wanting even greater power over Wales and the Marches.
In 1534 he passed an Act of Supremacy, making himself Head of the
Church in England and cutting away completely from Rome. But

Wales and England weren't yet legally one country, so the Act didn't apply to Wales. The situation was dangerous; religious protest might lead to violent opposition to the king; another Rhys ap Gruffudd might arise to canalise discontent. It was difficult for anyone to gauge the possibilities. So in 1536 Henry announced an act making all English law applicable in Wales, and within months of this the famous Act of Union followed. Some Welshmen welcomed this fateful Act of Union. Many of the Welsh gentry were already anglicised and the insinuation of English law into Wales had been going on for centuries, but the use of the word 'annexed' early in the document had sinister implications. Here are the words: 'That his said Country or Dominion of Wales shall be, stand and continue for ever from henceforth incorporated, united and annexed to and with this his realm of England.' A mighty blow was struck at the Welsh language. The king proposed 'utterly to extirp all and singular the sinister usages and customs' of the country, and this included the language, 'because the people of the said Dominion have and do daily use a speech nothing like or consonant to the natural mother tongue used within this realm'. Later on the Act stated 'that from henceforth no person or persons that use the Welsh speech or language shall have or enjoy any manner office or fees within this realm of England, Wales or other the King's Dominion upon pain of forfeiting the same offices or fees, unless he or they use and exercise the English speech or tongue'. Later in the century the poet Edmund Spenser, commenting on the very same policy as applied to Ireland, said, 'for it hath been ever the use of the conqueror to destroy the language of the conquered and to force him by all means to learn his. The speech being Irish, the heart must needs be Irish. For out of the abundance of heart the tongue speeketh.'

The all-English rule posed quite a problem for ambitious Welshmen in the Tudor administration, but for ordinary people the most easily observable result of all these changes, apart from the carting off of thousands to be hanged by Bishop Rowland Lee, was the destruction of the monasteries. Some religious houses disappeared completely, others remained as romantic ruins whose rounded or pointed arches offer a frame for agreeable vistas of meadow and mountain, for they are usually well placed in the landscape. Such are Tal-y-

Llychau, Tintern and Valle Crucis. The first Cistercian abbey to be founded in Glamorgan was in the lower valley of the Nedd, near Neath, the Nidum of the Romans. Its size and importance may be guessed at today from the immense floor area of its church. When Henry VIII applied his Act of Dissolution, Neath managed to keep open for a few years, perhaps because of the piety and scholarship of its abbot, Leyshon Thomas. (The Welsh names of the abbots and abbesses show to what degree these religious houses had become part of the life and culture of the country.) The king appointed callous 'visitors' who were required to look into the accounts of every religious house and to order the closure of any which had an income of less than £200 in the money of that day. This meant every monastic house in Wales. The order was for complete destruction, after the treasures had been removed for the king. But demolition was expensive. The roofs were stripped for the precious lead and useful or beautiful woodwork was removed for sale, or used to melt down the lead into convenient ingots for carrying away. The shell of the building became a quarry or was left to mellow to its present attractiveness. The story of the Abbey of Aberconwy is a sad one. Demolished by Edward I to provide stone and a strategic site for his castle and walled town of Conwy, it was rebuilt, with the king's help and encouragement, at Maenan, not far from Llanrwst. Llywelyn the Great had founded Aberconwy and had been buried there. In 1283 his sarcophagus, presumably with his remains, was transferred to Maenan. At the Dissolution it was carried to Llanrwst, where you will now see it, lidless and empty, in the Gwydir chapel attached to Llanrwst church. Nothing remains of Maenan Abbey, though a pleasant hotel on the site carries its name. The stones were removed by Henry VIII to repair his castle of Caernarfon. At Neath stones from the abbey were used to build an elegant manor house for the new Tudor owner. The bells of Strata Florida are thought now to ring out from the tower of Tregaron church.

One doesn't know by this time how much truth there was in the king's preamble to his Act, 'that manifest sin, vicious, carnal and abominable living is daily used and committed' in the monasteries. They were certainly in decline. They no longer farmed their land but rented it out. By 1536 the monks of Strata Florida had stopped exploiting the lead mines they owned in the upper Ystwyth valley but they still had sheep on the hills and still profited from their wool. The monks were said to spend more on their food and drink than on charity. At the time of the Dissolution the great and respected abbey of Neath, with its cathedral of a church, had only eight monks in residence. Wealthier Margam had only nine. Throughout Wales the number of inmates to mourn the passing of the monasteries was small. Abbesses and nuns, abbots and monks were pensioned off and the *Letters and Papers, Foreign and Domestic*, of Henry VIII record these transactions in great detail. The learned Leyshon of Neath got a pension of £40 a year and was made Rector of nearby Cadoxton, so that he was comfortably off at least. The abbess of Llanllugan, north of Newtown, got less than £4 a year, say £250 in today's money. Poor Rose Lewis, what a fall was hers from prestige and security to such a pittance! The monastic lands were sold and this was where the king raked in the money. Much of the best agricultural and mineral-bearing land in Wales was thus redistributed and became the property of new landlords, many of whom had previously rented the land. The great Margam estate was bought piecemeal, over a period of twenty years, for £2,482 by Sir Rice Mansel of Gower. Already in the 1540s this included coalmines, the abbey church and fishpond, a water-mill and any number of granges and fertile farms. The fishpond remains, as well as the gaunt ruin of a church the monks built on the hill above for the use of the people. The abbey church, with its façade italianised early in the last century, is still in use, and within the walls of the park there are picturesque chunks of building. When I was a boy, at a time when the Talbots were still in residence, I had a secret way over the wall, under cover of trees and rhododendrons, and I used to make an adventure of dashing across stretches of lawn when the gardener's back was turned in order to hide in the old chapter house and wonder at the beauty of the eighteenth-century orangery. It was here that I first saw oranges ripen, for the trees were taken out in their tubs into the summer sunshine. The local belief was that these trees had been intended as a present to Elizabeth from the king of Spain but that the ship that carried them had been wrecked on the Margam sands. Much varied glory has passed away in places like Penmon, Maenan, Ystrad Fflur and Margam and many of the great estates which came into being at the Dissolution have disintegrated in our own century. Margam is one of these.

During the last years of the life of the abbey of Neath an accomplished poet of Glamorgan, Lewys Morgannwg, wrote a skilful ode to Abbot Leyshon and his monastery. I translate a few lines from his description of the abbey as it was just before the Dissolution.

> Heavy is the lead that tops this mansion,
> the dark grey roof of the houses of the godly . . .
> every colour in the glass, each picture suitably sunny,
> through which, like the sun's ray,
> shine the gates of treasure-keepers . . .
> The great high ceiling sparkles in the heavens
> above, in the sight of archangels;
> the floor for the folk of all Babylon's people
> below was worked with speckled stones . . .
> the bells and the monks and the sweet worship
> of the constant glory of the White Monks . . .
> Wine-warmed dishes are served,
> the stag from the high parks of the hill
> and salmon from the oceans
> and wheat and every kind of wine . . .
> University of Neath, that's the talk of England,
> a lantern for France and Ireland,
> a school frequented by scolars,
> Arithmetic, Music, Disputation, Wisdom,
> Rhetoric, Civil Law and Canon.

W. Ambrose Bebb suggests, in his *Machlud y Mynachlogydd*, that under Abbot Leyshon the renaissance had come to Wales.

Certainly, not all religious houses were in decline when the Dissolution came, nor did the dreaded 'visitors' report unfavourably on them all. The priory of St. John, at Carmarthen, seemed still, in the 1530s, to fulfil all the functions traditionally expected of such an institution. Carmarthen at that time was an important market town and trading harbour but, according to the king's spies, 'As there is but little good lodging for noblemen resorting to these parts on the King's and other business, the house is an open lodging for all such.

. . . Hospitality is daily kept for poor and rich, which is a great relief to the country, being poor and bare. . . . Strangers and merchantmen resorting to these parts are honestly received and entertained, whereby they are gladder to bring their commodities to that country. The King of Portugal thanked the house under the great seal for entertaining his merchants.' What company the brothers had in those days!

So the priory managed to survive for a few years, but the blow fell in 1539. The buildings became an Elizabethan gentleman's house. This in turn fell into checkered decline and the ruins were cleared away. According to George Owen in his *Description of Pembrokeshire* Carmarthen under Elizabeth was 'the largest towne in Wales, fair and in good state'. But the present church of St. Peter is all that remains of a great institution where our oldest complete manuscript of Welsh poetry was written, *Llyfr Du Caerfyrddin*, the *Black Book of Carmarthen*. Even in decline these religious houses played an important part in the social, cultural and economic life of the communities about them and their elimination left sad gaps. At one blow Wales lost its most beautiful buildings and acquired instead its most picturesque ruins.

More than the passing of the monasteries the people of Wales regretted the destruction of the popular shrines and the ancient miracleworking relics. The order of the Black Friars at Bangor owned the ear of Malchus, the high priest's servant, sliced off by the impetuous Peter in his defence of Jesus. It took three days to pull down the priory and the ear was destroyed. It had brought the order a regular and considerable income, for according to Richard Ingworth, Bishop of Dover, the 'visitor' concerned, it was 'the holiest relyke in all North Wales. There may no man kiss that but he must kneel so sone as he se yt, tho it was in the foulest place in all the country, and he must kiss every stone, for in each is great pardon. After he hath kissed it he must pay a met [a measure, that is] of corn, or a chese of a grote or IVd for it.'

All pilgrimages to holy wells were now forbidden, but the urges of the old faith remained powerful and people travelled long distances to visit these curative waters at night, by moonlight or taper light. Such a well, designed for partial immersion, is that of St. Beuno on the road-side south-west of Clynnog-fawr as one drives from Caernarfon down into Llŷn. Whatever you may think of such cures, it's sad that a place which has meant so much to our forbears should be so unhonoured and unregarded. There is a similar well in a charming grotto behind the ruins of Penmon Priory in the eastern corner of Anglesey, a remote spot where the sixth-century St. Seiriol established his cell. The land beyond the ruins of the priory and the delightful dovecote is still owned by the family which took it over at the Dissolution. If you pay the small fee to be allowed to go on foot or by car (no, I think perhaps you only pay to take and park a car) you'll get a good view of Ynys Seiriol, the island named after the saint, called Priestholm by the Vikings, who couldn't have found much to pick up there, and Puffin Island by English-speakers who find the island as the breeding place of the handsome and unusual bird more interesting than in its older associations.

Another famous curative well is that of St. Winifred at Holywell in Flintshire. Winifred is the English form of the saint's name, Gwenffrewi, and her holy day was 3rd November. It is said that she was brought back to life by her uncle, St. Beuno, and that Beuno built a chapel at the spot where this happened. This simpler chapel was replaced, soon after the victory at Bosworth, by Margaret, widow of Edmund Tudor and mother of Henry VII, by a much more splendid building. Was it an act of family piety by the ruthless king to spare his grandmother's gift to Treffynnon, or Holywell? The building still stands near the parish church and the well is still frequented by those in search of a miraculous cure.

Another famous place of pilgrimage was the church of Llandderfel, a peaceful village in a lovely corner of the Vale of Edeirnion, where Afon Dyfrdwy, the River Dee, sweeps away from the main road to rejoin it near Corwen, curving gracefully past rich meadows and varied woodland which rises to the bare heights of the Berwyn Mountains. Grotesque stone heads built into the wall of the present church and its outbuilding remember the older edifice where pilgrims gathered to salute the wooden image of Derfel Gadarn, a more than life-sized figure which was perched on the rood screen and which opened its arms and rolled its eyes when appealed to. He was believed to have the power to move a soul from hell and heaven. It must have inspired much awe. Derfel's wooden horse, of mountain pony size, is still kept on a bench in the church porch. Every Easter Monday it was taken out on the shoulders of strong local lads for pilgrims to be given a ride, for which no doubt they paid handsomely, up the adjoining hill which is still called Bryn Derfel, Derfel's Hill. I think it must for them have symbolised the ascent to heaven. Derfel was one of Arthur's men; hence the horse. He fought with Arthur at the battle of Camlan, but later took to religion, came to this lovely spot and founded the church named after him. All that was in the sixth century, but his huge image was taken down by Henry VIII's agents in 1538, carried to London and used at Smithfield to burn a monk. An old prophecy, so tradition has it, though it sounds suspiciously like an invention after the event, said that this image would one day destroy a woodland. The name of the monk burnt at Smithfield was Friar Forest.

I examined Derfel's horse rather carefully, the first time I saw it, and found that it could still swivel its head. Then I found hollows cut into the wood and through the head to the eyeballs which could have concealed some simple mechanism, perhaps only cord or wire, to control the movement of the head and the eyes. This was without doubt how the great figure of Derfel worked. Then the vicar drew my attention to another strange feature of the church. The stone main doorway to the church was built in 1539, the year after the fire, and the stone-work was almost immediately attacked by some senseless vandal. The hitherto unexplained gashes and pock-marks in the stone are still there for you to see. I had time to be alone and ponder the problem and suddenly I saw what had been done to the stone. At the base of each pillar of the doorway the hacked lines lay criss-cross like faggots, the bundles of wood of an *auto-da-fé*. Then long wavy lines showed flames rising toward the pointed arch but, before they met, pockmarks in the stone above the door represented sparks spattering the sky. This was not vandalism but sculpture of protest. Some unknown artist in stone had felt very strongly about the burning of Derfel's image or the burning of Friar Forest and his like, or about all these things, for they were all aspects of an old faith which was now being banned. Llandderfel church could become a place of pilgrimage for those who are interested in Welsh hagiology, in medieval sculpture in wood, or in political and religious protest in art.

Readjustment

Matters decided in London now brought burnings and disembowellings to Wales too. Mary came to the throne in 1553 and tried to swing England and Wales back to Roman Catholicism, faithful as she was to the religion of her Spanish mother, not to that of the upstart who had taken her mother's place in the king's bed and on the throne. Few people in Wales, except for those near to Henry VIII, resisted this swing, for there had been much unwillingness to abandon the old faith. But Protestantism had been in existence long enough to have become a faith and not just a political manoeuvre, and one who did resist was Robert Ferrar, Yorkshireman and Bishop of St. Davids. He was brought to Carmarthen and several times tried by his successor, the Catholic bishop, in the consistory court in St. Peter's church there. The court room is still there, in the right-hand corner of the church as you look toward the altar, quietly grim in appearance but difficult in its simplicity for people to relate today, in the imagination, with the stubborn prelate and his persistent tormentors. Ferrar refused to revert to Rome and was condemned to be burnt. He was taken into the town. A stake had been erected in what is today Nott Square, near where the old market cross once stood. Before going to the stake Ferrar told a young Welshman called Richard Jones that if he saw him once to stir in the pains of his burning he should give no credit to his doctrine. Tied to the stake he stood, unflinching, until he was cut down to fall into the fire. A monument on the spot today recalls his martyrdom.

But bigotry, cruelty and ferocity in religious persecution are never the monopoly of one faith. Under Elizabeth Protestantism returned and now it was the turn of stubborn Catholics to suffer torture and fearful death. For Elizabeth the new faith was bound up with the legality of her father's first divorce and her legitimacy as the daughter of Anne Boleyn. She passed a series of Acts making it treason to suggest that she was the defender of an heretical faith. Recusants who refused to attend Anglican services were heavily fined and eventually lost all their land. These were strong inducements to the Catholic gentry of Wales to fall into line, and anything the Tudors did was still apt to be accepted in Wales. But not by everyone. There was Richard Gwyn of Llanidloes, for instance, sometimes known in translation as Richard White. He studied at Oxford and Cambridge and became a teacher and a poet. In his *Carolau*, written in a popular Welsh verse form, he spoke with nostalgia of the old ceremonies and holy days, and attacked those who:

> Gwadu aberth Crist yn llwyr
> a gwrthod cwyr yn olau;
> llosgu'r delwau, cablu'r saint
> a gostwng braint y gwyliau.

> Quite deny Christ's sacrifice,
> refuse the lighted taper,
> burn the images, curse the saints,
> give holy days less honour.

In Wrexham, in an open place known as the Beast Market and where the pleasure fairs are held, Richard Gwyn was hanged in 1584 until he was half-dead. He was then let down, his genitals were cut off and his belly sliced open for the drawing out of his intestines. At this point the Sheriff took pity and told the executioner to go for his heart to end his agony, before the final removal of his head. These were horrors which were to give the glorious Elizabethan age a nastier side. There is to my knowledge no monument to this martyr, but in 1970 he was canonised by the Church of Rome and he is now St. Richard Gwyn.

There was trouble in the world of poetry too, trouble which reflected the changes in the social order in Wales. Not all the new gentry were prepared to employ a house poet or to welcome an itinerant one and, to make matters worse, unqualified poets were wandering about the country and putting the trained bards out of business. Elizabeth issued an order to some gentlemen of North Wales that they should hold an eisteddfod at Caerwys to set matters right. It went thus: 'Elizabeth by the Grace of God, of England, France and Ireland, Queen, and Defender of the Faith . . . to our trusty and right well beloved Sir Richard Bulkely, Knight; Ellis Price, Doctor in Civil Law and one of our Council in the Marches of Wales; William Mostyn . . .

and to every of them greeting. Whereas it is come to the knowledge of the Lord President and other our council in the Marches of Wales that vagrant and idle persons, naming themselves Minstrels, Rythmers and Bards, are lately grown into such intolerable multitude within the Principality of North Wales, that not only gentlemen and others are often disquieted in their habitations but also the expert minstrels and musicians . . . much discouraged in the Practice of their knowledge, and also not a little hindered of livings and preferment; the reformation thereof and putting these people in order, the said Lord President and Council have thought very necessary . . . Our said Council have therefore appointed the execution of this commission to be at the town of Caerwys, the Monday next after the Feast of the Blessed Trinity, which shall be in the year of our Lord, 1568. And, therefore, to require and command you, by the authority of these presents, to cause open proclamation to be made that all and every person and persons that intend to maintain their living by name or colour of Minstrels, Rythmers and Bards appear before you, the said day and place to show their Leanings accordingly . . .

'Also that you Sir Richard Bulkeley, Ellis Price and William Mostyn, Esquires, repair to the place the day aforesaid . . . to admit such as by your wisdom and knowledges you shall find worthy to use, exercise and follow the Sciences and Faculties of their Professions . . . giving straight monition and commendment in our name to the rest not worthy, that they return to some honest labour . . . upon pain to be taken as sturdy and idle vagabonds . . . Given under our signet at our City of Chester the 23rd of October, in the ninth year of our reign, 1567.'

Elis Prys, the Ellis Price of this document, was known as *Y Doctor Coch*, the Red Doctor, because of his Cambridge gown, and was one of the most feared men in North Wales. He had been one of Henry VIII's 'visitors' for the dissolution of the monasteries and was a ruthless land-grabber, both for himself and his great friend, Robert Dudley, Earl of Leicester. He was the father of Thomas Prys, Plas Iolyn, the pirate poet. The Mostyn family had long been notable patrons of poetry and the queen's commission reminded William Mostyn that 'his ancestors have had the gift and bestowing of the silver harp appertaining to the Chief of that faculty'. On this occasion the silver harp went to

Simwnt Fychan, a scholarly poet who did much to carry on the traditions of the classical Welsh metres and who must often have recited his verse to the company in the noble hall which William Mostyn built and which today stands at a higher level than the bigger and more splendid Mostyn Hall.

Caerwys is today a sleepy little place and unlikely as a setting for a National Eisteddfod, which today depends on the common people of Wales for support, not on its gentry.

In another way too Queen Elizabeth undermined her father's policy toward Wales by unwittingly helping to preserve and dignify the Welsh language. She saw that the Welsh people would never accept Protestantism while it was presented in English, a language which most of them didn't understand. The break with Rome brought with it a break with Latin, but the ordinary people of Wales could hardly be expected to listen to the lessons, prayers and psalms in English as a replacement. In 1563 the queen commanded a translation of the Bible into Welsh. *The Book of Common Prayer* was also to be done and the impatient monarch required all this within three years. The work was undertaken by Richard Davies, Bishop of St. Davids, who recruited the help of William Salesbury, a gentleman of Llanrwst who twenty years before that had urged his fellow countrymen to beg the king and the Council to give them the Bible in their own language. Salesbury had started on the work before Henry VIII's death and had published in 1551 a book entitled *Kynniver llith a ban*, a translation of the lessons of the communion service. Mary's advent to the throne put a check to his work but in 1663 he welcomed the new opportunity. A certain Thomas Huet, precentor at St. Davids, helped with his version of Revelations. The translations were brilliant, though Salesbury's Oxford education and knowledge of Hebrew, Greek and Latin had given him strange notions of orthography in Welsh. Even before 1551 Salesbury had published books to help the Welsh learn English and the English learn Welsh, as well as a remarkable book called *Oll Synnwyr pen Kembero ygyd*, which means roughly 'all the common sense in a Welshman's head'. This was a collection of Welsh proverbs and the author's purpose was to get his readers to appreciate the richness of their folk traditions. We owe a very great deal to William Salesbury. It is said that he began to tackle the Old Testament too, but that he and Bishop Davies disagreed about the etymology of a word and the work was given up.

At this point the work of translating the whole of the Bible into Welsh was undertaken by Dr. William Morgan, a farmer's son of Penmachno, in the mountains south of Betws-y-Coed, who managed to get to St. John's College, Cambridge, where he took a series of degrees. Most of this great work was performed while he was vicar of Llanrhaeadr-ym-Mochnant, a quiet little town which stands at the entrance to a spectacular valley. Follow the stream a few miles up the valley and you will come to what is for me the most beautiful water-fall in Wales. The water falls abruptly over the lip of a high plateau and falls 240 feet in a series of slim, lace-like cascades. The stream is still lively as it passes the village church. Yet William Morgan's life was not entirely happy here. He was involved in intrigues and quar-rels over getting a rich heiress to marry Robert Wynn of Gwydir; he was taken before the Court of the Star Chamber and the Council of the Marches without his name ever being sullied; he fell foul of the grasping Sir John Wynn of Gwydir over the seizure of church lands. Yet back he'd come from the tension and anxieties of the courts to the beauty of Llanrhaeadr, even though its peace was disturbed by a squabble with his parishioners, and to the daily thunder and sweet-ness of his Bible in Welsh.

The work was published in London in 1588. In his Latin dedica-tion to the queen Dr. Morgan speaks with approval of the New Testament of 1567 and of his debt to Salesbury, Davies and Huet. He is very tactful in his assessment of the importance of having the Bible in Welsh, seeming to accept the Tudor ideal of one language to be spoken throughout the island but claiming linguistic uniformity to be less necessary than an understanding of the Bible and of the principles of the Christian faith, something which could be reached only in one's own language. William Morgan was not such a great scholar as Salesbury but he was familiar with the extensive vocabulary of the Welsh poetic tradition in the *cywyddau* written over the two centuries from Dafydd ap Gwilym. It was this that gave power and variety and beauty to his writing. He created a prose style which has continued to influence writers of Welsh to this day. It was not the language of the people, but William Morgan's Bible, with the revised edition by Dr.

Parry in 1620 and the cheaper edition, *Y Beibl Bach* (The Little Bible) of 1630, brought great prose into the homes of Wales and was the foundation of Welsh literacy. It immeasurably raised the standard of spoken and written Welsh.

It is ironical that the first great step toward this achievement should have been made by a descendant of a Norman invader, Salesbury, and that the command for the translation which did more than anything else to perpetuate the use of Welsh should have come from a queen whose father had insisted on the extirpation of that tongue.

The National Library of Wales at Aberystwyth is the place to see these early printed books to which we owe the perpetuation of Welsh and many of them are laid out there in glass cases for your immediate inspection. You may be surprised to observe from title pages that some of them were printed in places farther away even than London —in Milan, for instance. In fact, much of the work of sustaining Welsh culture was done outside Wales during the second half of the sixteenth century. Jesus College, Oxford, was founded in 1571 to encourage more Welshmen and make it easier for them to go up to that University, and to this day the college continues to nurture Welsh scholars. But Welsh Catholics had to cross over to the Continent to continue their studies, at colleges in Belgium or in Italy, where Welsh scholars and clerics taught and administered.

Morys Clynnog was a Caernarfonshire man who took a degree at Christ Church, Oxford, and who by 1558, when he was thirty-three years of age, had become Bishop of Bangor. With the death of Mary and the switch of faiths he escaped to Italy and became rector of the English College there. There he was accused of favouring Welsh students, but a more likely reason for his dismissal from the post was the ambition of his Jesuit subordinates to control the college. Once more a refugee, he set sail from Rouen for Spain and was drowned on the way. In 1568 he had a book called *Athraviaeth Gristnogavl* (Christian Doctrine) published in Milan, with an introduction by Gruffudd Robert and a sub-title which states that it contains compactly all the main topics a man will meet on his way to paradise.

Gruffudd Robert, too, had become Archdeacon of Anglesey just before Mary's death and he fled to the Continent with Morys Clynnog, staying in Brussels and Louvain on the way to Rome, to work at the English College there. In Italy these Welsh scholars met the full flood of the renaissance and they tried to convey some of the ideas of this great movement to their compatriots through the medium of Welsh. One of these ideas was the importance of the vernacular languages. (Dante had been one of the first to use contemporary Italian instead of Latin for serious writing.) Gruffudd Robert was the first to attempt a full-scale analysis of the Welsh language and the first part of this immensely important work was published in Milan in 1567, under the title *Dosparth Byrr ar y rhan gyntaf i ramadeg cymraeg* (*A short exposition of the first part of Welsh grammar*). The book can be seen at Aberystwyth and it is worth looking at if only for the beauty of its italic printing. This was followed by the second part, on the parts of speech, the third part, on *cynghanedd* (the complex system of alliteration and assonance used in the twenty-four strict Welsh metres), and the fourth part, on the verse forms. Gruffudd Robert took the European view that literature should be in the contemporary language of the people it was intended for. He slated the Welsh poets of his day for their conservative, backward-looking attitude to language. Bring in foreign words, he said, if they're useful, and make them feel at home in the language. Dafydd ap Gwilym, also aware of what was being done outside Wales, had done this successfully two hundred years before. William Morgan probably came in for the same condemnation. Whilst insisting on this natural, comprehensible way of writing, Gruffudd Robert was not unaware of the glories of classical literature and he has been shown by Mr. Saunders Lewis to have been the first and the greatest exponent in Welsh of that essentially renaissance mode, the Ciceronian style in prose.

Ambitious Welshmen who were prepared to toe the political and religious line of Queen Elizabeth found plenty of opportunity in London, by-passing Ludlow and its stranglehold on Wales. There, at the head of things, was William Cecil, Lord Burleigh, the queen's most trusted servant and the architect of England's growth and stability, building on the foundation laid down by Henry VII. Burleigh was the grandson of that Richard Cecil, or Seisyll, who had served Henry Tudor and who reaped his reward. Burleigh still retained some Welshness and a letter of his in Welsh is kept amongst the manuscripts in the Cardiff City Library, but the Cecils quickly became a great English family and Earls of Salisbury. Many of those who followed Henry Tudor, and their descendants, stayed on in England and became English. Dr. John Dee, of Radnorshire descent, became an outstanding mathematician and astronomer but financial and occupational rewards were slow in coming to him. He was more than prepared to apply science to practical problems, as is shown by his introduction to the first English edition of Euclid and by his astonishing production of a comedy of Aristophanes at Cambridge. His interest in alchemy and astrology were acceptable in his time but he was clearly tricked into involvement in spiritualism by the impostor Edward Kelly.

Other Welshmen were prominent in the queen's service. Sir Roger Williams was one of her most experienced and trusted generals at a time when young men like Sir Philip Sidney and the Earls of Southampton and Essex went to war in search of personal honour rather than for the sake of their country. Shakespeare gives us a reflection of Roger Williams and his book on the art of war in Captain Fluellen and satirises the pursuit of honour by Hotspur, with his counterpart, Falstaff. Morris Kyffin was a poet in English and Welsh, a great writer of Welsh prose, witness his *Deffynniad Ffydd Eglwys Loegr* (1594), which was a translation of Bishop Jewel's *Apologia* or defence of the Anglican faith, but he had his practical side too, for he was Comptroller of the Musters in Ireland till his death in 1598. There his task was the unpopular one of keeping an eye on dishonest officials of the queen and preventing the oppression of the Irish people. He was buried in Christ Church, Dublin. The Myddeltons of Denbighshire became great London merchants and Sir Hugh Myddelton, as Lord Mayor of London, became famous early in the seventeenth century for his construction of the New River which brought London a good water supply. His brother, Sir Thomas Myddelton, was a businessman on a very wide scale, an original shareholder in the East India Company and the Virginia Company. As a banker he worked together with John Williams, goldsmith and jeweller to James I, a man deeply versed in Welsh history and traditions, who supplied Michael Drayton with information for the Welsh section of his poem 'Polyolbion'. It was no doubt he who convinced Drayton of the devotion to poetry of the Welsh, a people, according to the Fourth Song of this poem:

Addicted from their birth so much to Poesy.

But not all the activities of Welshmen outside their native land were as law-abiding and useful as the few I have chosen to write about. Amongst the Welsh gentlemen of the Elizabethan age there were at least two prominent pirates. Of course, piracy was allowed to verge on respectability when the queen's coffers benefited from the robbing of Spanish ships, but there is no record of Thomas Prys, Plas Iolyn, or his cousin Pirs Gruffydd, of Penrhyn, near Bangor, ever contributing to the queen's funds, though Prys was at Tilbury at the Earl of Leicester's side to be inspected by the queen in 1588, in preparation for a possible landing of the Armada. Captain Thomas Prys was the son of the notorious Red Doctor and became the most interesting poet of the sixteenth century in Welsh. He built himself a house from the ruins of an old monastery on Enlli (Bardsey Island) and used it as a secure base for his piratical voyages. Smuggling, too, I imagine. But for Thomas Prys the dangers and costs of a pirate's life seem to have outbalanced the profits and he got out of it in time. An extraordinary *cywydd* in mixed English and Welsh recounts a disastrous attempt on a Spanish ship. It ends:

> bee ffor I will pil or part
> bei a shipp Il bee shepart.

In modern English:

> Before I will pillage, or part
> buy a ship, I'll be a shepherd.

Buying a share in a ship was the custom in those days and Shakespeare refers to such an investor as a putter-out. Having withdrawn from piracy and the dissipations of London before squandering his considerable inheritance Thomas Prys appealed to Pirs Gruffydd to do likewise. For this purpose he used the old convention of *y llatai*, a bird or beast as a messenger, and no one ever chose more aptly, for he asked the porpoise to seek out Pirs Gruffydd at 'the edge of Spain, bosom of the world':

133

It is six weary years
since he took ship abroad
to the seas beyond the estuary,
over the bar, across the world.
It's time for the gallant giver
to turn away from salt water
and come, ending anxiety,
to his own hall from that foul place . . .

The description of the porpoise is inventive and spirited and these are
the best sea poems in Welsh, for Welsh poets have rarely been seen
even ankle-deep in sea water. Prys grew to hate London, having
known its taverns, gaols and brothels as well as the court, and wrote
scathingly of the city and its officials. Part of his advice to his son is:

Beware the official, second Judas,
his dog's shanks and his evil ways.
No official, treacherous breast,
with his foxy smile can be honest.
Don't trust your blood brother with a loan
if today he's an official.

Most of Thomas Prys's poems are still unprinted but the manuscripts that carry his poems at Aberystwyth and in the British Museum
show that bitter experiences on sea and in London did nothing to
blunt his delight in life, and I know of no poet more likely to stir the
interest of young people in the tradition that is theirs. As a renaissance
man he abandons the overworked Welsh comparisons for a pretty
girl, Olwen, Gwenhwyfar, Indeg and the others, and likens her to
Fenws, Minerfa, Deiana, Palas, Medea, Lwcresia and Cresyd and
Elen of Troy, for that is how they appear in Welsh. He sends a flea
with a message of love and no creature can get nearer to a girl than a
flea, nor perhaps be less acceptable, which makes one doubt the
seriousness of the message. He sends a mouse from London with a
greeting to his friends at Llanrwst, carefully detailing the way. And
Llanrwst was to be the centre of his activities once he settled down to
his estates.

Llanrwst is worth a visit and, if you can, go there on Tuesday, for
this is market day and the lovely little town is at its liveliest. It's a

Welsh town, never having known a Norman castle, and it's a natural centre for the fertile Conwy valley. It had suffered fearful destruction in Owain Glyndŵr's wars and during the Wars of the Roses, and there wasn't much standing there when the Wynns took it over in the sixteenth century.

The most famous member of this family was Sir John Wynn (1553–1627), partly so because of his *History of the Gwydir Family*, a document of the greatest interest which was not published until 1770. He was at Oxford and then read law in London, where he continued to live until his father's death in 1580. He then made his base at Gwydir Castle, which was built by his grandfather outside Llanrwst, and entered fully and sometimes violently into public life in North Wales. Though quick-tempered, given to litigation, selfish and ruthless in the acquisition of property, he brought benefits to the district. Llanrwst owes its fine buildings to him, the free school, the solid and impressive almshouses near the church, the fine bridge which he is said to have commissioned Inigo Jones to build and the chapel he planned to build alongside the church which was actually put up by his son, to a design, so tradition has it, by Inigo Jones. Llanrwst claims this great architect as one of its illustrious sons. The details of the Wynn family tree are spelled on the wall of the chapel, there are fine brasses and a colourful memorial to Sir John and his wife Sidney, as well as to his grandfather, John Wyn ap Maredudd, with Llywelyn Fawr's empty sarcophagus on the floor, as though to boost the family's claim to royal blood. Sir John Wynn continued this tradition of patronage of literature by the Welsh gentry by supporting and encouraging Thomas Wiliems of Trefriw in his work of copying manuscripts and in his compilation of a Latin-Welsh dictionary.

Sir John brought the making of Welsh frieze, a woollen cloth, to the valley and he was interested in the copper-mining at Mynydd Parys in Anglesey. He proposed the reclamation of land on the Traeth Mawr in the Porthmadoc Estuary, a project carried out by Madocks, with some help from the poet Shelley, in the early years of the nineteenth century. The great landowners now had money to invest in industry and under Elizabeth Wales witnessed a great drive to exploit the vast mineral resources of the country, but much of the money behind this exploitation came from the rich merchants of the City of

London. One of these was the Welshman Sir Hugh Myddelton, who brought water to London and to whom Sir John Wynn proposed the drying of Traeth Mawr. In 1617 he took over Cwmsymlog, east of Aberystwyth, and mined silver and lead there. In 1568 Queen Elizabeth had made all mining her monopoly and she set up the Mines Royal Society to control mining and to lease areas to speculators. This was unpopular among the gentry, for any landowner who planned to mine on his land had to come to terms with this society before setting to work legally. Many of course mined surreptitiously. Fortunes were made in places like Cwmsymlog, but the only benefit to Wales, except where local gentry took to mining, was the low wages paid to the miners.

Cwmsymlog today is a palimpsest of mining methods and this is part of the fascination of the place. Lead had been mixed in Wales by the Celts, then by the Romans, who had processed and exported it. In the Middle Ages much lead had been mined for the roofing of religious houses, to be stripped off at the Dissolution. The lead roof of the lovely Bishop's Palace at St. Davids was removed by Bishop Barlow in the sixteenth century. At first, enough ore-bearing seams were found at the surface for a kind of open-cast mining to be possible. Fires were lit on the seam to crack the rock ready for crushing. When the seam was worked out at the surface a trench was dug to follow it at a lower level. Such a trench is to be seen alongside the road which leads uphill at Cwmsymlog. When that ran out, or it was no longer possible to dig a deeper trench, levels were driven into the mountain and shafts down into the rock. The ore obtained was first of all broken up with an iron mallet known as a buckler, a work that was usually performed by women and girls, and then it was sieved and washed to separate the good ore from the dross. A constant flow of water was needed for this and to supply it leets, or channels, were cut in the rock to bring the water down from reservoirs to the machines and washing floors below. You can still see how skilfully these channels were engineered if you search for them as they zigzag down through the woods to the left of the road up to the reservoir at Cwmsymlog.

A later development was the water-wheel for power and a wheel-pit at Cwmsymlog gives you some idea of how big these could be, a good forty feet in diameter in this case. Then for better ventilation a tall stone chimney-stack was built to suck up the foul air from the tunnels below, for these levels and shafts created new problems. Water gathered in the shafts and had to be channelled off or lifted to the surface with chain pumps, worked at first by hand. The further a level was cut into the mountain the fouler the air got and the thicker the poisonous lead dust. Until the workings got too deep, ventilation shafts could be driven down at intervals, but when this method failed a German device was introduced whereby a great bellows puffed fresh air along lead pipes to where the men were working. In spite of all these devices the ordinary lead miner's life was brief and unhealthy. But others grew rich from their labours. Thomas Bushell, who took over the Cwmsymlog mines from Sir Hugh Myddelton's widow, was allowed to set up a mint at Aberystwyth in 1637 to produce silver coinage which helped Charles I finance his struggle to keep his throne. Near Furnace Bridge and its fine waterfall, at Eglwys Fach on the road between Aberystwyth and Machynlleth, there is a great mill and forge built to process the silver from the mines at that time. It was destroyed by Cromwell, together with the mint in Aberystwyth Castle and the castle itself, because of this help given to the king. It is now being restored.

Lead and silver, these usually in conjunction, were not the only metals mined. Castell Nedd, or Neath, is at the mouth of the once lovely Nedd valley which is now happily recovering its verdant charm. From 1568 on it was Tintern that had the largest copper works in Wales, but Neath became important too. Its ruined abbey and castle indicated its older prominence but now it was seen to have wood, coal, running water to turn machinery and a navigable estuary for commerce. Once the copper works were established, ore was brought here by sea from Cornwall and from as far away as Keswick in the north of England. Capitalism thus brought the beginnings of industrial areas to South Wales.

Iron too was in great demand towards the end of the sixteenth century and one use of it was to cast it into guns to keep the Spaniards at bay. Richard Hanbury, a London goldsmith who ran the Tintern copper works, was one of the first ironmasters. The Elizabethan ironworks should not be thought of as something localised, like Margam or Shotton. They were small and there were two hundred of them in Wales in 1613. And they moved about. When all the woods in the district had been cut down and burnt the furnace was picked up and rebuilt in a new, unspoiled area. The popular poets expressed what the Welsh people thought of this stripping of their woodlands, and the extent of the deprivation which resulted from this destruction of an environment is amusingly detailed by a wandering poet of the lower order, a *clerwr* called Robin Clidro, in a 'poem on behalf of the squirrels who went to London to file and make an affidavit on the bill for the cutting down of Marchan Wood, near Rhuthun'. I translate a part of what their leader, a matronly red squirrel, says on oath to the Bailiff, whom she refers to as Sir Bribem:

> All Rhuthun's woods are ravaged;
> my house and barn were taken
> one dark night, and all my nuts.
> The squirrels are all calling
> for the trees; they fear the dog.
> Up there remains of the hill wood
> only grey ash of oak-trees;
> there's not a stump unstolen
> nor a crow's nest left in our land.
> The owls are all the time hooting
> for trees, they send the children mad.
> The poor owl catches cold,
> left cold without her hollow trunk.

Another spirited poem, by an anonymous writer complains of the felling of Glyn Cynon Wood in Glamorgan. I quote one stanza, again in translation.

> Many a birch-tree green of cloak
> (I'd like to choke the Saxon!)
> is now a flaming heap of fire
> where iron-workers blacken.

As timber was exhausted, and this was happening rapidly towards the end of the sixteenth century, coal took its place as fuel for industry. Coal mines, too, were very small in those days, rather like some of the one-family or small partnership levels and shafts which are still worked in South Wales today, in the Nedd Valley, for instance, where you will find them high up on the hill-sides. One I visited, the Graig Lwyd mine above Glynneath, is run by nine men, including the owners, with two horses for power and a lorry to distribute the coal. The Elizabethan colliers of Wales were said to be clannish, superstitious, a race apart. They are still a tough, independent body of men. And they were said to take every possible holiday. They still do that too, and it's difficult to blame them when one thinks of the work they do.

So these precious ores were melted down and carried out of Wales. Sir Henry Sidney, Lord President of Wales and the Marches and father of Sir Philip Sidney, poet and author of the *Arcadia*, owned a furnace and a forge near Cardiff, but the iron produced there was carried off to his works in Sussex to be processed into steel. Wales had become a valuable source country for England.

Slates had been quarried in Snowdonia since the fifteenth century and the high quality of that slate (the rose-tinted ones have long been favoured in Wales) led to much export from Caernarfon and Beaumaris to Liverpool and the north of England. Poets, though craftsmen in words, have a critical eye for other crafts as well, and a fifteenth-century poet, Guto'r Glyn, in a poem of asking, this time for slates to roof his house, *I Ofyn Ysglats*, says:

> *Er dwyn gwŷr i doi'n gywrain*
> *gwellt rhyg mawr, gwell y trig main.*

> Though you bring men to thatch skilfully
> with long rye straw, stone lasts longer.

From central Wales much went by land over the border to England: wool, woollen cloth and animals on the hoof. But in Wales we have water on three sides of us and since prehistory the sea had been a great highway not only for imports and exports but also for coastal traffic. Places like Beaumaris (Biwmares to the Welsh) and Cei Newydd, the Welsh New Quay, are holiday places today, their harbours bright with beflagged yachts and dinghies in summer. There may be a few lobster pots about and some tanned characters selling mackerel they claim to have caught, but in Elizabethan and Jacobean days all kinds of things were unloaded on their quays. There would be basic necessities, grain, lime, coal, slate and salt, and more exotic luxuries such as spices, wine and silk. Out from these ports would go the products of industry and agriculture. The port books of the time make interesting reading. Welsh wheat went from Swansea to Venice; out from Beaumaris went butter, hides and leather as well as slates. Welsh leather was in great demand in the English markets. From Carmarthen and the ports of Pembrokeshire the main export was frieze, the strong Welsh woollen cloth which was napped on one side. Imports were similar in North and South Wales, brass and worked pewter, alum, wine, hops, white and black soap, honey and raisins. The seaways of the Celtic saints had become lanes of convenience and profit. Today, with our railways being closed and our roads cluttered with heavy vehicles, it's surely time to re-open the ports and use our empty seas once more.

When Elizabeth came to the throne the population of Wales was less than a quarter of a million, but as it grew and as the new Tudor freedoms made the towns more possible places for the Welsh to be in, more people lived in what were once Anglo-Norman townships. The old town of Caernarfon within the walls is peaceful and sleepy today. Seagulls land in the middle of the streets and boys bicycle safely down the hills where there was once the busy noise of craftsmen and the coming and going of men with carts and women with baskets. The town slowly expanded and spilled out of its stone enclosure as the bustle of the shopping area moved to roomier places outside the walls, places where the country people had laid out their produce for the town-dwellers to come out and inspect and buy. Other towns, like Tenby and Conwy, managed to contain this new growth within their protective walls.

West of the great Border estates the farms were often small, many of them from ten to thirty acres, as they still are today, but the right to graze animals on common land enabled the farmer to plough his few acres. But now, in the sixteenth century, great expanses of common were enclosed by sharp-eyed estate-builders. The ordinary Welshman had little defence against this, for he was no longer certain of his rights as he had been under the laws of Hywel Dda, and he was unlikely to go to Ludlow or London to seek redress. There were some violent reactions. In Breconshire hedges were pulled down and angry countrymen tied the land-grabbers to the tails of their horses and made them taste the land they were stealing. Bitterness is still roused by the misuse of our few remaining commons. In these conditions the land had to be carefully farmed, and the Welsh were changing from a pastoral people to a partly agricultural one. Apart from the main grain crops, the farmer would set aside small patches in his ploughed land for peas, beans, hops for brewing and flax and hemp for spinning and home-weaving. Even today the hill farmer often prefers to grow peas, beans and carrots in a potato field rather than bother with a garden. A family had then to be as self-sufficient as possible, and bad harvests meant much suffering. Marl, a mixture of lime and earth, was used to improve the soil. Production increased and early in the seventeenth century great quantities of butter went from Wales to the west of England, Ireland and France. But life was still very hard for the hill farmers, their labourers and servant girls.

Yet even this life below a poverty line which is difficult for us to conceive had its moments of gaiety. The Puritans hadn't yet come to kill all Sunday and holy day fun and there's one annual excitement we know about in great detail, since there's a vivid account of it in George Owen's *Description of Pembrokeshire* (1603). It's the ancient Welsh game of *cnapan*, a kind of primitive rugby. At Cilgeran, on the border between Ceredigion and Pembrokeshire, just beyond the castle as you walk to it from the centre of the little town, there's a patch of green which looks precipitously down into a gorge cut by the River Teifi. It's still called Parc y Cnapan. A certain Doctor Thayer, who lived at Cilgeran in 1603, described how he used to sit at this spot to watch the start of a *cnapan* match. The game was played with a wooden ball about the size of a large apple, made of a hard wood, box or crab-apple or holly, and boiled in tallow to make it harder to handle. The handling of a greasy ball is an old tradition in Wales, for a handling game it was, played between all the able-bodied men of two parishes, or two larger areas, all stripped to the waist to save their shirts from tearing and wearing leather breeches. It was a spring and early summer game, played, at Cilgeran, on Ascension Day and Corpus Christi. To start the match the ball, the *cnapan*, was flung up in the air or, at Cilgeran, tossed down from the cliff-top, and they were off, each side

141

trying to pass and carry the *cnapan* as far as they could toward their own home base, often the porch of their parish church. It was rough, tumultuous, exciting.

The new gentry prospered and, as we saw in the case of the Gwydir family, were anxious to establish their descent from the native princely rulers of the Wales that had passed. In the church at Y Fenni (Abergavenny) there is a carved wooden figure of Jesse which dates from this time; the Tree of Jesse was a concept which appealed to these new Tudor families. The fact that Christ had been given a genealogy made more respectable their attempts to claim noble forebears. There were poets, like Rhys Cain at Llanrwst, who specialised in genealogies and who were not averse to the exercise of their imagination where their considerable store of knowledge of past generations failed to provide secure enough links. Funerary sculptors too did a good trade and the church at Montgomery is worth a visit for the splendid memorials to the Herbert family of that region, a family which supported the Tudor policy in Wales and became tremendously powerful. Not that this Herbert family, and others like them, became immediately anglicised. Lord Edward Herbert of Cherbury, eldest son of Richard Herbert of Montgomery Castle, makes it clear in his most interesting *Autobiography* that English was the language of the home but that he was sent by his parents to Edward Thelwall, of Place-Ward in Denbighshire, 'to learn the Welsh tongue, as believing it necessary to enable me to treat with those my friends and tenants who understood no other language'. He describes his father as 'blackhaired and bearded, as all my ancestors of his side are said to have been'. In education Lord Herbert held that Greek should come first and then Latin. He had great faith in herbal medicines and cured many people in this way. For exercise he advocated riding, fencing and dancing, for ease of movement, but he preferred hawking to hunting on horseback, which he considered to be a waste of time. He condemned dicing and card-playing but was open-minded in the matter of religion, a subject on which he wrote several treatises and which in his day was becoming a dangerously controversial matter. Lord Orford, in *Royal and Noble Authors*, sums up his position thus: 'Lord Herbert's chief argument against revealed religion is the improbability that Heaven should reveal its will to only a portion of the earth, which he terms *particular* religion.' One of the new school of metaphysical poets (the name was applied to them later), Lord Herbert says that his brother George, better known as a poet, studied languages in the hope of becoming Secretary of State but he was disappointed and so took holy orders. Another metaphysical poet, John Donne, was at Montgomery to preach the funeral sermon of the mother of these two poets. Donne seems to have been descended from the Welsh Dwnn family which produced poets in Welsh at this time, the best known being the heraldic poet, Lewys Dwnn. The connection between Welsh descent and the metaphysical movement is intriguing. Could this new and exciting vision of the world and of the human condition have sprung from a blending of blood, a blending of cultures? The Breconshire Henry Vaughan was to follow, later in the seventeenth century.

CHAPTER IV

Involvement with England

Only during the second half of this present century have we in Wales seriously and in growing numbers begun to doubt the justice and wisdom of our continued involvement in decisions taken at Westminster or in even more remote centres of power, increasingly aware as we are that the playing of war games and the training for war in our otherwise peaceful skies and on our bombarded and tank-torn uplands are no part of our view of life and of the world we live in, and that the prestige spending of a decayed empire has nothing to do with our simpler needs. During the seventeenth century Wales took the impact of this involvement with the experience of a destructive civil war and with the slow penetration of a new movement, Puritanism. There had of course been shocks before, and even though the Welsh gentry were heavily committed, on one side or the other, in the Wars of the Roses, the ordinary people of Wales must have regarded the ravaging of their country with nothing but horror, until Henry Tudor came along to claim their allegiance. They had seen the sad removal of the religious houses, the prohibition of recourse to popular shrines, and there had been the enforced abandonment of the Catholic faith, a loss which was mitigated by the gift of the Bible in Welsh. Now there was more destruction to come and more interference from outside with their life.

There had been developments in agriculture, and in commerce based on agriculture, which must have brought some degree of prosperity to those concerned. There had been a great increase in mining and quarrying, but most of the resulting profits had gone out of Wales with the processed metals. Government was remote and incomprehensible. There was a decline in the patronage of poetry, the foremost of the Welsh arts, by the great houses, and the craft of poetry itself suffered a kind of fossilisation. In many ways the country had grown stagnant and lifeless and we have seen how some livelier and more ambitious spirits had escaped to the opportunities of London, as they still do today. But some went further. Hugh Holland was born in Denbigh and educated at Westminster School and Cambridge. From the university he set out at once on his travels, by way of Rome as far as Jerusalem. In Rome he got into trouble over some remarks he made about Queen Elizabeth and in Constantinople, on the way back from Jerusalem, he annoyed the English ambassador to the Sultan with the freedom of his language. Hugh Holland was a poet in Welsh and English, a friend of poets and dramatists, a member of the Mermaid Club and the contributor of a commendatory sonnet to the *First Folio* of Shakespeare's works in 1623. For Coryat's *Crudities* he wrote an *englyn* (four-line poem) in Welsh. Like George Herbert he had hoped for and prepared himself for high office, but was disappointed. He was buried in Westminster Abbey in 1633. Could it have been the 'freedom' of his words about the queen which wrecked his hope of preferment? The title of a long poem which he published in 1603 is intriguing. It runs: *Pancharis: the first Booke. Containing the Preparation of the Love between Owen Tudyr and the Queene, long since intended to her Maiden Majestie and now dedicated to the Invincible James.* But he fared little better under the new monarch. In a poem in later life, *To a Private Friend*, which he calls

> This sad distracted abstract of my woe

he recounts his many griefs, the chief being the death of his wife, Ursula, and thinks back to the happy, studious innocence of his university days, from which he emerged into a corrupt world.

> I gave my wild, unsteady youth the reins,
> And saw all vicious and polluted strains
> That man was prone to (Heaven forgive me for them,
> Which now can witness how much I abhor them).

Hugh Holland is an interesting person, in many ways an emblem of his kind and his age, and a writer of astonishingly modern English.

The way to Jerusalem had already been pointed by another Denbigh man, this time of the prosperous craftsman class. Sir Richard Clough was the son of a glover of Denbigh and as a boy he was sent to sing in the cathedral choir in Chester. He went up to London and from there made a pilgrimage to Palestine, where he was made Knight of the Holy Sepulchre in Jerusalem. Hence the Sir in his name. He became Sir Thomas Gresham's agent in Antwerp and is said to have suggested to Gresham the advisability of setting up an Exchange in London on the lines of the Antwerp Bourse. He married Catherine of Berain, a second marriage for each of them, and travelled with her in Spain, Denmark and Germany on his profitable business ventures. In the Netherlands he got to know Abraham Ortelius and it was he who introduced Humphrey Lhuyd to the famous map-maker, a meeting which inspired Lhuyd to produce his own pioneering maps of Wales and England. With all his business interests on the Continent, Clough never lost contact with Wales, and his early death was lamented in traditional manner by some of the best poets of the age. Wiliam Cynwal, author of a lively poem 'In Defence of Woman', used the *llatai* (message-bearer) convention to ask a hawk to carry his greetings to Clough and his wife at Antwerp, *Kowydd i yrru y gwalch i annerch mr Ric. Klwch a meistres Catrin penn oeddynt yn Anwarp*. This and other poem titles indicate how the name Clough was then pronounced. Clough died in Hamburg and was buried there, but his heart was brought home for burial in Yr Eglwys Wen, the quiet Whitechurch, a mile east of Denbigh, where his friend Humphrey Lhuyd had been buried and where Twm o'r Nant was to lie. Clough had great plans for Wales, one of them to make the River Clwyd navigable for small ships up as far as Rhuthun. He seems to have had a town house in Denbigh and to have been building two houses not far from the town, Plas Clough and Bachygraig, for his eventual retirement.

Another notable traveller in Europe, James Howell, left the beautifully situated village of Llangamarch, where his father was curate, with little intention of returning. He went to school at Hereford and then to Jesus College, Oxford, where he took his degree in 1613. He went into business and, with his knowledge of languages, he was employed on various commercial and diplomatic missions. He was a kind of professional information gatherer, a foreign correspondent before newspapers began. Here is a specimen of his news reporting, written in 1623, a detailed account of the murder, and the causes and effects of the murder of Sultan Osman II in a palace revolution in Constantinople. 'Sultan Osman, the Grand Turk, a man according to the humour of that nation, warlike and fleshed in blood and a violent hater of Christians, was in the flower of his years, in the heat and height of his courage, knocked in the head by one of his own slaves, and one of the meanest of them, with a battle-axe, and the murderer never after proceeded against or questioned. . . . This Osman was a man of goodly constitution, an amiable aspect, and of excess of courage, but sordidly covetous. . . . He used also to make his person too cheap, for he would go ordinarily in the night time with two men after him like a petty constable and peep into the cauph-houses and carabets [cabarets] and apprehend soldiers there. And these two things it seems were the cause, that when he was so assaulted in the Seraglio, not one of his domestic servants, whereof he had 3,000, would lift an arm to help him.' (These are very early references to coffee-houses and cabarets in English. I myself have seen and touched the blood-stained sheepskin kaftan of the murdered sultan in Istanbul, and thought of James Howell in doing so.)

James Howell published his letters as *Familiar Letters* or *Epistolae Ho-elianae* and today they are still of endless interest, dealing as they do with the characteristics of nations, the origin and nature of languages from Turkish to Welsh, the favourite drinks of the different nations, including the Turks' coffee, the occurrence of *cynghanedd* in Welsh and Italian, football, tobacco, scientific method, the value of libraries and a host of other subjects. He was an accomplished poet in English and consoled himself with the writing of verse during the eight years he spent in the Fleet prison for acting as secret agent to the Earl of Strafford. His support of the Stuarts was rewarded in 1661, when Charles II made him Historiographer Royal. He was buried in the Temple Church in London, where his memorial was damaged but not made illegible by German bombing in 1941. He never returned to Wales but he paid his respects to his native culture by appending a delightful collection of Welsh proverbs and sayings to his immense *Lexicon Tetraglotton*, a dictionary of four European languages.

But not even London, Antwerp, Rome, Constantinople and Jerusalem were enough for some dissatisfied Welshmen. There was William Vaughan, son of Walter Vaughan of Gelli Aur near Llandeilo. He went to Jesus College, Oxford, and took his B.A. and M.A. degrees there. He too travelled in Europe, came back to be Sheriff of Carmarthenshire and to be knighted. He claimed descent from the princes of Powys. He married an heiress of Llangyndeyrn, between Carmarthen and Llanelli, and settled there at Torcoed Fawr. This is a farm today but the old house still stands, though much altered, and some of the outhouses have hardly changed since the early years of the seventeenth century. The farmyard is Italian in its situation, terraced high over the lovely Gwendraeth Fach valley. But though William Vaughan had done well enough for himself he took a poor view of the economic state of Britain and favoured emigration to some new country. In 1617 he bought land from The Company of Adventurers to Newfoundland, and sent Welsh settlers out there at his own expense. He called the colony, which was on the south coast of the island, near Tripaney Bay, Cambriol, and gave Welsh place names to the settlements there. Ill health prevented him from following his settlers, difficulties arose for them, the climate was much harder than had been expected and the venture failed. Vaughan died at home in Llangyndeyrn and is buried in the churchyard there. If you have occasion to go to Llangyndeyrn, don't miss the charming hamlet of Pontantwn, a few miles down river. Who the Antwn, Antony or Antonius was who gave his name to the bridge I have no idea.

Adventurous Welshmen had been leaving a Wales in which little seemed to be happening, but there was soon to be a nasty stirring up, an English revolution which was to cause Wales to be harried once more, a king to lose his head, with two Welshmen amongst those who signed his death warrant. After eleven years of despotic rule Charles I called parliaments between 1640 and 1642 and Welshmen were prominent as members of them. They came from the new Tudor land-owning class and they were faithful to the king, though they didn't approve of his court or of his powerful favourites. Rumours of the gathering of Catholic power once more were rife in Powys and they centred round the splendid castle of Rhaglan in the south-east.

The seaways of the west and the beaches and harbours of south-west Wales once more loomed large in men's thoughts and fears and in the anxieties of the government. Help for the Catholics might come from Ireland or Spain and the coasts were vulnerable. Hadn't Henry Tudor come to the throne through such a landing? So, until the use of that money became suspect, the Welsh at first willingly paid the tax of ship money which the king raised to build up his navy. No one in Wales wanted the ravaging advance of an invading army through their land, nor any kind of war, civil or otherwise. James Howell summed up the feeling that civil war could endanger that rare conjuncture of peace, security, honour and wealth which he said the Welsh had enjoyed under the Tudors and the Stuarts. A true conservative, he believed 'that changes in government are commonly fatal, for seldom comes a better'.

Castles and walled towns too began to assume an importance they had lost for centuries. The king made for the Welsh border to recruit men. On the whole the Welsh gentry frowned upon the new Puritanism which had sprung up within the Anglican Church itself and the Parliamentary party was Puritan. In their country houses up and down the land some waited to see how the tide would flow before committing themselves and even after making up their minds some of them changed sides during the conflict. It must have been very confusing for anyone who was not in touch with happenings in London. There were some who strongly disapproved of Charles's way of governing, while others had already come under the Puritan influence. But the king had passionate and unswerving supporters. There was old William Salesbury of Rhug, near Corwen, not of the family of the great translator but known as *Hen Hosannau Gleision*, old Blue Stockings, presumably because he favoured that unfashionable colour. Salesbury repaired the castle of Denbigh at his own expense to hold it against Cromwell's forces. Marching and countermarching armies brought the noises of war to the unaccustomed Welsh countryside. After his defeat at Naseby Charles made for South Wales and the castle of Rhaglan, which four years earlier had gathered an army together for him and which now held out till August 1646.

Up in the north, Holt, Conwy, Harlech and Denbigh still held out, harbouring the last desperate Welsh Royalists whilst the Roundheads occupied the country all round. Charles, on the run, came to Denbigh Castle and made a rendezvous with his followers in the hamlet of Cyffylliog, in a quiet valley a few miles west of Rhuthun. You can visit the tower where he lodged in Denbigh Castle and where he was lectured for two hours on end by old Blue Stockings. The king said afterwards, 'Never did a prince hear so much truth at once', but it was too late for good advice to save him. Salesbury stubbornly defended the castle even when the walled town below was taken, for he'd sworn never to yield it except at the king's command. The six months' siege was conducted with as much decency as bombardment, for Thomas Mytton, now general of Cromwell's forces in North Wales, knew and respected Salesbury. He sent him letters begging him to give in, to save his people from further suffering. Mytton was a Border man whose family had married into the Welsh gentry and if for Salesbury King Charles was the Lord's anointed, Mytton himself was seriously concerned with reform in Wales. There could only be one end for the beleaguered fortress. A contemporary note says: 'Mr. William Salesbury of Rhug, after he had sent to the king to show in what case the country stood and what misery they suffered by reason of the leaguer, and also how his soldiers in the castle were infected with divers diseases, was commanded by the king and delivered up the castle to them upon 26th October.' That was in 1646. There was to be no insulting, no robbing of the defeated garrison. Salesbury and his men were allowed to march out of the castle with colours flying and drums beating.

The castle of Conwy, still today in remarkably good condition, fell to Mytton in the following month. It had been defended by another tough character and much more notable soldier, Sir John Owen of Clenennau. Owen was taken from Conwy to Denbigh Castle, now parliament's prison for captured Welsh Royalists. From there he was taken to London, tried and condemned to death, but someone intervened at top parliamentary level, perhaps because of the high regard in which Sir John was held in Wales, and he was pardoned and given a restricted freedom. Not long after his release John Evelyn, the diarist, records that Sir John entertained him in London with a Welsh harpist. He retired to his estate of Clenennau, at Dolbenmaen, five miles north of Cricieth, and spent his days out with his gun and his hawks. His reward at the Restoration was the post of vice-admiral of North Wales. He died in 1666. A worn memorial in the church of Penmorfa records his passing. Mytton's campaign ended triumphantly with the taking of Harlech in 1647.

The last and most important battle of the Civil War in Wales was fought in a wide, still unspoilt valley north-west of St. Fagans. A disused railway embankment gives a point of vantage from which the landscape somehow offers an unlikely site for an important battle and the choice between river bank and hill-top a puzzle for the amateur tactician. (Nearby is St. Fagans Castle, a sixteenth-century house with spacious grounds which now house the well-established Welsh Folk Museum. The main types of Welsh domestic architecture may be studied here and the tannery and cockpit are of particular interest. Some of the traditional crafts are still practised here.) Parliament now controlled the whole of Wales but in 1648 discontent led to protest and a call for the return of the king. John Poyer, merchant and mayor of Pembroke, who had become governor of Pembroke Castle for parliament, now declared for the king. He was joined by Rice Powell and Major-General Rowland Laugharne, another Pembrokeshire Parliamentarian. They marched eastwards, gathering forces, though Carmarthen, Swansea and Neath. At St. Fagans they were met by the Roundheads under Horton, who disposed his men on the higher ground while the Royalists ranged themselves along the brook. They were defeated. Poyer, Powell and Laugharne were condemned to death but only one sentence was carried out and they were asked to draw lots to make the choice. It fell to Poyer and he was shot at Covent Garden. Charles II was to grant his widow a good pension.

In the north the Welsh Royalists were defeated at Barmouth, Llandegai and the Red Hill Fields in Anglesey. Showing his strength and emulating William the Conqueror in a similar situation, Cromwell marched through Cardiff and Swansea to take Tenby and Pembroke. In all this he gave no indication of awareness of his Welsh ancestry. The triumph of the Commonwealth marked the winding-up of the Tudor bandwaggon for the Welsh gentry. They lost their seats in parliament as a result of the change in government and the vigour and influence of the Welsh Members of Parliament were not recaptured with the Restoration of 1660. Aberystwyth Castle may stand as a sign of the calamity which the Civil War was for Wales. Here Cromwell wreaked his vengeance for the mint which had supplied the king with silver money and only today is there talk of making its tumbled masonry more attractive and comprehensible.

While things had been moving toward this fearful upheaval something else that was foreign had slowly been invading Wales. John Penry, the early Puritan and Nonconformist reformer and propagandist, was born at Cefn Brith on the north-westerly slope of Mynydd Epynt, today an army training area, took degrees at Cambridge and then Oxford and quickly plunged into controversial writing about the Anglican Church. He was involved, no one knows to what extent, with the publication of the Marprelate tracts and may himself have been Martin Marprelate, and with the secret press he was pursued from town to town by the queen's government. After several trials he was condemned under Elizabeth's Law of Uniformity, condemned to death and executed in 1593, when only thirty years of age. His writing and publishing was done entirely in English and drew little immediate reaction from the Welsh people, who were only beginning to accustom themselves to Anglicanism, but John Penry did direct one pamphlet to Wales, *An Exhortation unto the Gouernours and pe ple of hir Maiesties countrie of Wales*, published in 1588. I know of a monument to him, but my Methodist upbringing rai vaguely ered him as a kind of hero.

It was at Llan alongside the main road between Caerleon and Caerwent, that Puritanism in Wales established its first breakaway chapel, leaving the lovely parish church from which it seceded. In 1611, William Wroth, a member of a family which had settled in Wales, was appointed rector of Llanfaches. He was an easy-going man and a scholar, but he paid no great attention to his clerical duties, an attitude not uncommon among the clergy of his day. Then an extraordinary thing happened. A friend of his won a law-suit in London and to celebrate his triumphant return Wroth bought a new fiddle to play in the entertainment he'd planned. All was ready when Wroth heard that his friend had dropped dead on his way home. Wroth took this as a sign from God, threw away the new fiddle, went down on his knees and promised to reform. He now devoted himself strictly to his calling and got into trouble under Charles I for refusing to accept the restored holy days, which he took to be occasions for immorality. He was forced to give up his rectorship of the church on its peaceful hill. But he stayed on in the locality preaching the simple, godly life. In 1639 he founded the Independent chapel and at first it took in Baptists and Presbyterians as well. It became a cathedral of Nonconformity and people flocked here from the adjacent counties of Wales and England to hear Wroth preach. He once claimed to have a congregation of eight hundred.

The story of Llanfaches shows that Puritanism was at first a movement within the Anglican Church, a movement of reform intended to fit the Church for the task of raising the moral standards of the people. And the help and encouragement which Wroth got from the Independents of London show that as a prospective separate Church it was a movement from outside Wales. The breakaway to dissent or nonconformity came when Puritan teaching within the Protestant Church was stopped by Charles I and his Archbishop Laud. The prohibitions, however, did nothing to interfere with the sturdy, simple admonitions to the Welsh people which Rhys Prichard, vicar of Llanymddyfri (Llandovery), his birthplace, couched in the popular, easily comprehensible stanzas of his *Canwyll y Cymry*, *The Candle of the Welsh*, in which he attacked the current immorality of his fellow-countrymen. These thousands of stanzas of buoyant verse, thumping away at every kind of over-indulgence, became widely known but were never printed in his lifetime. Here are a couple of early stanzas, in translation:

> The parson, the farmer, head farmhand and craftsman,
> the bailiff, the justice, the gentry right through,
> each one does his best to annoy the All Highest,
> not knowing whose ways are the worst.

> The parson is loitering, the justice is bribing,
> the gentry are tippling from tavern to sty;
> head farmhands who yesterday couldn't keep company
> smoke endless tobacco today.

There is even stronger stuff than this farther on in the book, but it's hard for us today to credit that rural Wales knew all the sauces and delicacies that the Old Vicar accuses his contemporaries of substituting for the simple food of their forefathers. He is still affectionately known in Welsh as *Yr Hen Ficer*, the Old Vicar.

This body of moral and religious verse in the old *clerwr* or popular poet tradition was gathered together for printing in 1659, fifteen years after the Old Vicar's death, by Stephen Hughes, the son of a silk-weaver of Carmarthen. Hughes's intention was to provide improving books for those Welsh people who could read, and he was a staunch Nonconformist. For ten years after the Restoration he was forced to suspend his publishing operations, but he returned to them once more until his death. In 1688, the year of his death, he published the first Welsh translation of Bunyan's *Pilgrim's Progress*, under the title *Taith neu Siwrnai y Pererin*, a work in which he had collaborated with others. Stephen Hughes's work is of the greatest importance in the history of the use and status of the Welsh language.

The break with the Anglican Church was accelerating and the largely foreign movement of dissent pushed into Wales much as the Romans and the Normans had done, from bases at Chester, Shrewsbury, Gloucester and Bristol. The first Puritan communities were formed in the anglicised parts of Wales and through the medium of English, in Radnorshire, at Wrexham, Oswestry, Brecon, Abergavenny and in south Glamorgan. A missionary would come to a place and try to convert enough people to start meetings in a temporary building, a barn or a house, in the hope that this would lead to a regular meeting-house. But like Protestantism itself this new way of living and worshipping had to find expression in Welsh before it could hope to overrun the whole country. Morgan Llwyd was one of those who provided it. He was born at Cynfal Fawr, in a lovely valley surrounded by mountains and between Ffestiniog, Trawsfynydd and Maentwrog. A plaque in Welsh commemorates his birth at the door of the house, which is now a riding-school. (A rock in the River Cynfal nearby is known as *Pulpud Huw Llwyd*, Huw Llwyd's Pulpit, because it is said that Morgan Llwyd's grandfather, Huw Llwyd, a poet, a soldier, a noted sportsman and something of a wizard, used to stand on it to declaim his accomplished verse in the strict and free metres.) Morgan Llwyd was a poet too, wrote Welsh hymns and translated some of the Psalms and part of the Song of Solomon. He had his schooling at Wrexham in the 1630s and there he met Quaker missionaries and was profoundly affected by them and by the preaching of Walter Cradoc, curate at the fine church in the town. He was impelled to write one of the great books of Welsh prose, *Llyfr y Tri Aderyn*, the *Book of the Three Birds*. The birds were the eagle, the dove and the raven and they represented Cromwell, a Puritan and an Episcopalian. It's difficult to convey the power of his writing in translation, but I attempt a passage: 'He who has two faces, one of the two is devilish. He who flatters men is rotten in his heart. It's easy to eat, drink and play too much and to dance in the flesh after the devil's pipe. The spirit of the blood is a cloud for the mind. The way of the world is the wide gateway to destruction and he who never climbs above his own hand will never sit in heaven. The amusing, laughing man is out of his mind and within the mind of the serpent.' Those are not excerpts strung together but a piece of continuous writing. A memorial was set up in the Rhosddu Cemetery, Wrexham, in 1912 to commemorate this great Welsh Puritan and writer.

Cromwell's parliament needed shorter ways than the publication of books to bring the Welsh to accept its doctrines. It passed an Act for the Better Propagation of the Gospel in Wales and established a commission to impose Puritanism on the country. Anglican clergy not up to standard were ejected from their livings, but suitable ministers to replace them were in short supply and some of these had to become itinerant in order to cover the country. In this way Morgan Llwyd, who played an important part in this campaign, preached from Wrexham past his birthplace well into Llŷn. A writer in English, Vavasor Powell, took mid-Wales as his parish during one period of his stormy career of political and religious controversy.

State subsidised education in Wales has always been controlled from outside and it is sad but not surprising for me to note in the *Western Mail*, just before typing this page, that some non-Welsh professors at the University of Wales are opposing any suggestion of devolving control of the University's finances from London to a Welsh assembly. Cromwell's new commission, which consisted mostly of English and anglicised Welsh members, not only set up sixty-three schools in Wales but became effectively responsible for local government. The schools were mostly in the anglicised areas, with Cardigan, Lampeter, Dolgellau and Ffestiniog as exceptions. Local government officials were required to punish cursing and swearing and to discourage drinking, dancing, bear-baiting and all the fun of the fair.

With the prospect of all that gaiety returning and these little-understood prohibitions being raised, it's no wonder that there was jubilation in Wales when the news swept across the country that the Commonwealth had collapsed and that Charles II had returned to the throne. But for some Welshmen it brought suffering. Colonel John Jones was executed for having signed Charles I's death warrant; Vavasor Powell spent most of the last ten years of his life in different prisons and died in the Fleet in 1670. At Ilston, today an inhumanly spotless commuter village in the Gower Peninsula, John Miles, who came from a Welsh-speaking part of Herefordshire, set up a chapel to be his headquarters in the spreading of the Baptist faith in South Wales. If you follow a path down a secret valley from Ilston to Parkmill you will come to the meagre remains of this chapel and a pulpit monument to its founder. Dissenters were now being persecuted so, soon after the Restoration, Miles gathered his flock together and took them away to America, where he formed a community in Massachusetts and called it Swansey. The Conventicle Act of 1664 and the Five-Mile Act of 1665 made it difficult for the Puritans to worship in gatherings of more than five. They could be dragged off from their homes, made to walk to prison, were forced into taverns on the way to pay for drinks for their tormentors and ultimately condemned without trial by jury but simply on the oath of an informer. Yet the movement grew and the break-through of Baptism into rural, Welsh-speaking Wales came with the founding of a chapel at Rhydwilym, near the boundary of Pembrokeshire and Carmarthenshire in 1668. A few years later an Act of Indulgence by Charles II freed Catholics and Dissenters to worship as they pleased, but we must remember that in 1670 there were still only four thousand Dissenters of any kind in the whole of Wales and they were mostly in the south-east. Puritanism was still far from sweeping the country.

The movement needed well-qualified Welsh preachers and that was what Samuel Jones set out to provide. After being ejected from his hill-top church at Llangynwyd in mid-Glamorgan, a village worth visiting for its old-time atmosphere and its tradition of the ritual of *Mari Lwyd*, Samuel Jones settled down to live at Brynllywarch, a house which his wife had brought him as part of her dowry, and still in the parish of Llangynwyd. It's still a fine house, much of it un-changed since Samuel Jones's time, and I found the present owners, Mr. and Mrs. Cowdray, most welcoming and prepared to show it. I think they must be used to visitors, particularly members of the In-dependent denomination who wish to visit the home of a great and famous member of their persuasion. Samuel Jones had been a fellow of Jesus College, Oxford, and had lectured there. Now, under the shadow of an Act of Uniformity of 1662, he opened an academy at Brynllywarch and gathered together young men of all classes, in-cluding the sons of local gentry. He gave them a thorough grounding in the classics and in philosophy and sent them out preaching, first of all in the meeting-house he established in his home and then in other meeting-houses. The Act of Toleration of 1672 gave him greater freedom to teach and to preach and he became greatly respected in Wales, though he himself moved very little from his academy of Dissent, the more so because, like Stephen Hughes, he was open-minded and saw little difference between the Presbyterian and the Independent.

Samuel Jones thus worked from within to consolidate the gains made by Puritanism in Wales. For others it seemed best to get out and start afresh in some more tolerant atmosphere, as John Miles and his flock had done. In 1681 William Penn got the grant of Pennsylvania from the king and Welsh Quakers bought forty thousand acres of this land from him. Penn sold some of the land to English settlers too. And in 1683 a company of Baptists from Radnorshire settled near Philadelphia, a town which still has strong Welsh associ-ations. The dangerous pendulum of religion still swung over the land. In 1686 James II made a pilgrimage to St. Winifred's Well at Holy-well, but Wales was to see no official return to the old faith. James was peacefully deposed in 1688 and the new reign brought a new Toleration Act which did away with religious strife. The green hand of nature slowly healed the scars of the Civil War and grass and weeds softened the rubble heaps of Aberystwyth Castle. The Court of the Marches had been done away with and Wales no longer had a centre of administration or a political voice. Nothing had come of the suggestion that Ludlow should be incorporated in Wales, to serve as an administrative capital. We should have been spared the remoteness of Cardiff from Gwynedd. The country sank back into political lethargy and religious torpor from which it was to be roused in the next century.

This chapter has dealt mainly with politics and religion, but the most remarkable Welshman of this Restoration period kept clear of both these disturbing distractions and made invaluable contributions to the world of science whilst focusing his main attention on every conceivable aspect of Wales. Once having reached Oxford he made it his lifelong home, not as a cloistered retreat or ivory tower but as a base from which to pursue his interests in the Celtic countries of western Europe. Edward Lhuyd was the illegitimate son of Edward Lloyd of Llanforda, near Oswestry, and Bridget Pryse of Glanffraid, overlooking Afon Leri, a little to the east of Dolybont in north Cardiganshire. (Ffraid, of course, is the Welsh form of Bridget and of her name.) In 1682, then aged twenty-two, he became a student at Jesus College, Oxford, well informed already, according to his father, in heraldry and genealogy, surely further proof that the father acknowledged the son. In 1683 the Ashmolean Museum was opened and Lhuyd became assistant to Dr. Plot, its first curator. He later succeeded Plot in that post. His interests were already widening; he invented a non-inflammable paper made of asbestos and made a descriptive list of the plants of North Wales. In the summer of 1688 he made a collection of the wild plants of Snowdonia and his list was included in Ray's *Synopsis Methodica* of British plants. He never lost his interest in botany but once he became curator of the Ashmolean he turned more to rocks and fossils and he published a Catalogue of British fossils under the title *Lithophylacii Brittanici Ichnographia*. Now came the preparation of his magnum opus, and in order to win the support of subscribers for the projected publication he issued a plan of its intended contents, with the title *A Design of a British Dictionary, Historical and Geographical; With an Essay entitl'd 'Archaeologia*

Britannica,' and a Natural History of Wales. In May 1697 he set out, with three Welsh friends, on a journey that was to take two years, to gather material for his great book. Much of the time was spent in Wales, two months, for instance at Bontfaen (Cowbridge) in Glamorgan, but many months too in Cornwall, Ireland, Scotland and Brittany. They copied manuscripts and inscriptions and collected all kinds of antiquities. In Brittany they spent eighteen days in prison at St. Pol de Léon, under suspicion of being spies. The first volume of Lhuyd's *Archaeologia* was ready by 1703 and out in 1707, dedicated to Sir Thomas Mansel of Margam. It was called *Glossography* and dealt with the comparative study of languages, particularly of the Celtic tongues. He thus laid the foundation of Celtic studies, but the work was perhaps too arcane and specialised for most of his subscribers, who were baulked by his death in 1709 of parts of the encyclopedic work which would have been more to their taste. He was buried in the Welsh Walk in the Church of St. Michael, the nearest to Jesus College. There is no memorial to him there but in 1905 a brass plaque to commemorate him was placed on the wall of Jesus College chapel. Disaster fell upon much of his work in manuscript; his college and university refused to buy his papers after his death; they were acquired by Sir Thomas Sebright and then distributed in a further sale; those bought by Sir Watkin Williams Wynn of Wynnstay, the second of that name, were destroyed by fire at a bookbinder's in London, where they had been sent for binding. Another important batch, bought by Thomas Johnes, scholar and experimenter in agriculture and afforestation, were lost in a fire at his house, Hafod, in the upper Ystwyth valley, in 1807, but not before they were seen and used by the compilers of the *Myvyrian Archaiology of Wales.* Could there have been some strange foreknowledge in Edward Lhuyd's interest in the development of asbestos paper?

CHAPTER V

Self Help

The land doesn't always remember its past and the happiest times for ordinary people have been those which left no monuments, times when no castles or prisons were built, when there were no new battle-fields to scar the land and enrich it with blood, when even the towns were static and the countryside largely undisturbed, when men didn't quarrel or despise and persecute each other over politics or religion. Wales at the beginning of the eighteenth century was like that, but before the end of the century things were to come which are not easy to forget and which still condition much of our living today.

In the year 1700 there were about half a million people in Wales, three-fifths of them living on the land. The towns of Wales were still small. In 1720 Rhuthun had only three hundred people, Denbigh four hundred. Brecon was considered to be the richest town and Wrexham the biggest in Wales. Carmarthen was important and had a great name for cheerful weddings. The harbours were busy, the most important being Caernarfon, Pwllheli, Cardigan, Milford Haven, Swansea and Chepstow. In 1701 Beaumaris had only one deep-sea ship recorded but by the end of the century the number had increased to 327. In the same period the number at Aberystwyth had gone up from 1 to 99. The average size of these deep-sea sailing ships was about thirty tons. The Aberystwyth number does not include the smaller coastal fishing-boats, for Aberystwyth had, until the end of the eighteenth century, the busiest fishing harbour in Wales. Herman Moll, in his *New Description of England and Wales*, published in 1724, writes: 'What it is chiefly resorted to for, and contributes to its wealth, is its Fishing Trade for Cod, Whitings, but principally Herrings. . .

160

The Herring Fishery here is so exceedingly abundant that a thousand barrels have been taken in one night. . . . In addition to Herrings, they have such an abundance of Cod, Pollack, Pollack Whiting, Common Whiting, Ray and other fish that they set but little value upon them. Bottlenoses and porpoises sometimes run on shore in shoals and blue sharks are frequently caught upon the coast, from all of which they make considerable quantities of Oil.' During the nineteenth century the fishing moved southwards to Aberaeron, New Quay, Aberporth and Llandudoch (St. Dogmaels), adjoining Cardigan. The last, probably because of the easily navigable Teifi Estuary, had exceptionally big fishing-boats, of from eight to twenty tons, with masts and sails, but open, without decks, for convenience of hauling in fish, and with a crew of six to eight men. Ship-building was a necessary industry and went on at Aberystwyth into this present century. This brought the ancillary crafts of sail-making and rope-making and Ropewalk Farm, on the right at the top of the first hill as you leave the town towards Penparcau, marks the spot from which the rope was twisted, uphill towards Pen Dinas.

Farming in the Welsh countryside in the early eighteenth century was still unscientific, for the smallholding was not the place for experiment. Good land was often divided into strips known as *lleiniau*. This word, or its singular *llain*, still occurs in farm names, and between Llannon in Ceredigion and the sea, on land still known as *Tir yr Esgob*, the Bishop's land, if you walk southwards from the pretty little village of Llansantffraid, you can still see these medieval strips, mostly in separate ownership, running towards the storm beach. Farming was based on inherited methods and sometimes on old sayings which enshrined accumulated experience. These were more apt to fossilise tradition than to inspire new ways of working, but there was some traditional wisdom in them that must have done good if followed, such as:

Aur dan yr eithin	Gold under gorse
arian dan y rhedyn	silver under bracken
newyn dan y grug.	famine under heather.

This would at least have told the young farmer where to clear for ploughing if he managed to enclose a piece of rough common. The main food of the country people was oats, reaped with the sickle, for the scythe hadn't yet penetrated the hill country. The *car llusg*, a wheel-less cart or flat sledge, was used to harvest oats, hay, rushes and peat. Oxen, rather than horses, were used for ploughing, and songs have been recorded in Ceredigion which were sung to encourage the oxen as they plodded over the ground.

Llymru, an oat porridge, also known as *bwdran* or *sucan* when it was thinned down, and *cawl*, a vegetable hot-pot into which a bone or a piece of bacon might be thrown, these were the staple dishes, for potatoes had but newly arrived in Wales and had not yet become an essential element in *cawl*, as it did in the nineteenth century and continues today. John Owen, a member of the Morris family of Anglesey, complains in a letter written in 1757 how expensive things are in Aberystwyth market. The prices he quotes are interesting, and staggeringly high if you multiply by something like twenty or thirty, or whatever the plunging equivalent is, to account for the fall in value of the pound. Here are some of them, and I remind you that a peck was a two-gallon measure, roughly sixteen pounds weight.

Wheat	6/–	the peck
Rye	4/–	the peck
Peas	5/–	the peck
Barley	3/–	the peck
Potatoes	2/6d	the peck
Cheese	2½d	the pound
Butter	4d	the pound

So potatoes were almost the price of cheese and that's perhaps the comparison we should make today to realise how dear they were. Cheese for home consumption was made of skimmed milk after the cream had been taken off to make butter. Such was the cheese of Welsh hill farms until well into this century, and I remember enjoying great hunks of it when it was fresh, but also how hard and leathery it became if the huge round cheese was started and not eaten up fairly quickly. Thin beer was brewed at home from malted barley and a way for a widow to raise money, perhaps to pay for a funeral, was to make a brew of beer and invite neighbours in to drink it and pay for what they drank.

Most houses were earth-walled and thatched and have therefore mostly disappeared since the time when building in stone became commoner in the eighteenth century. There is one, in a progressively ruined state, at Trefilan in Ceredigion, still with wattled partition and open, wattle-canopied hearth. Kitchen gardens were rare and so they still are in the hill farms of Wales, though much oftener to be found in the more fertile lowlands and valleys of the north and the south. The Welsh farmer often prefers to plant peas, beans and carrots in rows in his potato or swede field and they are thought to do better there. There was no money to be made on a smallholding, only a desperate clinging to life and an unsuccessful clinging on the part of many children. Cattle could be sold, very often had to be sold because there was little winter food for them, since they were cattle which grazed chiefly on common land until the ruinous enclosures came. The cattle drovers were the middlemen in this trade and Archbishop John Williams, who came back from York to help defend North Wales against Cromwell's men, called them *llongau Sbaen*, ships of Spain, because their return from England in the late summer or autumn, with the money they'd got for the cattle, was the nearest to treasure that the Welsh farmer would ever get. The drovers gathered the cattle and met at assembly points for the departure. The little black or red cows and bullocks, little because they hadn't then been developed into the beefy, hornless creatures we know today, were shod for the long trek to Barnet Fair, or St. Bartholemew's Fair in London. Halfway between Dolgellau and Trawsfynydd, north of the only bridge on this piece of road and near a Forestry Commission picnicking place, is a riverside meadow known as *Maes y Gofaint*, the Blacksmiths' Meadow, where such shoeing was done. The trade was considerable. Lewis Morris estimated, in the middle of the eighteenth century, that from Anglesey alone fifteen thousand cattle, five thousand pigs and thousands of sheep went to England every year. The sheep and cattle had to swim the Menai Straits while the pigs were carried in boats, unable as they are to swim far without cutting their throats. Geese were shod by dipping their feet in pitch and then walking them over fine sand. The din of lowing, bleating, squealing and honking which accompanied the high hopes of the senders must have equalled the uproar raised on the same shores to frighten the Romans many centuries before. In Wales, partly in order to avoid tolls, the drovers kept to the green ways which may still be traced across our moorlands; in England they followed roads built by the Romans which had deteriorated ever since. It was a tough assignment but it had its moments of cheerfulness when the drovers and their flocks rested at a familiar inn. Their ways are still remembered in pub and road names, the Drovers' Arms, Drovers' Roads, Welsh Ways and Welsh Runs that mark their passage through Wales and England.

These drovers did business for people, paid bills in London and became bankers. Many such banks were established in the eighteenth century at places like Carmarthen and Llandovery and their bank-notes usually carried the head of an ox or a sheep. Tregaron had its *Banc y Ddafad Ddu*, Bank of the Black Sheep. By the early nineteenth century banking had passed out of the hands of the drovers and covered a wider economic field. Every town in Wales then had its local bank, but by the middle of the century these too were being swallowed up by the big banks we are familiar with today. But droving itself went on, in spite of the spread and decline of the railway, well into our present century, and the last of the drovers of Ceredigion lives near me today.

Another way to make life possible on a smallholding was the practice of rural crafts, and in this way the standard of living of a scattered community could be raised by the exchange of the products of their different skills. Wool was spun at home and then often knitted into stockings which fetched a good price when gathered by agents for the English market, slung into panniers and taken off on horseback. The more specialised crafts of the bootmaker, saddler, locksmith, wheelwright, blacksmith and coppersmith were in the eighteenth century centred in the towns and villages, where the craftsman had access to the materials he needed, but those who followed any one of these necessary crafts were rarely if ever sufficiently numerous to form a guild in any of the Welsh towns. From the middle of the eighteenth century on, enclosures of the commons resulted in the spread of rented smallholdings up into the hills. And there were many squatters' enclosures, *tai unnos*, one-night houses, a custom by which if you hedged a small parcel of land and built a house on it which had smoke in its chimney between sunset and dawn, then it was yours. You could recruit your friends and build it of turves, with a wood and turf roof. Then at your leisure you could build a stone house round it and throw the turf house out of the window. There is such a house near me, its square little plot of land and tiny house like a patch on a garment in a great sweep of common. This pushing up toward the hills meant even poorer and more remote homesteads and scattered communities which learnt even to do without the nearest village for their essential craft products. So, in my locality of Trefenter in Ceredigion, there were during the last century, according to the chapel baptism record book, children born to weavers, tailors, masons, hatters, shoemakers, grocers, butchers and blacksmiths. Of those who had gone away to work, leaving their families at home, there were colliers, a sailor and a cowkeeper in London. The cowkeeper must have worked for an early Cardiganshire dairyman in London who produced the milk in his backyard.

There was poverty in the countryside but there was pride too and few 'went on the parish'. There was cheerfulness and dancing at the inn and at *twmpathau dawns*, or country dance meetings, in barns or in the open air in May and June. The word *twmpath* means a cairn or mound, a tump in South Wales, and its use in this context is difficult to explain unless such a hillock or small tumulus in the middle of the dance was convenient for the musicians and the caller of the dances. *Twmpath* is much used today for a folk dance gathering which continues into the international disco. The fiddle and the harp provided the music and there were jigs and clog dances and shovel dances for the men. Ballads were sung and the *hen benillion*, the old anonymous stanzas written to be sung to the harp. The harp itself is praised in these stanzas. I translate one in which a girl speaks:

> Many a time I've thought a harper
> would make the most untiring lover
> for his plucking of the strings
> would sweeten dawns and evenings.

There was gaiety in private houses too. William Morris, writing to his brother Richard in 1754, describes a farewell party at the end of a visit to his father in Anglesey. There was a man present who was 'the best violin perhaps in Wales'. He says that his niece played the harp 'very pretty', while William Morris, his father and a parson sang the old stanzas in the traditional Welsh way of descanting. The term he uses for this evening's entertainment, *noswaith* or *noson lawen*, a cheerful evening, is still used today for this regular combination of song, poetry and story. Lewis Morris, William's other brother, describes the rye harvest on 22nd August at his farm, Penbryn, near Aberystwyth. I translate, except for the first word, his favourite exclamation: 'Wawch! There were 45 people here yesterday reaping my rye, and some peas too—breakfast of bread and cheese and milk and whey; dinner of *llymru* and bread and butter, but supper was the big meal, a brewing-vat full of beef and mutton, and carrots and potatoes and broth and wheat pudding and about twenty gallons of small beer and over twenty gallons of ale, and the stringing of the red wooden fiddle and the fiddler playing to them when they'd eaten their bellies full and then going to the barn with the wooden floor and they danced till the sweat poured from them, with a great jug of ale at their knees and a piece of tobacco for each one. What a life!'

The Morris brothers and their kind had little sympathy for the accelerating wave of Puritanism. There were still games played on Sunday and hymns hadn't yet replaced the old folk songs. There might not be the same general welcome for poets in the houses of the gentry, but the *hen benillion* brought true poetry into the homes of the poorest. It's no wonder, with his background of jollification, that William Morris's personal collection of songs should include so many about drinking, though many of these were connected with the *Mari Lwyd* tradition of Glamorgan, or with the Feast of Mary at the beginning of January, nearly all of them being a musical plea at the door of a house for entry into the house and participation in its entertainment. The occurrence of the word wassail in a variety of spellings in some of these carols and *Mari Lwyd* songs suggests a link with a similar English tradition. A seventeenth-century song, written to be sung at doors, begins (I translate):

It's a custom at Xmas time
to wander the night where it's worth while
to look for a place where there's good liquour,
made since March, before the summer,
and here, for that is what we've heard
as through the snow we fared,
is drink that warrants praise . . .

and if allowed in they offer to sing as they sit by the fire. The *Mari Lwyd* (Grey Mary or Grey Mare?) waits of Glamorgan carried before them a horse's skull on a pole, decorated with colourful ribbons, a practice continued well into our present century at Llangynwyd.

While thinking about this upland part of Glamorgan I remember that I have neglected to refer to a famous sporting event which is still much talked about in those parts and which is recorded on a tombstone in the churchyard of Llanwynno (horribly spelt Llanwonno in my *Bartholemew Road Atlas*), high up between the Cynon and Rhondda Fach valleys, on a road between Ferndale and Aberpennar (Mountain Ash), and surrounded today by forestry plantations. It records the death of Griffith Morgan, aged thirty-seven, in 1737. Griffith, known then and now as Guto (short for Griffith) Nyth-brân (Crow's Nest), the name of the farm where he lived and which still exists, was a famous runner and had won many races. His final exploit was to race against an Englishman named Prince over a twelve-mile course starting at Newport and finishing at Bedwas church, not far from Caerffili. Hundreds of pounds were wagered on the race but Guto, having, it is said, dawdled occasionally to give his opponent a chance, won the race on the last climb up to the church. He had done the twelve miles in a time which is cut on to the tombstone as seven minutes under the hour. So great was the delight of one of his greatest supporters, a woman who kept a shop and named Siani'r Siop, that she clapped him vigorously on the back. It was too much for Guto's heart, strained by the final pull up the hill after the long run, and he dropped dead on the spot. Poor Guto's reft heart is depicted inside the simple flower arrangement high up on this stone which was erected in his memory in 1866.

These were popular entertainments in a Wales ruled now by the gentry, for they were the locally all-powerful justices of the peace. For the most part they were anglicised and they provided no leadership for the people, but it was they who introduced the new agriculture which brought money to them and greater poverty to the country people. It was they who enclosed the commons to add to their estates and to deprive the commoners of their best grazing, all quite legally, by act of the remote parliament. Montgomeryshire suffered most, with over forty-three thousand acres enclosed between 1733 and the end of the century. In all these activities the stewards, usually foreign to the locality, were hated more than the masters. Twm o'r Nant, the popular dramatist of this age, says (I translate):

> Offend a gentleman and you'll be pardoned:
> offend the steward and you'll be ruined.

But a different kind of leadership was to come to the people from a different direction. Even before Methodism exploded on Wales, many Welsh clergymen had been concerned about the state of their parishioners' souls. One such was Griffith Jones, a Carmarthenshire man who in 1716 became rector of Llanddowror, a village on the A477, south-west of St. Clears. A fine plaque inside his church records his achievements. He had already become prominent in movements like the S.P.C.K. and had thought of going out to India as a missionary, but decided to stay at home and reform the Welsh. He realised that to make them good churchmen he must teach them to read, so that they could study the now available Bible and learn the catechism. And since their language was Welsh they must learn to read Welsh: his concern was simply that and not to educate or give life to any old tradition. Early in the 1730s he opened a school at Llanddowror and by 1737 he had organised circulating schools, so that teachers trained at Llanddowror could do the rounds of Wales. It was the patronage of the pious and well-to-do Sir John Phillips and Madam Bridget Bevan which enabled Griffith Jones to finance this project. The teachers would stay in a place for three months during the winter, a time when farm workers had comparatively little to do and wherever possible the teaching was done in the church and by the invitation of the vicar, even though higher dignitaries of the church disapproved of Griffith Jones, his campaign and his methods. They

168

disliked especially his occasional preaching in the open air wherever he found a congregation and no church. However narrow his intentions were, he made the Welsh the most literate country people in Europe, for in a quarter of a century his schools are said to have taught 158,000 people, a considerable percentage of the country's population. He left all his money to his schools and so did Madam Bevan her considerable fortune, but the latter was the subject of legal squabbles for twenty-five years before it was released for the purpose she intended. In 1854 the schools were taken over by the National Schools movement. Back in the eighteenth century another hero of nonconformity, Thomas Charles of Bala, carried on this movement towards literacy started in Llanddowror.

Griffith Jones was a great preacher as well as an educational visionary and it was while listening to him that Daniel Rowland was converted to a more passionate view of religion. He was born at Pant-y-beudy, at Nantcwnlle or Bwlchllan, between Talsarn and Llangeitho in mid-Ceredigion. The fine, solid farmhouse and out-buildings are well kept today. In 1735 Daniel Rowland became curate of Nantcwnlle and of the adjoining parish of Llangeitho, where his elder brother John was rector. (The weirdly situated Nantcwnlle church looks almost abandoned to its hill-side jungle today, but that of Llangeitho more serenely survives the fiery rise and apathetic fall of Methodism.) Daniel Rowland now went outside his parish boundaries to preach his new vision. He was an excitable man and is said on his preaching journeys to have kept his horse at a gallop, credibly, since he never went very far from home. These missionary efforts didn't go down well with his brother or with the church authorities and when this brother was drowned while sea-bathing at Aberystwyth it wasn't Daniel Rowland but Daniel Rowland's son who became vicar, while the great reformer and preacher remained a curate for some time. Across the river from the church at Llangeitho he built himself a place of worship at Y Gwynfil, just outside the village, called it the New Church and made it his base until his death. This action probably cost him his curacy but he refused a comfortable living at Trefdraeth, Newport, in Pembrokeshire. It must be remembered here that though Rowland is a founder of Welsh Methodism this movement was not established as a separate Church until 1811, twenty-one years after his death. The present spacious chapel is a later building on the same site. Daniel Rowland became famous as a preacher throughout Wales and people flocked from the Welsh-speaking parts to hear him, so that Llangeitho became a place of pilgrimage in his lifetime and of respectful resort afterwards. Forty-five Caernarfonshire men travelled by ship to attend a great meeting and to hear him preach. I imagine they landed at Aberarth, in which case they might well have stopped at Pennant to refresh themselves, as I have done, at the Ship Inn, which dates from that time. The wind was unfavourable for a return by sea and they had to go home on foot, to be jibed at by unconverted mockers in the small towns and villages of Meirionnydd. Daniel Rowland was buried in the cemetery of his New Church and an impressive statue honours him there today.

Not such a good preacher but a far better organiser than Daniel Rowland was his friend and co-founder of Methodism, Hywel Harris. Harris was deeply moved by a sermon preached by the vicar of Talgarth, a few miles down the valley from his home at Trefeca, in Breconshire. Having observed the Llanddowrór method he rebuilt his home to make it a great centre of religious education, and such it remains today, though I believe it now welcomes students from outside the Methodist denomination. The house is worth a visit for its unusual beauty, a charm somewhat impaired by a modern addition and by a huge Victorian chapel in Anglican style which shows signs of cracking. At the peak of his house he placed a weather-vane consisting of a gilded angel blowing his trump, with the words *Cyfodwch y meirw a dewch i'r farn*, Rise o you dead and come to judgement. This has recently been restored to its original position. Over the main entrance are the words *Initio sapientiae timor domini* and in the middle of the decorated ceiling of the present warden's living-room the eye of Iahveh once looked unblinkingly down. The method of the pioneers sent out from this place was to go somewhere, preach passionately and then set up a 'society' (*seiat*), still within the Anglican Church. In this way they benefited from the experience of English Methodists and especially of Whitefield, but the Welsh *seiat*, as it is still called, became much more powerful and influential in Wales than it ever did in England.

This Methodism, strange though this may seem to us today, was an early manifestation of the European romantic movement. Contrasting their methods with those of the already established Nonconformists, Quakers, Independents and Baptists, Harris said that he and his colleagues preached chiefly to the heart and to the spirit. They inspired faith in the hearts of their hearers rather than light in their minds. They stirred the soul to its depths, carrying conviction to its very foundation. The others, he said, leave the soul quiet and undisturbed, they don't search into the heart.

It's difficult by this time to judge how far Hywel Harris's own heart was involved in his curious relationship with Madam Sidney Griffith, wife of a drunken gentleman of Tudweiliog, Llŷn. Harris regarded her as a kind of divine mouthpiece whilst she thought of herself as the prophetess or spiritual mother of Methodism in Wales. It has recently been suggested that Williams Pantycelyn's great poem of epic length, *Bywyd a Marwolaeth Theomemphus* (The Life and Death of Theomemphus), was a study of the life experience of Hywel Harris, of whom the historian R. T. Jenkins said: 'It is difficult not to believe that he was the greatest Welshman of his century.' Philomela in the poem would then be Madam Griffith, rather than Harris's wife. I translate three stanzas of the section called *The Farewell Song of Theomemphus:*

Your beauty will no longer harm me,
   if there's beauty in your form,
for I now portray your visage
   as it will be in the tomb;
your precious soul's now my companion,
   where there's grace, that dearest worth,
and I'll have that as my company
   a million miles above this earth.

Be you married, be you widowed,
   be you married now in haste,
and let seven men in succession
   own the fairness of your face,
I will not be one amongst them,
   I have no desire to lie
under the power of such pleasure
   whilst stars orbit in the sky.

Come to me, my Philomela,
　　it won't harm me to remain
in your company for ever,
　　for I've trampled on my sin;
let's join hands, go out together,
　　innocently walking now
between the graves whilst meditating
　　from morning until afternoon.

.What we have is a poem which moves from an eighteenth-century elegiac mood to a romanticism which was to come much later in the work of Keats and Shelley, and in the opinion of Mr. Saunders Lewis this is the first great poem of the romantic movement in Europe. Its author, William Williams, was born at Llanfair-ar-y-bryn, north of Llandovery. After marrying and after being denied ordination as a priest by the Bishop of St. Davids, he moved to his mother's home at Pantycelyn, a few miles from his birthplace, and so acquired the name by which he is usually known. The impressive farmhouse is still there and is still owned by his family, some of whom still have the long, fine nose of the poet. Williams too ranged over Wales as a preacher and as co-worker with Daniel Rowland, but he is best known for his hymn-writing. From 1744 he published a series of little collections of hymns, some of which sold for a penny a volume. These were sung with the enthusiasm which characterised the movement and partly account for the rapid sweep of the fire of Methodism through the land. Here is my attempt to translate a hymn in which he longs for union with Christ:

I look across the distant hills
　　each hour for thy coming:
come, my loved one, for it's late
　　and my sun's near to setting.

Sweeter than the honey drops
　　a minute's joy in thee;
and I've no other pleasure that
　　lasts everlastingly.

And when the stars of heaven fall
like ripe figs to the sward,
there'll be no ebb to the delight
that's all in my great Lord.

Williams's famous English hymn, 'Guide me o thou great Jehovah',
having become dreadfully familiar at Cardiff Arms Park as a plea for
the bread of heaven of more points for Wales, has now, I believe,
been taken up by soccer supporters. Williams displays a curious
awareness of time, of the different parts of the day and night, which
contrasts with his sense of infinite space outside the atmosphere of
this earth, and hills play an important part in his imagery, the gentle
hills of north Carmarthenshire where lived and died one who has been
called the first poet of the modern mind in Europe.

Even more passionate were the hymns of Ann Griffiths, who was
born at Llanfihangel-yng-Ngwynfa, a few miles west of Llanfyllin,
and buried in its churchyard at the age of twenty-nine, a year after her
marriage to a farmer and soon after the birth of her first child. Llanfihangel-yng-Ngwynfa means St. Michael's in Paradise and a strange
place its hill-top church and churchyard is, especially if you visit it
for the first time, as I did, on a misty day which shut out the green hill
country and gave it an elegiac ghostliness. Ann Griffiths's father was a
farmer too, at a farm called Dolwar Fach in the parish, a man of
culture and a good church-goer. She herself was fond of what pleasures the quiet countryside had to offer, dances and *nosweithiau llawen*,
but once converted by a Methodist preacher she became religious to
an erotic degree. She too sang of Christ and of union with him. I
translate:

See him stand among the myrtles,
worthy object of my love,
though as yet I barely know
that he's all earthly things above.
Come the morning
I shall see him with no veil.

The reformists' insistence on the godhood of Christ, on the physical
suffering of God and the death of God in the crucifixion gave Ann
Griffiths some astonishing imagery. She speaks of:

> The universe moving in him
> and he dead in his grave

and of:

> putting the author of life to death
> and burying the great resurrection.

Though clearly a conscious artist she left no manuscript of her hymns and they were not printed in her lifetime. We owe our text of them to the good memory of her servant Ruth Evans and to the man Ruth married, the Reverend John Hughes, who wrote them down at his wife's dictation.

I may have given the impression that Methodism was mainly a South Wales and Border country affair, but this was not so, even though the leaders of the movement were South Walians. At Bryncroes, down toward the tip of Llŷn and some five miles from Aberdaron, a *seiat* had been established in 1748. The leading figure there was Siarl Marc, a carpenter and poet who became a powerful preacher and a man of great personal influence. When a young woman convert gave him the farm of Tŷ Mawr he went there to live and in 1752 a chapel was built near the farmhouse, the first Methodist chapel in Caernarfonshire. That little thatched meeting-house gave place to the present chapel in 1799.

Not everyone accepted Methodism and its attitude to life. Over in Môn, or Anglesey, an island tormented today by low-flying planes and heavy pipe-laying machinery, something very different was stirring. Three brothers, to whom I have already referred and who were to have an immense effect on the cultural history of Wales, were born in the early years of the eighteenth century at a farm called Y Fferem, in the parish of Llanfihangel Tre'r Beirdd, which most suitably means St. Michael's, Home of the Poets. The fine stone building in which they were born is now an outhouse of the present farmhouse and no plaque or memorial records its importance in our history. The brothers were Lewis, Richard and William Morris. If we were able to go back to the Wales of about the year 1720 we would find few people, even amongst the cultured, who knew much about the great literary traditions of their country. It was the Morris brothers of Anglesey who restored interest in these traditions and made possible the developments of the nineteenth and twentieth centuries. The fact that a young poet can today tackle contemporary problems in the old metres of Welsh verse and win the chair at the National Eisteddfod by so doing is largely due to these three remarkable men. They belonged to the *gwerin*, the common people of Wales, but they were descended from the old Welsh nobility and they were conscious of this. Lewis Morris studied to be a surveyor and became an official of the crown manors in Cardiganshire, attempting to control the search for lead and silver there. He suffered grievously at the hands of the land-grabbing squires of Nanteos, Trawscoed and Peterwell, who challenged the royal monopoly of mining, and he was for a while imprisoned by them in Cardigan. But he went on studying the old poetry, wrote some lovely lyrics and fascinating letters which rank high as lively Welsh prose. W. J. Gruffydd has pointed out that there were in Wales then no theatres, no coffee-houses, no clubs where ideas could be exchanged and judgements expressed, while the noble houses had ceased to entertain poets. So the letter became the main instrument of culture. Lewis Morris drew the attention of scholars to the antiquities of his country and he and his brother Richard founded the Honourable Society of Cymmrodorion, a scholarly body which continues to flourish. This was centred in London, for Wales had no metropolis. Other learned societies, the researches, inventions and plans of Iolo Morgannwg and the establishment of the modern Eisteddfod all follow from the vision of these brothers from Anglesey. A monument to the brothers stands on a hill overlooking the A5025, half-way between Benllech and Amlwch and a few hundred yards north of Brynrefail.

In this area too, a mile or so west of Benllech, is the lonely church of Llanfair Mathafarn Eithaf, charmingly perched above its quiet little valley. In a cottage in this parish was born Goronwy Owen, one of our great poets, who was encouraged and inspired by the Morrises. After a good grounding in the classics at Friars School, Bangor, he got into Jesus College, Oxford, as a servitor, but spent little time there and never took a degree. He worked as an usher in different schools in North Wales, then was for a short time curate in his native parish before drifting further and further away as curate and teacher. His vicar at Northolt recommended him as grammar school master and then professor of Humanity (the classics) at William and Mary College, Williamsburg, Virginia. From there he accepted a living at St. Andrews, Brunswick County, still in Virginia, bought a plantation to grow tobacco and cotton, married his third wife and lived till his death in 1769. He was buried in his plantation.

From what he considered as his exile, first in England, then in America, Goronwy Owen measured out with Augustan balance his nostalgia for his loved Anglesey. He had studied the poetry of Alexander Pope, Homer, Anacreon and Virgil and had modelled himself on the fifteenth-century Welsh poets. When, as a good clergyman, he ponders the last day and the final foretold destruction of the world by fire, he thinks of his home:

> Pan fo Môn a'i thirionwch
> o wres fflam yn eirias fflwch,
> a'i thorrog wythi arian,
> a'i phlwm a'i dur yn fflam dân.

> When Anglesey with its gentleness
> from the flame's heat will be one scorching,
> its pregnant veins of silver,
> its lead and steel one flame of fire.

But long before that cataclysm Goronwy Owen hoped to be reunited, after the long years of separation with his old friends, the *Monwysion*, the Men of Anglesey, and the culture they stood for.

All this scholarship went hand in hand with a happy involvement in folk culture. The cheerful sounds of the fiddle and harp were soon to be drowned with hymn-singing but the Morrises recorded and thus perpetuated the popular kinds of verse, the ballads and the lively stanzas for singing to the harp. Of Richard Morris it has been said: 'Like his brother Lewis he was in his younger days a jovial, rollicking young fellow.' He could play the harp and his list of tunes he could play on the fiddle include titles like '*Morfa Rhuddlan*', 'Five Pound Jig', '*Pen Rhaw*', 'Let Burgundy Flow', 'Collier's Daughter' and 'Noble Gracy Shenkin'.

Another mood of the eighteenth century was the elegiac lament for the passing of old houses where poets had once been welcome.

Ffynnon Bedr, or Peterwell, outside Lampeter, had fallen into ruin in the eighteenth century. I translate some stanzas from a lament by David Davis, Castell Hywel, in the *englyn* form:

> Silent the young girls' song, the music,
>   the spicy talk of the lads;
> sweet lovers no more wander
> nor a lone girl in this gay glade.

> No more harpists here, no chord,
>   no tune, no singers
> loved and contented, no pipers,
> no more sweetness of the tender song.

> To dust it went when its day came—the end
>   of its immense delighting;
> and it's the silent owl that now
> breeds within its walls.

> Its fine wide hearths are turned to gardens
>   and to green hedges,
> and many an ox from the yoke
> crops the floors of its parlours.

A fine avenue of trees still takes you down to the ruins and there's a good deal of interesting wall left. You may even find an ox grazing in the parlour.

Literature wasn't the only art that flourished. Richard Wilson was born at Penegoes, near Machynlleth, where his father was vicar. At the age of seventeen he was sent, with the help of a rich relative, Sir George Wynne, to London to study painting. He became a successful portrait painter. Then at the age of thirty-seven he went to Italy, first of all to Venice and then to Rome, where he stayed for six years, mixing with the painters of the day. It was here that he turned away from portrait painting to landscape. Back in London he was one of the founders of the Royal Academy and became librarian to the Academy. He painted wonderful views of Cader Idris and Snowdon, giving the Welsh mountains a limpid Italian light in which they are, in fact, often bathed. He retired to live with his brother near Yr

Wyddgrug, Mold, and died there. His tomb is at the north side of the church.

Another artist, by no means as great, was the water-colourist Moses Griffith, who was born at Bryncroes in Llŷn. He was discovered by the antiquarian and naturalist Thomas Pennant, whom he accompanied on all his journeys for twenty-one years, recording scenes in water-colour and then doing engravings of them for publication in Pennant's books. The National Library of Wales has a large collection of Moses Griffith's water-colours of Welsh churches, mansions and scenery. Others are in the National Museum, the British Museum, the Victoria and Albert Museum as well as in private collections.

There was a limited form of sculpture too, and one of the delights of wandering through old churchyards anywhere in Wales is the discovery of tombstones of the eighteenth and early nineteenth centuries on which inscriptions and simple designs have been cut on slate in classical good taste.

Wales was being discovered for tourism. Defoe had ventured into Wales and Dr. Johnson had deigned to visit us, in spite of his dislike of mountains. Our 'horrid mountains' and 'rushing torrents' (these were favourite expressions in visitors' accounts of their travels) were now opened up to the intrepid tourist. The 'natives', muttering in their strange tongue, gazed on these fashionable strangers setting up their easels in the rain from the doorways of their 'wretched hovels'.

Gwallter Mechain, reporting on conditions in Wales at the beginning of the nineteenth century, said: 'The Welsh have the labour and the strangers the profit.' In the second half of the eighteenth century what we now call the industrial revolution was well under way in Wales. Coal now supplied the power for industry and it was usually cheaper to take metal ores to the source of power than to carry vast quantities of coal to where it was needed for the smelting of copper and iron. Industry thus became concentrated where there was coal, a big population move resulted and industrial areas came into existence. Not all the profit went out. Mynydd Parys, near Amlwch in Anglesey, was the heart of the empire of a Welsh captain of industry. Copper had been mined there by the Celts and the Romans but the presence of this useful ore had gradually been forgotten. Lewis Morris knew about it and Goronwy Owen spoke of his beloved island as having wealth in every corner of its bosom, *mwnai ymhob cwrr o'i mynwes*. In 1768 a very rich vein of copper was found on Parys Mountain and it soon fell into the hands of a lawyer, Thomas Williams of Llanidan, who set about working it. He was popularly known as *Twm Chware Teg*, Fairplay Tom, probably because of the fairness of his dealings with his workmen. He left us interesting ruins, the first ruins of the industrial age, a windmill on the summit for power, buildings for the processing of the ore and, most impressive of all, a tremendous hole in the mountain, a hole which is now being used, like the common land near my house, for the dumping of old cars and of household and builders' rubbish in our vandal age. I should make it clear that Mynydd Parys, though unfenced, is privately owned.

Thomas Williams did very well for himself, for he broke the stranglehold the English smelters had on the copper industry and came to control half the copper production of England and Wales. He built his own smelting furnaces at Amlwch, the nearest port, and at Swansea, near the coalmines. Thomas Williams's influence on naval warfare and on trade is incalculable. Early in the eighteenth century it had been discovered that a sheathing of copper could protect the hulls of wooden ships, lengthen their working lives and allow them to slip more quickly through the water, unhampered by barnacles and other growths. But the bolts and screws used to fasten the copper to the hull were of iron, and iron rusts. The copper sheets sometimes opened and came away and ships were lost as a result, one of them a naval vessel. So the practice of copper sheathing was on the point of being given up, long before iron ships were thought of. Thomas Williams caused specially hardened copper nails and fittings to be manufactured and the sheets were made safe. The British Navy was not alone in being happy about this, for he sold his sheets, bolts and nails to all the navies of Europe. He had agents pushing these products in France, Holland and Spain, and workmen to show how to fit them. At the Battle of Trafalgar, the ships on both sides moved the more efficiently for his enterprise. And fewer slaves died on the crossing from Africa to America, because the ships got there so much more quickly.

He had his own bank and minted his own copper coinage, nearly nine million pennies in all, mostly for the payment of workmen. The coins could be exchanged for coin of the realm in Anglesey, Liverpool or at Williams's head office in London. They were better designed than the royal coinage of the day. One side carried a noble druid's head with a surround of oak leaves. The life of Thomas Williams is an epitome of capitalism and he left a vast fortune. His six great-grand-daughters, whatever other charms they may have possessed, had dowries desirable enough to entice a duke, two earls, a baronet and the younger sons of a duke and an earl to marry them.

Lead-mining in Cardiganshire still made fortunes and Thomas Johnes of Hafod poured his into astonishing experiments in farming and afforestation, into the collection of manuscripts, into fine printing and into the building of a fantastic house which was unhappily dismantled after the last war. Before the roof of lead came off I saw a splendidly horned wild billy-goat framed in the arch of one of its Georgian doorways. The grounds are now a camping site and the kite breeds in its trees.

Wales had not only advanced in the practice of capitalism but also in the evolution of its theory, theory which went hand in hand with political revolution, then very much in the air, and which in Wales found expression in the life and work of Dr. Richard Price. One of the most original and influential thinkers of his age, he was born at Tynton, Llangeinor, in mid-Glamorgan, a house which is still there but which has no sign or plaque to remind one of the fame he earned outside Wales. He foreshadowed the philosophy of Kant in his *Review of the Principal Questions in Morals*, published in 1758, and gave actuarial practice a scientific foundation which is the basis of insurance. He believed in human liberty and welcomed the French Revolution though he did not advocate the overthrow of the monarchy in Britain. He advised the Americans on the organisation of their finance and on the framing of their constitution and in 1781 was honoured with a doctorate at Yale. The only other recipient of a doctorate on that day was George Washington. He had been given a doctorate at Aberdeen, made freeman of the City of London and F.R.S., and is still remembered with honour in France and America but is rarely mentioned in his own country. A street was named after him in Paris. Much of what he wrote is apt today and deserves to be re-read. Here are some lines from his *Love of our Country*, published in 1789–90 to welcome the French Revolution:

'First, that by our country is meant, in this case, not the soil or the spot of earth on which we happen to have been born; not the forests and fields, but that community of which we are members. . . .

'Secondly, it is proper to observe that even in this sense of our country, that love of it, which is our duty, does not imply any conviction of the superior value of it to other countries. . . .

'Thirdly, it is proper I should desire you particularly to distinguish between the love of country and that spirit of rivalship and ambition which has been common among nations. . . . What has it been but a love of domination . . . ? What has it been but a blind and narrow principle, producing in every country a contempt for other countries and forming men into combinations and factions against their common rights and liberties? . . . What was the love of country among the old Romans? We have heard much of it; but I cannot hesitate in saying that, however great it appeared in some of its exertions, it was in general no better than a principle holding together a band of robbers in their attempts to crush all liberty but their own. . . . We ought to seek its good . . . but at the same time we ought to consider ourselves as citizens of the world . . . [with] . . . a just regard to the rights of other countries. . . . An enlightened and virtuous country must be a free country. It cannot suffer invasions of its rights, or bend to tyrants.'

Of the king and his authority Price says: 'His authority is the authority of the community; and the term Majesty, which it is usual to apply to him, is by no means *his own* majesty but The Majesty of the People.' How far we are from reaching his ideal of civil liberty may be seen from a passage in his *Observations on the Nature of Civil Liberty:* 'In every free state every man is his own Legislator.—All taxes are free-gifts for public services.—All laws are particular provisions or regulations established by COMMON CONSENT for gaining protection and safety. . . . '

The nineteenth century, with its hideous exploitation of the workers at home and the coloured peoples of Africa, was to make Richard Price seem to be an ineffective dreamer instead a man talking humane common sense.

CHAPTER VI

Radicalism

As we move through the nineteenth century and toward our present age in our view of Wales, the land offers us memorials, memorials which remind us of how we became what we are, which become uglier and more frequent as they near our own day, more difficult to select and more complex in their significance. Mynydd Parys has its deep and colourful hole which seems to make a shell of the mountain and which only the barbarians of today make ugly; the oldest tips of Merthyr Tudful are grassed over to a dignity and form which rival those of the great Celtic hill-forts; the terracing of the slate quarries of Llanberis seems to offer a stadium for the dark gods of the locality to observe our silly machines hurrying past places where we should pause; the jagged hacking suffered by the rocks of the abandoned slate quarry of Abereiddi in Pembrokeshire answers the occasional ferocity of the sea; and I for one regret the removal of the pyramids of Cross Hands in Carmarthenshire, which gave interest to an otherwise dull landscape. The scars of industry. When combined with wild scenery, the scars of industry appear as an impressive if violent statement of a necessary interaction between man and nature. But the devastation of the lower Tawe valley above Swansea by chemicals puffed into the air from plating processes gives us something much less picturesque, though again not without astonished interest to the comfortable traveller in his Pullman train. And even today the people of nearby Baglan get a whiff of something similar.

Industry had come to stay, unlike the peripatetic earlier ironworks; it had come to effect long-term pollution and a racking of the soil. There were greater fortunes than ever to be made and now more money stayed in Wales, though not in the hands of the people. The

Cyfarthfa Castle, Castell Coch, Cardiff Castle and Penrhyn Castle remain to show how and where the money was spent and the fact that these are all today in some kind of public ownership indicates a sort of revenge taken by economic processes, if not by the drive of radicalism. (My own radicalism springs not so much from awareness of the proximity of Margam Castle and of the remoteness of its occupants, toward whom I felt neither envy nor respect, nor from sympathy with colliers and other workers as from a story my mother told about her childhood in Groes, a village only this year barbarously wiped off the face of Glamorgan. She had come first in a needlework competition set by the lady of the castle but was denied the prize when it became known to the donor that my mother was of a Nonconformist family. The prize had to go to the child of an Anglican.)

By this time, of course, we realise that we owe a good deal to these masters of industry, not only the stately homes which now house useful activities or which please many people to visit, not only the ingenuity they showed and encouraged in the processing and use of metals, but also benefits in unexpected fields. The young Talbot ladies of Penrice Castle in Gower worked with Professor Buckland of Oxford in the 1820s on the excavation and interpretation of Paviland Cave with its Red Lady, later shown to have been a young man; and these excavations enabled Buckland to upset the Diluvian theory which held that prehistoric bones found in such a place were washed up there by Noah's Flood. Through Fox Talbot, Margam Castle was associated with early experiments in photography. Most remarkable was the work of Lady Charlotte Guest, wife of the grandson of the founder of the famous Guest ironworks at Dowlais. The daughter of the ninth Earl Lindsey, she learnt Welsh when she married Josiah John Guest and went to live in Dowlais, and eventually, with the help of some of the best Welsh scholars of her day, translated *The Mabinogion* into English, a translation which remained standard for a hundred years, which is still worth referring to, if only for the copious notes. She took a warm interest in the welfare of the workers, organised schools for children and adults and libraries for their use. Her collection of porcelain is at the Victoria and Albert Museum in South Kensington.

Such civilised activities, however, were on too small and local a scale to meet the general discontent. Protest in Wales came early and was much more violent here than in any other part of the United Kingdom, industrial protest in the form of the Merthyr riots and Chartism in Gwent, rural protest in the Rebecca Riots of Carmarthenshire and Pembrokeshire.

The Dissenter Richard Price had welcomed the French Revolution, but a French landing at Fishguard in 1797 was too much for the new Methodists, who, until 1811, were still technically members of the Anglican Church, and it made them anti-radical for half a century. (I take Radicalism to be the protest of Puritanism against Capitalism.) A pub in Abergwaun, or Fishguard, has a notice above its door in which it claims to have been the scene of the surrender of the last foreign force to land in Britain. The story is told that Welsh women marching round a hill in their red petticoats (as well, I have no doubt, as other garments) were taken by the French to be reinforcements for the militia.

The workers now called for the vote and for parliamentary reform, a demand in which they were joined by the growing middle class, and when the first Reform Bill failed in 1831 there were riots in Carmarthen and Merthyr Tudful, riots which produced heroes and a martyr. (The name *Merthyr* means martyr or, in this case, a martyr's shrine or place of martyrdom, from the Greek *martyrion*, which also gave the English word martyr. Tudful is said to have been the daughter of an early king of Brycheiniog.) The organiser and leader of the protest in Merthyr, in which the house of the clerk to the Court of Requests was destroyed, was Lewis Lewis of Penderyn, known as Lewsyn yr Heliwr or Haliwr, because his work was to haul coal from the mines to the lime kilns of Penderyn, a couple of miles north of Hirwaun. He was caught and condemned to death for his felony and disturbance of the peace but ultimately deported to Australia. To quell the riot the government sent down a company of Highland soldiers. In a scuffle between the soldiers and the crowd outside the Castle Inn shots were fired and a number of the protesters killed. One soldier was struck and injured and Richard Lewis, known as Dic Penderyn though he was born at Aberafan, was arrested and charged. He was tried and hanged in public in Cardiff. The following morning, a Sunday, his body was carried, followed by a growing crowd led by

Wesleyan ministers, to Aberafan, where he was buried by the vicar in the churchyard of St. Mary's. The present tombstone was erected by the trade unionists of the Afan Valley. Dic Penderyn is now thought to have been innocent of the deed for which he was hanged at the age of twenty-three.

Chartism now canalised this protest with a far-reaching and possibly too idealistic programme of reform. This too led to rioting. John Frost, a successful business man, and J.P., who addressed his followers in Welsh, led five thousand men from Blackwood to meet two other parties, from Pontypool and Glyn Ebwy (Ebbw Vale) at a protest meeting in Newport. John Frost hated violence and there is no evidence that he and his men intended any, but troops hurriedly sent to the Westgate Hotel fired to disperse the crowd and killed twenty of them. Frost was condemned to be hanged and quartered but was deported to Tasmania, and pardoned some years later. He came back via America to settle and die at Stapleton, near Bristol. Chartism achieved little and other ways had to be found in the drive toward equality and better conditions of living.

The people of the industrial towns were mostly new-comers, cut off from their rural traditions and without institutions to help them combat the exploitation to which they were exposed. There was much drunkenness and any number of pubs in Dowlais and Merthyr, many of them unlicensed and others owned by pit-owners who brewed the beer that was drunk. To the people of Cardiganshire the glow of the furnaces of Dowlais, which they could see in the night sky from their hill-tops, symbolised a kind of hell. But chapels were built too, and the great choirs and brass bands which have become typical of the mining valleys grew out of the newly formed communities, communities which were still Welsh-speaking. Merthyr at this time was the centre of Welsh culture, with flourishing eisteddfodau, its Cyfarthfa Philosophical Society, and the presence of men like Thomas Stephens and Taliesin, son of Iolo Morgannwg. Following an ancient Welsh tradition of mutual help, friendly societies were established throughout Wales to help members face financial crises in their lives. Notable amongst these was the Iforiaid, the Ivorites, founded in 1838.

One who reacted in a highly civilised as well as practical manner to the terrible conditions in which workers and their families were expected to live in the early decades of the nineteenth century was Robert Owen of Newtown in mid-Wales. He was the son of a saddle-maker and ironmonger in the town, learnt the drapery trade and at the age of eighteen borrowed a hundred pounds to set up as a cotton manufacturer in Manchester. Success enabled him to acquire the managing partnership of a cotton mill at New Lanark in the Scottish lowlands. Here he put his ideas on society into operation. He believed that character was formed by experience and environment and he proposed to give his workers and their families decent surroundings, two rooms for each family, schools, playrooms and gardens for their children. His ideas on education were astonishingly modern, lessons in the open air in fine weather, walks in the country, aids like pictures, maps and coloured blocks, singing and dancing. Russia and America showed interest in what he was doing and he spent five years in the U.S.A. establishing the utopian community of New Harmony, Indiana. He tried to get laws passed to govern factory conditions but the benefits for the workers which could be spared when times were good and profits high were the first things to be cut in any kind of slump. He then thought that the workers could get these for themselves through powerful trade unions and in 1833, with Owen's help, the Grand National Consolidated Trades Union was formed. But a trade slump frightened the owners and the government cracked down on the union by transporting to Australia six young Dorset farm labourers who tried to set up a branch and were subsequently known as the Tolpuddle Martyrs. Robert Owen ended his life at Newtown and was buried in the old churchyard there. In 1902 the Co-operative movement placed a memorial to him in the churchyard. When the International Labour Office was founded at Geneva the Welsh sent a statue of Owen by Goscombe John to stand in its library. There are two small museums in Newtown, one devoted to the local textile industry and the other, above the Midland Bank, to Robert Owen. The house where he was born was on this spot.

That was a quick view of the career of a Welshman who did well in England and Scotland. The reverse happened at Merthyr Tudful. It was Anthony Bacon, possibly of Cumberland and possibly of Sir Francis Bacon's family, who made Merthyr an iron-making centre and who built its famous Cyfarthfa works. This was developed by

Richard Crawshay, a poor Yorkshire boy who did well in business in London, married the boss's daughter, acquired Cyfarthfa Works and built Cyfarthfa Castle to symbolise his domination of the rapidly growing town. It was his grandson, William Crawshay II, who became known as the Iron King and whose amorous adventures and seignorial ways are still the subject of stories. But the most celebrated member of the family in verse was the original Richard Crawshay's nephew, Crawshay Bailey and a song about him, beginning 'Crawshay Bailey had an Engine', is still sung in the valley. Cyfarthfa Castle now belongs to Merthyr and houses a school and a museum.

The occurrence of coal, iron ore and limestone near each other created these industrial areas. Around 1800 coke replaced charcoal as fuel for the furnaces and bituminous coal was more suitable for turning into coke than the other coals, especially anthracite, that burn away. This was the reason for the development of the iron industry in the bituminous coal area, roughly between Aberdâr, Brynmawr and Pontypool. The Bessemer process of steel-making came in 1856 and steel was in much demand for the construction of ships and railways in particular. The iron foundries declined while steelworks rose to take their place, still at Dowlais, Ebbw Vale and Blaenavon. Then the local iron ore was found not to be suitable for steel-making and the ore was now brought to Wales from Spain, Algeria and even Russia. It was inevitable therefore that in the second half of the nineteenth century steelworks should spring up where there were ports. Iron ore could be unloaded from ships straight to the works, while coal was brought down from the valleys on the new railways. The Cornishman Trevithick's steam engine, the first to pull carriages along rails, had run from Dowlais to Abercynon as early as 1804. There was coal for export too and steam coal for ships. Llanelli, Swansea, Port Talbot, Cardiff and Newport became busy with all this trade, which included all kinds of manufactured articles sent out in the empty iron and copper ore ships, as well as steel rails from Port Talbot for the world's railways. In the early decades of this century the *Société Nationale d'Affrétement* had a fleet of thirty ships continually plying between Port Talbot and Rouen with coal to run the railways of France. In the 1870s, William Siemens, experimenting at Swansea, produced a steel capable of being rolled out into thin

sheets for tinning, or for coating with zinc. The Swansea and Llanelli
areas became the homes of these plating industries, and any number
of works from Carmarthen to Port Talbot turned out all the tinplate
the world needed. But in 1893 President McKinley placed a pro-
hibitive tariff on Welsh tinplate in order to boost the American industry and the tinplate workers of South Wales suffered widespread
and in those days unrelieved unemployment.

I have stayed long with industry, for one thinks of the nineteenth
century as a mainly industrial age. But there was protest and violence
in the farming world too. There was growing discontent with the
application of the law in the English language, the justices of the
peace were English or anglicised Welshmen and the Welsh were
treated with contempt in the implementing of the Poor Law. Toll
gates made it costly for the farmer to drive his cattle to market; the
payment of tithes and church rates seemed unjust to the majority of
the population, who had by now left the church; there was an increase in farm rents caused not only by the rapacity of landowners
but also by competition for good farms, one farmer going in secret
to the landlord to offer a higher rent than the occupying tenant was
paying; officials and estate agents were English, Scottish or anglicised Welsh and out of touch with the rural communities. Terrible
poverty, partly brought on by events outside Wales, the old involvement with an outside power, meant malnutrition and liability to
death from tuberculosis, typhus and other diseases when resistance
was weakened (nature's way of dealing with the problem of poverty
and overcrowding, some people might say) and infant mortality was
appallingly high. Discontent erupted in the form of the Rebecca
Riots of 1843. No one knows why this movement was known as
Rebecca or who its leaders were. It was a secret society started in
rural Carmarthenshire to right the many wrongs under which the
Welsh country people suffered, but it is popularly associated with its
most spectacular enterprise, the destruction of toll-gates. About one
hundred and twenty of these were broken and burnt by riders on
horseback, dressed as women and carrying axes and flaming torches.
The first to be attacked were those at Efail Wen, above Whitland,
and Maesgwyn, Llanboidy. Local people will show you where these
toll-gates were. In his book *Aros Mae*, translated as *Land of my*

Fathers, Dr. Gwynfor Evans tells us that for the government of the day the cause of Rebecca was ignorance, ignorance of English, that is to say, on the part of the Welsh people. A commission was set up in 1846 to report on the situation and it published its report in the following year. The commissioners sent down were three monoglot Englishmen. It was, the poet Ieuan Gwynedd said, like sending three monoglot Welshmen to inspect the condition of education in the east midlands of England, and Henry Richard, who disapproved of violence and whose statue as Apostle of Peace stands in the square at Tregaron, said of the three men: 'They came with a smile of scorn which never left their lips.' The commission recommended that all education in Wales should be through the medium of English and its report has since been known as the Treachery of the Blue Books, *Brad y Llyfrau Gleision*. We are still today fighting that recommendation, which has poisoned our educational system since that day. In 1847, as there were in Tudor times and there still are today, there were Welsh people who would be content to see the Welsh language disappear in the absorption of Wales into England. Matthew Arnold saw this as 'socially and politically desirable'!

Early in the nineteenth century two societies had been formed to run schools in Wales, the National Society, which was Anglican, and the British Society, which was Nonconformist. The National Society in Wales eventually obtained the Griffith Jones, Llanddowror, inheritance and its organisers were cleverer or more influential in getting government grants and the British schools faded away except in North Wales. The lovely little church hall at Llangwyryfon, Ceredigion, bears a circular slate plaque on which is cut the inscription: 'National School 1861'. It became the church hall when the local board school was opened. That was a change which resulted from the Education Act of 1870, a measure beneficial in some ways but infamous in others for Wales. It transferred the control of primary education to local boards authorised to draw upon local rates for their sustenance but at the same time it imposed an English system of education on the children of the country. Not only was English to be the sole medium of instruction for monoglot Welsh children but the use of Welsh in the schools was forbidden. Any child heard speaking Welsh was punished by having a wooden board with the words WELSH NOT cut on it hung round his neck, and there it remained until he reported another child for using his native language. The board was then transferred to the new offender. In his autobiography, *Clych Atgof*, Sir Owen M. Edwards wrote proudly of his reaction to this monstrous practice: 'Every day the token, as though by its own weight, from every corner of the school came to my neck. This is a comfort for me until today,—I never once tried to be rid of the token by transferring it to someone else. . . . It wasn't the fault of the school-mistress, but of the system. . . . I talked one language, my teacher talked another,—and I learnt nothing. But for the Welsh-language Sunday School I would today be illiterate.' The Sunday School had existed before Thomas Charles, Bala, became aware of its possibilities and organised it more thoroughly, and it slowly became an important feature of Methodism. I myself, though all my life agnostic or atheist, owe a great deal to it. It was not that it taught me to read and write Welsh; that was sufficiently encouraged at home. The class of big boys had no regular teacher but was taken by the visiting preacher of that Sunday and I got the opportunity to pit my wits and ideals against those of a man who often turned out to be learned and tolerant of my crystallising views. School gave me no such opportunity: there one had to accept and reproduce.

In 1872 a degree-awarding college, the University College of Wales, was founded at Aberystwyth with money collected from the people of Wales. In 1893 the University of Wales was founded by charter, with the stated purpose: 'There shall be and there is hereby constituted and founded a University in and for Wales.' I have been, as student or teacher, a member of six universities and the University of Wales is the only one of these which did not serve its own culture and language. In accordance with the Act of 1870, English was from the beginning the sole medium of instruction and even today only an infinitesimal proportion of the teaching is done in Welsh, each move toward the appointment of a lecturer or professor to teach in Welsh being opposed by the English and anglicised majority in control.

A grim picture of a nation unable to face up to powerful external forces, to which there were several possible reactions, apathy, acceptance, struggle or emigration. I say acceptance since for many

Welsh parents ambitious for their children an education in English alone could lead to well-paid jobs. Even today this attitude, which is not entirely superstitious, persists, and there are parents who are unwilling to accept for their children education in the excellent Welsh-language primary and secondary schools which are being set up.

Struggle there had been and it was to continue in different forms. There's an old Cardiganshire song, which was sung to me by my grandmother, which expresses the Welshman's deep urge to become master of a few acres of land, at least a smallholding. This is our land hunger which distinguishes us so sharply from the English, but which is being rapidly lost as our towndwellers lose their difference from the English urban population. In England there have always been many times more farm workers than farmers, but not so in Wales, for here it has for centuries been a practical possibility, owing to the smallness of the farms and the poorness of the soil, for a farm labourer to become a peasant farmer. (It is no longer possible, owing to the inflation of house and land values caused by buyers of second homes and investors of taxable income in farmland.) The song is called '*Y Cryman Bach*', 'The Little Sickle', and I translate it thus:

> From the sharp reaper's ugly path,
>   its woodwork all untidy,
> the little crooked sickle took
>   a leap into the rooftree.
> And there it now lies thick with rust,
>   by deepest dust it's covered,
> its handle shrunk, the blade all blunt,
>   by men no longer honoured.
>
> The sickle still has work to do,
>   a future shining splendid,
> in fields of oats throughout all Wales
>   until the years have ended.
> So let us boldly take it up
>   and cut the yoke of bondage,
> that every Welshman soon may own
>   his acres and his cottage.

Economic change caused this dream to fade and only a small minority of Welsh people own land today. There was a movement from the rural areas to the new industrial communities springing up in east Carmarthenshire, Glamorgan and Gwent. I have no statistics to support my belief but I have a strong impression that the manufacturing industries were largely manned from the rural areas of these counties, whereas men from farther afield, from over the border, from Cardiganshire and as far north as Caernarfonshire came in to dig the coal and to build the houses for these new communities. Young men, and sometimes older, married men, would venture to these places—it was a kind of emigration—and having decided that it gave a better life would send word to friends or move their families to join them. Thus began the depopulation of the countryside of which we complain today without being able to find a remedy.

Such families usually kept their links, for generation after generation, with their relatives in their places of origin, but emigration to America meant an almost complete break. Such a move was the one way in which it was hoped to possess a little land and to be free from landlords and tithes and the attitude of London toward Welshness. Emigration from Wales was far from new in the nineteenth century. Ever since the victory at Bosworth Welshmen had moved to England to better themselves in commerce or administration. In the seventeenth century it had been to find freedom from religious tyranny, but now in the nineteenth century it was a flight from poverty, but always with the hope of creating Welsh communities wherever these Welshmen went. The exception to this was the move from Radnorshire to England. (The new county names of Powys, Dyfed and the others are quite useless in a survey of this kind, so I continue to use the older, more significant names.) Radnorshire had long been anglicised and between 1851 and 1891 Radnor lost half its agricultural population to England. In 1891 more Radnor-born people lived in England than in Radnorshire. Further west in these poorer counties of mid-Wales the move was to North America first of all. Between January and June 1841 283 people went from Cardiganshire, 162 from Montgomeryshire and 128 from Meirionnydd. In June 1852, Samuel Roberts, known as S.R., wrote: 'This morning 70 persons, mostly young, left Llanbrynmair for America.' Many of these emigrants to America found what they wanted, a land where they could live and work in freedom, and they wrote home to say so. Other reports were not so good. John Evans wrote back in 1842 to say: 'The land in New York, Pennsylvania and Ohio is very poor, the banks sometimes fail, there are no laws protecting the Sabbath, the law is uneven in its punishment of violence and it is said that there isn't much of a penalty for killing an Irishman.' From such conditions came the urge to establish Welsh communities and attempts were made in upstate New York, Pennsylvania and, most notably, in Tennessee in 1865. The Tennessee venture was planned by S. R. and Michael D. Jones, a scholar and principal of the Independent College at Bala, on behalf of Montgomeryshire men. One thousand acres were bought but the planners were cheated, for the farms turned out to be scattered holdings and not the compact territory needed for the dream of a Welsh community to come true. S.R., also an Independent minister and radical reformer, went with his family to live for ten years in Tennessee and during those years the Civil War raged back and forth over the Welsh farms, destroying stock and property and scattering the emigrants. By 1870 there were 115,000 Welsh-speaking people in the U.S.A. but hope of a Welsh colony was abandoned as, by the last years of the century, a million Welsh homes conformed to the new American way of living and helped, in fact, to form it. Information and advice to intending emigrants was given in a book entitled *Hanes Cymry America*, (A History of the Welsh of America), published in 1872 by a Welsh printer in Utica, N.Y. and put together by R. D. Thomas, whose bardic name was Iorthryn Gwynedd, an Independent minister from Llanrwst who spent the last thirty-three years of his life in the U.S.A. and was buried in Gray Cemetery, Knoxville, Tennessee in 1888.

From the failure in Tennessee was born the plan for a Welsh colony in Patagonia, in Argentina. In 1833 Admiral Fitzroy had reported in *Voyages of the Adventure and the Beagle* on the Chubut Valley and New Bay, places more familiar to us in Wales as Dyffryn Camwy and Porth Madryn, that the shores seemed fit for cultivation and that the river and the country around had a beautiful appearance. Again Michael D. Jones was to the fore in the establishing and financing of the Patagonian Welsh colony. On 28th May 1865 153 Welsh men and women set sail from Liverpool to Patagonia in the sailing ship *Mimosa*. This was a Welsh community at last, so long as the Argentinian government showed little interest in what went on in their southernly and comparatively unproductive province, but the notion of cultural autonomy for the immigrants proved ultimately unacceptable. The majority of young Welsh Patagonians are now mostly monoglot Spanish speakers and are merging into the Argentinian population. Welsh is still spoken by older people and the links between Patagonia and Wales have been tightened in recent years. A large delegation from Y Wladfa, the Colony, as it is known in Welsh, attended this year's National Eisteddfod at Cricieth, but apart from that week they were disappointed with what they found in Wales, especially with the status of the Welsh language. A nation which does not control its own affairs can hardly expect a colony to perpetuate its culture. It can in fact now be seen that these Welsh emigrants were really pioneering on behalf of the Argentine government, which had no intention of allowing an independent Welsh state to arise on its southern border. Their attitude to the Falkland Islands is similar and understandable.

So much for attempts to escape and set up a new Wales. For those who remained, and who had been horrified by the way Chartism had been suppressed and by the way the admirable Rebecca movement had turned ugly in such activities as those of the paid terrorist John Jones, Shoni Ysgubor Fawr, a saner and more peaceful way was pointed by Thomas Gee, Methodist preacher and editor. This was by contesting parliamentary elections. Henry Richard sums up how such elections had been held in Wales up to about 1850: 'Certain great families, who by tradition or accident rather than from conviction had come to espouse one side or the other in politics, held it a matter of hereditary honour to contest the representation with each other, far less as a means of giving effect to any particular views of State policy than of asserting and maintaining their own family consequence against rival claimants in a county or neighbourhood.' Any interest common people had in supporting such candidates was sporting or tribal rather than political. Thomas Gee deliberately drew attention to the fact that he was voting Liberal in the Denbigh election in 1852. As a result the gentry stopped ordering their stationery from his shop and he turned all his attention to his new paper, *Banner Cymru*.

By the election of 1859 the farmers were waking up to the possibilities of Liberalism and genuine representation in Parliament. The landlords were worried and began to put on the screw. Veiled threats came first, a request to their tenants to vote for a certain person, a Tory, of course. In 1860 Mary Morrice, owner of the Carrog estate at Llanddeiniol in Ceredigion, sent this circular letter to her tenants: 'I feel a moral obligation in myself to offer you two things to choose between—you and your family must attend our church and uphold its principles, or if your conscience will not allow you to agree to my request, you must give up your farm to me. My conscience too forbids me to allow you to use the advantages which come to you as my tenants to support principles which are contrary to those of the lady who owns your land.' Liberalism had become associated with Nonconformity, while the Tory landlords made a bastion of the Anglican Church. In the adjoining parish of Llanrhystyd the medieval church was pulled down and replaced with a stylish new structure, with a spire, unusual in these parts, to draw attention to it, partly to enable the Church to put a more flourishing face on matters in view of the rapid increase in tidy, spacious, large-windowed chapels. It is not unconnected that a religious revival in 1859 was accompanied by an increase in the Liberal representation to fourteen out of the thirty-two seats. In the election of 1868 it became twenty-one seats to the Tory twelve, evictions and open threats of eviction increased, at Gwydir, Rhiwlas, Glanllyn, Nanteos, Crosswood, Derry Ormond and any number of other great estates. Henry Richard of Tregaron, elected as Liberal member for Merthyr Tudful with a big majority, called attention in the House 'to the proceedings of certain landlords in Wales toward their tenants on account of the free exercise of their franchise.' The landlords hit back. A meeting of landowners and agents of the county of Cardiganshire was held at Aberaeron in the spring of 1869, at which it was agreed: '(1) that all tenants who voted for a Liberal candidate on the November previous should be evicted, (2) that all who remained at home that day should have their rents raised, (3) that, where possible, no farm should be let to Nonconformists, and (4) that new churches should be built in several districts.' That is the reason why, as one travels around Ceredigion today, one sees few medieval churches but many of the undistinguished Victorian structures which replaced them.

Some evictions were effected by a brief notice to quit; others were attended with the most exquisite cruelty. People who had spent a lifetime on a farm were turned adrift; young people just started in life were made homeless; women within a month of their confinement had nowhere to see it through. In the Report of the Royal Commission on Land in Wales and Monmouthshire you will find story after story to exemplify these injustices. This commission was appointed in 1893, had Welshmen as members and published its findings in 1896. It asked 79,062 questions of witnesses from all over Wales and it gathered a vast amount of first-hand information which is there for any student of Welsh social history. No government commission ever found the whole truth and this one, honest and conscientious though it was, was faced with a particular impediment. On page nine of the Report the commissioners explain what this was: 'In our judgement, we feel bound to say that not simply a small number of exceptionally timid men but a very large proportion of the tenant-farmers in each district were deterred from coming forward to give evidence by fear of incurring the displeasure of the landlord, and therefore possibly of receiving notice to quit, or at any rate, being placed in a disadvantageous relation to him and his agent.' The commission tried to give confidence to witnesses by quoting the Witnesses' Protection Act of 1892, but when some witnesses later complained of having been victimised, the Home Secretary decided that there were not sufficient grounds for prosecution. Even after the Ballot Act of 1872 introduced the secret ballot the tenants were right in fearing victimisation. These things come very close to us in time, to within living memory in fact, and I have talked with a man who was evicted from his home in those terrible days.

A blacksmith of Aberhafhesp was evicted, he believed, for voting for Stuart Rendel, afterwards Lord Rendel, an Eton and Oxford man and a barrister. Now Stuart Rendel was English and an Anglican and after winning Montgomeryshire for the Liberals, thus breaking the Wynnstay family hold on the seat, he so closely identified himself with Welsh affairs that he became known as 'the member for Wales'. He was instrumental in pushing through the Intermediate Education Act, a measure by which Wales opened a path which England was to follow; he gave generously to the University College of Wales at Aberystwyth and saved that college from an early death; and in 1897 he bought land on the hill above Aberystwyth which he gave as a site for the envisaged National Library of Wales. One should therefore not draw too hard and fast a line between Anglican and Nonconformist or English and Welsh in these matters. Nor were all landlords cruel despots. Consider Sir Watkin Williams Wynn of Wynnstay, the fourth of that name. The Land Commission found that in 1856 he had acquired from the Crown some 23,000 acres of common land in the counties of Denbigh and Meirionnydd for a sum the commissioners considered absurdly small. That was quite legal, but he was accused of illegal enclosure of commons in 1870 and of tricking squatters on the common, who lived in the traditional *tai unnos*, or one-night houses, into paying him rent. Yet some witnesses testified that this same man was a kindly and excellent landlord. The variation in treatment was no doubt due to the character of the agents in different parts of an estate and the direct responsibility of the landowner for some cases of hardship may thus be open to dispute. But the ultimate responsibility was that of the landlords and grave and widespread injustice must be laid at the doors of those who once lived in the beautifully situated *plasau* of rural Wales. The triumph of radicalism had opened exciting vistas for the future and it is significant that the first chairman of the Denbighshire County Council, set up after the Act of 1888, was Thomas Gee, the redoubtable radical and founder-editor of *Baner ac Amserau Cymru*, a weekly paper which is still sold in our increasing Welsh language bookshops.

CHAPTER VII

Summing up

I have suggested that radicalism in Wales was the protest of Puritanism against capitalism. To come closer to the Welsh rural experience would be to say that it has been the confrontation of landlordism by Nonconformity. Now that Liberalism has won us the secret ballot and Socialism has gained good wages and better living and working conditions for the worker, radicalism, with little more to go to the root of, is yielding to nationalism in Wales. Methodism opened up a passionate relationship between the poorest individual and God or Christ, something which Catholicism had offered through the intervention of the saints and Mary; the Welsh had voted Liberal because of the contempt with which landlords and the education authorities in London had treated the people of Wales; the Labour Party gradually bettered the lot of the worker. These are splendid achievements but they have been reached at some cost. The new establishment is in many ways less humane and more difficult to approach than the old; nationalisation has not given the workers control of industry and the nationalisation of land would destroy the freedom of the small farmer. The National Coal Board and the British Steel Corporation are more remote and more powerful than the Guests and Crawshays ever were, and with ultimate control moving to even more faceless authorities in Brussels, the Welsh farmer fears for his few acres and his future. So Nationalism is replacing radicalism as protagonist in the struggle for the freedom of the individual in a planned society, since the nation is, as I have tried to show, an organic stage in the relationship between the individual and the universe, a link which must be there if there is to be any two-way exchange of interests between man and his fellowman. Experiment and beneficial change can only be based on already

198

acquired experience and knowledge, and the Welshman is essentially conservative in his attitude to tradition. It is in this sense that I mean that nationalism is conservative while very far from being Conservative. (The English Conservative Party which appears to most Welsh people to be the party of big business, the landlords and owners, the Church, the aristocracy and the monarchy, has little appeal and little support in Wales. It would never win a general election in Wales, just as the Labour Party finds it difficult and often impossible to win a general election in England without the Scottish and Welsh Labour vote.)

I have shown how, under capitalism, profits and products either went out of Wales or were not used primarily for the benefit of the Welsh people. Under state ownership and continued union with England, Welsh industry is now peripheral to that country and to the other countries of the European Economic Community. Coal mines and steelworks have recently been closed in Wales by decision from outside Wales, without reference to our good. The farther away from the centre of administration the more quickly the effects of recession in industry are felt, rather like a film of a stone dropping into a pond played in violent reverse, with the heaviest impact in the outer rim lessening as it approaches the centre. The result has been more nationalist feeling among the workers and the establishing of a Welsh T.U.C., much against the will of the London-centred T.U.C. Until recently, nationalist feeling in industrial South Wales has been side-tracked or sublimated in rugby enthusiasm at Cardiff Arms Park and in the annual coalminers' Eisteddfod at Porthcawl, but awareness of nationhood is now being felt necessary in less poetic, everyday activities. All this makes for greater unity within Wales and one is glad to note that archbishops of Wales have joined in the struggle for the status of the Welsh language, particularly when one remembers how far most clergymen were a hundred years ago from sympathy with their dwindling flock.

To be civilised the individual must have roots and a decent and established relationship with the rest of mankind. Nationalism in Wales, as I see it, sets out, or should set out, to cling to what we have that is good and, on the foundation of conserved tradition and culture, to build something new. The danger of socialism has been its urge, understandable in some ways, to make a clean sweep of the past, to demolish in order to build. There are signs that the movement is growing out of this destructive phase, which now characterises smaller, splinter groups of disillusioned young people, perhaps because it is becoming more aware of its own martyrs, its own history, its own traditions. But I cannot forget that during recent years, and under socialist control, my birthplace, the borough of Port Talbot, now more happily known as Aberafan, has demolished or allowed to be demolished the only buildings of architectural and historic interest which it possessed, the old town hall of Aberafan, the romantic thatched cottage of Twll yn y Wal and, during this very year in which I write, the lovely village of Groes, with the charming house where my mother was born. This recent vandalism can be claimed not to be a deliberate act but a too ready acquiescence to a higher and purely philistine authority.

The mood, then, for those Welsh people who believe they are a nation, is toward conservation, toward the assertion of a difference in an age when a crushing international uniformity has brought about a lowering of taste, a break-up of communities, an acceptance of violence and a resulting disrespect for the decencies of life within a community. What is there by this time to conserve? I shall try to sum up the value of our heritage as I see it, drawing together lines which I hope I have been seen to follow in the preceding chapters of this book.

The Language

Welsh has a claim to be the oldest modern European language, with its continuous literary tradition from the sixth century till today. Just as English has evolved from a number of different languages within the Germanic family of Indo-European languages, Welsh has come down to us from the Brittonic group within the Celtic family. I have already dealt with different attempts on the part of English administration to kill the Welsh language and how by some miracle these attempts have until now failed. There are signs that this persistent linguacide may at last be succeeding. Not long before his death the philosopher J. R. Jones crystallised the feeling of thoughtful Welsh men and women in the face of our present situation (I quote from Cynog Davies's translation in his chapter in *The Welsh Language Today*, edited by Meic Stephens, a book which should be read by anyone interested in the possible future of the language): 'It is said of one experience that it is one of the most agonising possible . . . that of having to leave the soil of your country for ever, of turning your back on your heritage, being torn away by the roots from your familiar land. I have not suffered that experience. But I know of an experience equally agonising, and more irreversible (for you could return to your home), and that is the experience of knowing, not that you are leaving your country, but that your country is leaving you, is ceasing to exist under your very feet, being sucked away from you, as it were by a consuming, swallowing wind, into the hands and the possession of another country and civilisation.'

It was Saunders Lewis who analysed the situation and suggested what could be done about it, in a powerful radio talk entitled *Tynged yr Iaith* (The Fate of the Language) in 1962. (An English translation of the broadcast was published in the magazine *Planet 4* for February–March 1971.) Inspired by this, young Welsh people realised that it was time to do something, not just sentimentalise or be satisfied with the patriotic effusions of ambitious Welsh politicians. They formed a society known as *Cymdeithas yr Iaith* with the intention of gaining equal status with English for the Welsh language in Wales. The report of the Hughes Parry commission of 1965 appeared to recommend this but the resulting Welsh Language Act of 1967 showed that the battle was far from won. As Cynog Davies puts it: 'What was needed was a statement incorporated in legislation of a Welshman's *right* to conduct his official affairs in his own language.' The use of Welsh was made a matter of administrative judgement rather than legislation. From that time the struggle has been to win recognition of the equal validity of Welsh from such bodies as the Post Office, the BBC, the income tax and road tax authorities, the chain stores and the University of Wales. Reluctance to grant this has come sometimes from administrative inertia, sometimes from contemptuous opposition, but the campaign has gone on, winning not the general acceptance of the equality of Welsh but the piecemeal granting of unwilling concessions. During the course of this continuous campaign, hundreds of the best of our young people have seen the inside of prisons, mostly in England, and the young campaigners have gradually won the approval and gratitude of older, responsible members of our society.

The new concessions have not only been difficult to gain but difficult to put into operation. Welsh has not been an official language in Wales since 1536 and there was a great deal of leeway to be made up in officialese. Terms for banking, insurance, taxation and local government had to be invented or recovered from near oblivion, and middle-aged and elderly people, conditioned to dealing with these matters in English, found it easier to continue to do so. But the bilingual forms helped and the Welsh terminology and jargon of the law and of administration is slowly becoming familiar.

For all these centuries the use of Welsh has been confined to the home, to the chapel and to the public houses and to the eisteddfod, together with a few journals dealing with religious and literary matters. Broadcasting has helped to right the balance, particularly radio, which now gives us fat stock prices, rugby commentaries, pop music, comedy programmes and gardening programmes in Welsh. The effects of television are a matter of controversy. The popularity of such programmes as 'Match of the Day', 'Top of the Pops', the western films and science and travel documentaries continues to condition children and young people to expect these things in English, and the monstrous overloading of BBC Wales with these English favourites can only be answered by the provision of the long-wished-for Welsh-language channels in radio and television, channels which administration from London shows the usual reluctance to grant. But good has come of television too. The BBC and Harlech ITV both present lively news and news commentaries in Welsh, attractive serial programmes have been produced and commentators, entertainers and singers have become household names in Wales as a result. I am told that in Gwent, the most English-speaking part of Wales, some of the TV programmes have captured the attention and interest of non-Welsh-speaking people who as a result are learning Welsh in order to understand them. In other ways too radio and television have done good in familiarising people in the different parts of the country with each other's local accent and in gradually levelling the age-long wall of suspicion and misunderstanding which has separated North and South Wales.

The limitation in the general use of Welsh has been reflected in literature, where in the main it has been the language of poetry and religion. That balance too is being righted today, largely by the subsidising of publishers of books and journals by the Welsh Arts Council, but opinion is divided on the question of whether we can, with our limited reading public and resources of writing and publishing, ever hope to cover the range we find in contemporary English, French or German publishing. A new field in Welsh is the refreshing near-pornography of *Lol*, a magazine which combines some of the features of *Men Only* and *Private Eye*.

Welsh is spoken today by about 550,000 people in Wales, twenty per cent of the present population. The number of people who speak it outside Wales is not known, since there is no provision for the entry of such information in census forms in England. Neither is this the percentage of Welsh people who speak the language, but of the recent English immigrants as well, and it is as well to remember that while the depopulation of rural areas and the high unemployment in industrial areas has led to the movement out of Wales of young people, there has been a corresponding influx from England of retired people and of workers and specialised technicians for the new industries and engineering projects. The percentage of Welsh speakers in the rural areas, hitherto the fortresses of the language, has therefore fallen, but again there has been a compensatory development in the English-speaking areas where many people and, a hopeful feature, young children are learning the language. Out of this springs a controversial issue, whether it is better to establish a mainly Welsh-language area, in the manner of the Irish *Gaeltacht*, and to concentrate on the preservation of Welsh in that area, or whether this would be to disregard the widespread Welsh-language activities and Welsh learning in the predominantly English-speaking areas. Our situation, after all, is very different from that of Ireland or of Brittany. While only one-fifth of the inhabitants of Wales regularly speak Welsh, they do it over a much larger proportion of the country, and it is today the language of politicians, archbishops, rugby players and innumerable poets as well as of the farming population of half our land surface.

But the situation is alarming, perhaps desperate, for I believe, with many others, that the death of Welsh would mean the end of the *Cymry* as a nation. The passing of Welsh would mean the end of direct access to one of the great literatures of the world and to the treasure-house of our traditions, since it is to be doubted whether a so-called Anglo-Welsh culture could incorporate enough traditional elements to justify separateness as a nation. Anglo-Welsh writing and feeling can only exist so long as there is writing and living through the medium of our national language. The anglicisation of Anglesey, traditionally known as *Môn Mam Cymru*, Anglesey the Mother of Wales, is a kind of cancer in our nationhood and I am told that a body known as the Lancastrian Society threatens to dominate the island. One is strongly reminded of Ogden Nash's little poem, 'The Japanese', and its last line:

So sorry, this my garden now.

Other English newcomers, more especially the younger ones, show more respect for our traditions and our identity as a nation, and many of them are learning Welsh. For them, and for those Welsh people who wish to recover their native language, there are classes organised all over Wales. At the University College, Bangor, in October 1975, 260 new students asked to join Welsh-learner classes run by older undergraduates. Radio and television have helped by producing lively and well-planned series of programmes for learners of the language. Visitors to Wales will certainly notice the increase in the public, visible use of Welsh, on buses in Cardiff, inside post offices and outside some, on shops, county council vehicles and footpath signs. Meirionnydd (old Merionethshire) has gone so far as to put up footpath signs in Welsh only and it surely doesn't take a visitor long to learn that *Llwybr Cyhoeddus* means Public Footpath, even if he fails to pronounce the words. These are signs of the times and they give a new dignity to the language. The more foreign a country is the more interesting it is to visit and these signs of the difference of Wales should give pleasure to the intelligent tourist. Road signs are still a matter of controversy. The Bowen Commission, set up to examine the question, recommended bilingual signs with the Welsh form of a place name uppermost. The Welsh name is usually the older, original name and the English name is often a garbled version of this. But the present Secretary for Wales and his Welsh Office have decided that the English form must come uppermost, out of an unsubstantiated fear that delay in seeing the English form might cause accidents. There are indications that the sign-destroying campaign which preceded the Bowen Commission may start up again. The language is the nation.

Literature

I have occasionally endeavoured, during the course of this book, to give some idea of the nature and significance of what was being written at different times. Space now permits me only the sketchiest outline of the history of Welsh writing. The earliest extant poetry in Welsh was composed toward the end of the sixth century in southern Scotland, where an early form of Welsh was then the spoken language. The known poets were Taliesin and Aneirin, and the poetry was heroic. Another age of heroism and suffering came in the ninth century, with the running warfare between Powys and Mercia, and heroic and elegiac verse was composed about Llywarch Hen, Llywarch the Old, and his family, and about the princely girl Heledd and her brothers. Some prophetic verse may conceivably go back to an actual sixth-century warrior-poet Myrddin (the Merlin of Arthurian legend) but other poems in the same manner are linked with eleventh- and twelfth-century events and persons, old material revamped to meet a new situation. From the pre-Norman centuries we also have religious verse, gnomic verse carrying traditional wisdom and poetry full of sharp observation of the moods of nature. Unique survivals, like the short poem expressing the gloom of the benighted warrior, the mother's song for her little son Dinogad, and the spirited praise of Tenby, suggest a wider scope in the literature of the to us dark ages, in poems which have been lost. We have the names of such apparently famous poets as Arofan, Bluchbardd and Cian, but nothing remains which is attributable to them.

We do not know how much of the old prose has been lost. Names of heroes occur in the Triads and in the *Stanzas of the Graves* but there are no longer any tales to tell us who they were or what they did. It is to the second half of the eleventh century and the early part of the twelfth that we are thought to owe some of the glories of Welsh prose. They are the stories known to English readers as *The Mabinogion*, and available to them in two translations. The material of the first four, known as *Y Pedair Cainc, The Four Branches*, is ancient and mythological; then there are four heroic British tales and three romances. We do not know the names of the writers who put these magical tales into their final form.

Struggle against the Anglo-Normans brought yet another heroic age of poetry which was full of awareness of earlier struggle as far back as the sixth century, but this time in the twelfth and thirteenth centuries with new elements, a delight in the beauty of the Welsh landscape and in the loveliness of women. Dafydd ap Gwilym dominates the fourteenth century, with his mastery of language and form, his very personal view of nature and his dependence on friendship and the love of women in a Wales dispirited after the disaster of 1282. The fifteenth was a great century of poetry, but in the sixteenth century the continuing tradition of writing in the old metres is overshadowed by the great translation of the Bible into Welsh, in language which owed much to the poetic tradition. At the same time it was probably the experience of Welshmen at the Tudor court which made respectable the writing of lyrics in the free metres, that is in stanza forms of either Welsh or English origin.

The seventeenth century saw religious and moral propaganda in popular verse forms and in splendid prose. In the eighteenth century Welsh poetry came more into line with other literatures with its own Augustan Movement, but the Morris brothers and their circle also saw the value of folk poetry, the *Hen Benillion* or *Penillion Telyn*, Old Stanzas or Stanzas for the Harp. The Methodist Revival gave us the passionate hymns of Ann Griffiths and the Romantic poetry of William Williams, Pantycelyn, whilst Twm o'r Nant gave the people moral and satirical interludes which delighted them. Toward the end of the eighteenth century scholars were busy with dictionaries and the publishing of old poetry, and Iolo Morgannwg invented and grafted on to the National Eisteddfod the *Gorsedd* (the guild of poets who organise and control the poetry side of the festival). The eisteddfod dominated nineteenth-century versifying and works of monumental dullness were produced, but the scene was enlivened by satirical and lyrical verse outside Druidic competitiveness. And we had our first and great novelist, Daniel Owen.

The twentieth century has seen a renaissance of Welsh writing and may come to be considered another great century of poetry, as is the fifteenth, with names like those of T. Gwynn Jones and R. Williams Parry in the earlier part and a host of names to follow. It is to be noted that the National Eisteddfod has during our present century elicited far greater poems than those honoured in the last. In Wales the essay remains a valid literary form, mainly owing to the pungent and racy readability of Sir T. H. Parry-Williams, whose astringent verse has proved a corrective to slack romanticism. We have still to produce a steady flow of readable novels and now that television has established its grip perhaps we never will, but drama, a form of writing in which we had little to show until recently, has suddenly flourished, most notably in the plays of Saunders Lewis. More and more, and he is still writing, does this many-sided man appear to dominate the century, in poetry, fiction, drama, political and critical writing, for everything he writes is economical, powerful and deeply original. Arts Council subsidies to magazines and to publishers give young Welsh writers a better chance of being published than they have ever had before and they are meeting their opportunity in a variety of exciting ways.

During this century a far greater body of work than ever before has been produced by Welsh men and women writing in English, the greatest among them being David Jones and Dylan Thomas. Not all these writers agree to be classified as Anglo-Welsh, but the term has its uses so long as it is confined to literature. One of the best of our contemporary writers in English, Glyn Jones, has said, and I translate: 'I am a Welshman, not an Englishman and not an Anglo-Welshman either. For me Anglo-Welsh is a literary term and nothing more.'

Architecture

Architecture is the most public of the arts, the one you cannot fail to observe as you travel through a country. Carefully noted it provides the symptoms from which the current state of a country may be judged; it shows where the money is being spent and with what degree of taste; it will reveal how far a nation is reinforcing and how far sur-rendering its individuality. Prosperity during recent years in the farms of Ceredigion is reflected not only in the number of vehicles and machines—and west Wales has more cars per head than any other part of Britain—but also in the amount of paint lavished annually on houses, outbuildings and gates. I expect that with the current falling-off of profitability on the land the cars will get older and fewer and the houses less fresh and dazzling.

I have talked of chambered tombs, hill-forts, classical St. Justin-ian's Chapel, castles fantastic or tough, churches, the timber hall, the long house, the lovely Bishop's Palace at St. Davids, half-timbering, Tudor light for medieval darkness, Nonconformist chapels simple to ornate, the imitation castles of the kings of industry, but I have said nothing of the architecture of industry itself, which is conspicuous enough in South Wales, if confined to a relatively small part of the North. Most of the old water-driven mills, which used to be found throughout Wales, have lost their wheels, but some still have them and some are being restored, as museum pieces rather than for use. Ceredigion is a good area (it would please me to say county) for mills and there are woollen mills still working at Talybont, near Aberys-twyth, and in the lower Teifi valley. These were a happy adaptation of the industrial age to village life and the rural landscape. There is nothing, to my inexpert eye, particularly Welsh about our coalmines, our steel and tinplate works, our oil refineries and car component or vacuum cleaner factories, or the tidy homes of the new smaller in-dustries, nothing but their situation. But when one is suddenly con-fronted by the Skewen oil refinery and its satellite gas works, their fantastic piping traced on the sky between two green hills and spouting steam or flame, one has the right to a feeling of excitement; or if one looks down on the squat, dark, solid mass of steelworks bang in the middle of Ebbw Vale, or along the articulated mileage of the Margam Steelworks, ribbon-developed between the rounded, ravaged moun-tains and the duned seashore, polluting a large chunk of Glamorgan with its varied exhalations. There's a certain grandeur in the mon-strosity of these things, a grandeur which is the gift of the poisoned landscape, the shrivelled hills and the adulterated rivers. And, corres-pondingly, it's a stygian grandeur which comes from the very magnitude of the exploitation for which these once-lovely hills, rivers and beaches have provided the décor.

Rural Wales too offers similar shocks of linked horror and delight; the windmill and the ruined works buildings on the lip of the enormous, colourful hole scooped out of Mynydd Parys in Anglesey, the intriguing remains of leadmining at Cwmsymlog and the hidden slate quarry at Abereiddi, north of St. Davids. To me Abereiddi is the most astonishing place in Wales. Slate quarrying was begun here in the nineteenth century and continued into the early years of this present century and then abruptly dropped. The slate doesn't look to me like roofing slate but was used for the other purposes of this fine material, flooring, lintels, gravestones and the panels used in industry for mounting electrical equipment. Some thirty years ago a great storm swept in from the sea and flooded the houses on the valley's edge and the people were evacuated and resettled at Groesgoch. Three years ago it was an abandoned hamlet, but now the houses have been spruced up and look like holiday homes. The county council has built a sea wall across the storm beach; cars can be parked and the ice-cream vendor is there on summer afternoons. But on the northern side there are puzzling black ruins of industrial buildings and if you walk around the point you will suddenly come upon the little gulf of deep bottle-green water which the quarrymen blasted and scooped out of the cliff. Here too there are almost black buildings, built with the slate quarried here. It seems to be friable stuff and the walls are all crumbling. A narrow rock ledge will take you into the quarry itself. It's a grim, jagged, frightening place, and the holiday-makers' brightly painted boats at anchor look like incongruous toys.

Our castles and abbeys were Norman, many of our mansions are Georgian in style and our civic buildings are hardly distinguishable from those of England, but our domestic architecture up to the last century has been native and local in design and materials, though occasionally showing the influence of the Georgian style. It's well worth while noticing these local differences on a journey through Wales. The houses built as homes for the families who came to the industrial valleys and, later, to the coastal towns of South Wales, present little of architectural interest though their interiors were snug enough, and that after all was the first consideration of their occupants. I have known no warmer hearts to houses than the kitchens of workers' homes, a black-leaded grate kept spotless and a glowing five-barred coal fire warming the room, nor any front doorsteps scoured so clean. The street names are of great interest. Many of the streets built at Port Talbot during the late nineteenth and early twentieth centuries commemorate members of the Margam family which owned the land and owners and managers of the different works, but some of them carry the names of the fields and farms on which they were erected. Such are Tydraw Street and Cwrt Ucha, after farms, Grange Street after the Court Farm, which was once a grange of Margam Abbey, and Grugos Terrace, built on a field known as Cae Grugos.

In Pembrokeshire some householders still follow the old custom of giving not only the house but the roof as well an annual pink, yellow or white lime wash; it's a windy county and such a roof is not only rain-proof but gives the wind nothing to get hold of, unlike rattling slates. Llandudoch, or St. Dogmael's, on the south shore of the Teifi Estuary, has a unique and very attractive pointing for its stone houses. Llandybie, in Carmarthenshire, has houses of the local multi-coloured stone, with oddly shaped pieces of white limestone to decorate the pillars of front gates. Elegant Aberaeron, a new town in 1807, when the harbour was made and the river deflected to it, was built in one style, late Georgian or Regency, and the houses in the centre of the little town offer the purest and most balanced exteriors of any in Wales. There are similar houses in this, surely the most agreeable urban style ever invented, at Aberystwyth too, but there they have to be sought out, whereas at Aberaeron they are all about you. Aberaeron is a planned town laid out with almost Roman exactness, with streets running parallel or at right-angles to each other between the square and the harbour. How different are the yet newer towns in valleys which finger their way into the uplands of Glamorgan and Gwent. Here the narrowness of the valleys and the steepness of their sides dictated the arrangement of the streets into parallel terraces that rise, step above step, like the ledges of a slate quarry. Yet in these regimented dwellings there came into existence a new corporate life that was like nothing Wales had seen before, a life which turned about choral singing, brass bands and ragtime bands, rugby, left-wing politics, drinking and hare-coursing, a life which has been well recorded and sometimes travestied by our Welsh novelists who write in English.

Going northward from Machynlleth you will pass through Corris, where almost everything is made of slate, where there are fences which are upright slabs of slate wired together and a dignified chapel at Corris Ucha made of the same material. There are millions of tons of good building stone left here as a frightening scree on the hill-sides and I can never understand what prevents it from avalanching across the road. The road leads to Dolgellau, a town of well-proportioned ruggedness, with buildings made of huge, dark, trimmed blocks of local stone, set off by white-painted woodwork. In rain or sunshine, and it gets quite a lot of both, this is a very impressive town. Further north still, Maentwrog is much smaller but built of the same stone, with greater elegance. While you are here, make an excuse to go to Plas Tanybwlch, across the valley, where a road goes off to Rhiw. This magnificently situated house, once the home of the slate-quarrying Oakeley family, is now a National Parks study centre and offers an interesting list of short courses connected with Snowdonia. The view of Maentwrog, surrounded by deciduous woodland, and of the Ffestiniog valley, is one of the best in Wales. Slates were once exported from a quay below the house. Between Dolgellau and Maentwrog you will have passed the Trawsfynydd Atomic power station, doing its best to look like a castle in the landscape of mountains and man-made lake, which is full of trout.

If you take the A487 from Trawsfynydd to Caernarfon you will run along Madocks's great sea wall, locally called the *cob*, with its fine view up the Glaslyn valley to Snowdon, and then on to his well-planned little town of Tremadoc. As you approach the town from the south notice on the left the bland, classical-faced Peniel chapel, sited, no doubt deliberately, since Madocks was a good churchman, at some distance from the town. His church is perched on a rock across the road and rather nearer the town, whilst the chapel, as he is said to have assured the Bishop of Bangor, is on land reclaimed from the sea and not so solidly founded. Four miles to the east, at the village of Carrog, are the charming and more recent architectural inventions of Clough Williams-Ellis, whilst between Penrhyndeudraeth and Porthmadoc a road turns off southward to the same architect's Italianate hotel complex and harbour of Portmeirion.

Farther north there's another village I must mention, Talysarn, south of Caernarfon and on the B4418 from Penygroes to Rhyd-ddu, a lovely road. Talysarn was ribbon-developed during the last century to house workers in the nearby slate quarries, some of which produce the pink slate so highly thought of for roofing as far south as Ceredigion. Slate has been beautifully used here to face the fronts of houses by a method known as slate-hanging, to produce a fish-scale or diamond effect. Some houses have been roofed in a pattern of multi-coloured slate. (And in the middle of Bethesda, five miles south of Bangor, there is a huge chapel marvellously slate-hung in two colours.) While you are in Talysarn, go to the eastern end of the village, where there is a dead end and a turning place, to see a remarkable house at the corner of Cavour Street, built on the lines of a classical temple, with cast-iron Corinthian columns on the balcony and painted pilasters on the ground floor.

This section is in danger of becoming a haphazard tour of Wales, but I hope I have conveyed my feeling that the main architectural appeal of Wales is not in castles, ancient or bogus, not in the mansions of the disappearing gentry, nor in the ostentatious 'North Road' villas of successful lawyers and business men, but in the farmhouses and in the regionally diverse styles of the older houses in our small towns and villages. The county council and speculative building of today is indistinguishable from that of England.

There is in Wales today more concern with the preservation of the more spectacular old buildings than there is for the evolution of styles which suit the nature of our towns and countryside and which do not break too violently or too insipidly away from the building materials and domestic architecture of the past. The National Trust (*Yr Ymddiriedolaeth Genedlaethol*) is the third greatest landowner in Britain, after the Crown and the Forestry Commission, and its properties in Wales are run by a Welsh committee. It owns castles such as Powis, Penrhyn and Cilgeran, mansions such as Plas-yn-Rhiw, in Llŷn, and Erddig, near Wrexham, outstanding urban residences, Aberconwy House in Conwy, the Tudor Merchant's House in Tenby and Tu Hwnt i'r Bont at Llanrwst. Gardens, like those of Bodnant and Powis Castle attract many thousands of visitors, whose entrance fees provide an income, but access to the coastal property of the Trust is free and here the Trust depends on the annual subscriptions of members.

Another source of financial help in the conservation of buildings is the Historic Buildings Council for Wales. Government money is made available, through the Welsh Office, for the repair and preservation of the structure of a building of historical and architectural interest but not for its decoration. Two other bodies come nearer to the everyday needs of ordinary people in Wales, *Adfer*, which means to restore, and *Tai Gwynedd*, which means Houses of Gwynedd. These were set up, in mid- and North Wales, by members of *Cymdeithas yr Iaith*, the Welsh Language Society, as a positive gesture in the face of the buying up of rural cottages by strangers for redecoration as second or holiday homes, a practice which has swept through Wales in recent years and which has not only gravely reduced the number of houses available to young Welsh couples but has also artificially raised prices to a level beyond their reach. These new organisations invite loans or money to be invested in them; they buy old homes, renovate them, often with volunteer labour and craftsmanship, and then let them at a reasonable rent to young Welsh couples. It is a small beginning but a movement in a desirable direction and it may, one hopes, open the eyes of county councils to what they should be doing to check the depopulation of the rural areas of Wales.

Sculpture

Nothing much has been made of such public sculpture as we have in Wales and even if one includes wood carving and epigraphy it is difficult to discover any continuous tradition in this art. Yet what we have is of the greatest interest and is worth hunting out. Five thousand years ago we had men cutting strange abstract patterns on stone in the chambered tombs of Anglesey. The patterns are abstract to us but to those who cut them they may have carried important symbolised meanings. The triskele motif was the basic element in Celtic design in gold, bronze and iron. Characteristic Celtic design, abstract, interweaving, centrifugal, is to be seen on the many lovely crosses of the pre-Norman period, on the tall stone in Nevern churchyard and the splendid one on the roadside near Carew Castle, again in Pembrokeshire. The National Museum at Cardiff is a good place to study these crosses. Some have been gathered in there and there are plaster facsimiles of most of the best ones. I have referred to the two contrasting ones in Llanbadarn church. I hope someone will soon carbon-date Derfel's wooden horse at Llandderfel. It and Derfel's wooden effigy were famous in Wales for long years before the statue was burnt in 1538. And I hope that no one ever removes the agonisingly hacked stone pillars of the doorway to the church. The wood carving of rood screens has suffered from two attacks, the demolitions of Henry VIII and the wholesale rebuilding of churches in the Victorian age. I have been told that this happened in Llangwyryfon just over a hundred years ago when a wooden rood screen was destroyed. But some remain and are of great beauty, repaying a detour to such places as Llanegryn, Llananno and Partrishow. Llanrwst and Abergavenny have such screens and Abergavenny has the great wooden figure of Jesse, with Christ's family tree. With the rebuilding of churches we may have lost many gargoyles and grotesques, but I have a feeling that they were never common in Wales. For the best examples in a Welsh church you have today to cross the Border to Kilpeck in Herefordshire, Welsh because when its wealth of sculpture was cut it belonged to the diocese of Llandaf and because the work was done by a Border school of Celtic sculptors. In the eighteenth and early nineteenth centuries lovely lettering was cut on the slate of gravestones which are to be found in old churchyards throughout the country, often embellished with designs which echo Celtic tracery in a simple, unambitious manner. The last hundred years has given us some respectable portrait sculpture but the statues most Welsh people are familiar with are the pathetic mass-produced khaki-clad soldiers with reversed bayonets. The Aberystwyth war memorial is much more splendid and I know people who still go round the point on which it stands to view once more what is thought to be the finest backside in Cardiganshire.

Painting

Painting in Wales has a much more meagre and brief history than sculpture, no history, in fact, until Richard Wilson went to Rome and learnt how to paint Welsh mountains. In prehistoric times life was too hard in Wales for there to have been cave-wall painting like that of Lascaux, and in historical times domestic buildings were too short-lived for such decoration to survive. Poetry can outlive the burning-down of a chieftain's hall but painting can't. Therefore no tradition of patronage developed for such an ephemeral art.

Welsh men and women have, until recently, had to go outside Wales, to London, Paris and Rome, to learn to paint and, because of the situation at home, to live and work abroad. An interesting case is that of Penry Williams (1800–85), the son of a Merthyr stone-mason, whose ability was spotted by Sir John Guest, ironmaster of Dowlais and husband of the enlightened Lady Charlotte. The young man was sent to London to study under Fuseli at the Royal Academy. From there he went to Rome, stayed there, though exhibiting regularly in London, and died there. Most of his work is of the Roman scene, human and architectural, but he painted portraits of John Gibson, the sculptor from Conwy, and Lady Charlotte Guest. He was clearly a traditionalist, for a hostess said of him: 'He suspects the Italians will soon be down on the Eternal City and destroy the antique and picturesque to make room for modern railway stations and Government buildings.'

I have considerable regard for a Welsh painter of the second half of the nineteenth century, whose work I have never seen, even in reproduction, simply because of his reported subject matter. He is S. Maurice Jones, of Mochdre in Denbighshire, who did a series of pictures of Homes of Welsh Worthies, including those of John Gibson, Dewi Wyn, Ieuan Glan Geirionnydd, Dafydd y Garreg Wen, Dic Aberdaron, John Elias, Williams o'r Wern, John Jones Talysarn, Glasynys and Ceiriog. I have long thought that something like this should be undertaken say once every fifty years and a plaque placed on the building in question. Another painter to whom I feel similarly indebted (but some of whose work I have seen), is the enlightened Lady Llanover, founder of the Welsh Manuscript Society and replacer of inns by coffee taverns, who painted a beautiful series of women in the costumes of the different parts of Wales. The series has been reproduced as postcards and these are on sale at the National Library at Aberystwyth.

Welsh painters of our present century have shown even more interest in the landscape and people of Wales. J. D. Innes, of Llanelli, painted Wales in a Provençal light and Augustus John, like his sister Gwen Tenby-born, made what I see as a prophetic remark: 'I guess the hidden soul of Welsh art will be found crouching under those grey *cromlechs*, the only monuments of Wales, upon the slopes of her immemorial hills.' A brilliant guess it turns out to have been, now that we have been able to study the designs of Bryn Celli Ddu and Barclodiad y Gawres and relate them to the Celtic tradition of design in sculpture, woodcarving and manuscript decoration, a tradition which has been caught up in our own day in the paintings of David Jones, where the same subtle, centrifugal vision is perpetuated.

Ceri Richards has given us sensitive studies of Welsh tinplate workers, illustrations to Dylan Thomas which are as strange and pulsating as the poems, and a series of piano-playing studies which must have a special appeal for Wales, a country which has more pianos per house than any other part of Britain. Kyffin Williams has depicted the mountains of North Wales in a blacker, more threatening mood than that in which they appeared to Richard Wilson, a vision similar to that which the Polish immigrant Josef Hermann has given us of our industrial scene. Brenda Chamberlain's interest in islands and the sea has linked Wales visually with Greece. Welsh painting today is full of experiment in the current international styles.

The Crafts

A hundred years ago, and especially in the scattered rural communities, there were craftsmen everywhere, craftsmen who could between them clothe you from head to foot, build your house or your outhouses and process your wool and barley. All that's left now is a handful of carpenters, blacksmiths and masons, not enough of them. The craftsmanship of the rural Welshman has been canalised into new directions, mostly concerned with the repair of cars, tractors and agricultural machinery, electro-welding, TV and vacuum cleaner repairs, post office engineering, electrical installations and repairs, and plumbing, in other words to servicing factory-produced things, not actually making anything. Nor can an urban industrial worker who helps turn out sheets of steel or brake linings really feel that he is making a car. The very old tradition of making things by hand and with simple tools has been broken. The new Do-It-Yourself practice and evening classes in pottery and weaving, together with the development of creative craft teaching in schools, have to some degree restored the dignity and attraction of making useful things by hand.

Crafts are today being revived and all over Wales people are setting up workshops to do pottery, weaving, jewellery, postcard designing and printing and woodcarving. Some of these craftsmen are beginners and many of them are strangers to Wales. Again, as in the case of the apparent reluctance of many young Welsh people to live in the country, it is unusual for young Welsh men and women to stick to or return to an old craft. Of the few young craftsmen who live within two or three miles of me, one, a carpenter, is Welsh, the other two, a blacksmith and a potter, are American. Their advent is welcome, but for me there is a danger in this situation. These newcomers, excellent though they are as craftsmen and craftswomen and eager as they are to enter into community life, are inadequately aware of the older traditional crafts and techniques of their localities. The danger is that their products could be vaguely international in style or, in an effort to avoid this, too much a caricature of Welshness and too 'Welsh-costume' in type, if only by a deliberate limitation to Celtic motifs. These Celtic motifs come from too distant a past, while there are nearer traditions only recently dead or dying, such as the making of the Ceredigion long-handled spade, the *rhaw*, at Aberaeron, or the lip-work basket-making at Penuwch in the same county, traditions which a kiss of life might yet revive. I am not suggesting a wholesale return to products and designs which have passed out of usefulness, but a search, at the St. Fagans Folk Museum and in the many other craft and local museums, for suggestions for home industries which could once again be profitable and useful, and which give the craftsman the pride and pleasure of making something with his own hands.

Neither in poetry nor in the visual or palpable arts do we in Wales strictly separate art from craft.

Music

I find it difficult to write about Welsh music since I know so little about it and since there's so little to write about. We are often said to be a musical nation and yet musical taste in Wales is as low as it could be, due, I like to think, not to any inherent inability but to the lack of musical education. There's no lack of the teaching of the techniques of producing lovely sounds, whether from voice or instrument, but little enquiry into or appreciation of the nature of the music to be presented. It is true that a high percentage of Welsh people have good voices, but they are just as happy singing rubbish as they are with good music, happier perhaps. The thrill of music is for us most often a physical one, in the throbbing of the larynx, the reverberations in the head, the pulsing of the blood, and the greatest thrill is that of harmonising, plain, uncomplicated harmony, with the tenors hitting the roof, in group singing. In this way Welsh singing in chapels, at rugby matches, on trains or in pubs is a healthy manifestation, for it demonstrates a sense of community, of shared effort and shared pleasure. And I think that people who sing under the influence of drink are less likely to quarrel and fight.

Since the beginning of history the Celts have been famous for their love of music, and by the Middle Ages, the tradition being then so old, Welsh music was probably as complex as the poetry, and there are indications that this was so, in the poetry of the fourteenth and fifteenth centuries, where the poets talk of their entertainment at great houses. But the music was not recorded, save in a few uncertainly deciphered manuscripts, and today it is only to be guessed at from the varied and charming detritus of our folk music. One traditional form of music has survived, through continued use over the centuries, a form which is unique to us and which is our chief glory in this art, a method of singing to the harp which is known as *cerdd dant* or *canu penillion*. The harp, or if not available the piano, plays a well-known air, a folk tune or an old or modern hymn tune (and many of our loveliest hymns are old folk tunes). Then the voice or group of voices breaks in, well after the start of the music, to descant to the air, singing a given poem, often in a different tempo but, and this is essential, ending with the air. Traditionally and in theory the singer or singers should be sufficiently expert to do this extempore, but in fact this kind of singing is today carefully rehearsed since, in the case of the National Eisteddfod, the poem to be sung and the air to which it must be sung are announced a year before the competition takes place. Mr. Saunders Lewis has suggested that the Welsh device of *sangiad*, or parenthetical writing of verse, derives from the *tropus* of medieval liturgical singing. It is possible that our *cerdd dant* comes from the same source, or could it have come from the practice of the old poets of accompanying themselves on the Celtic harp, providing an uncomplicated background to their words, playing a few bars to silence the chatter in the hall and seize the attention, and seeing to it that the music ended with the words? What music did Homer play on his lyre as he recited his epics? Aren't Bob Dylan's words more important than his music? Whatever the origin of this singing to the harp, the taste for it must be an acquired one for anyone who doesn't inherit it naturally. But for any music-lover it is the prime offering of Wales.

Music takes less notice of frontiers than any other art, though it often shows strong national characteristics, and in the sixteenth, seventeenth and eighteenth centuries Welsh words were being written to popular English airs, just as they are today to foreign popular music, as well as to old Welsh tunes and original Welsh music. The influence of the German *lieder* wasn't entirely happy on our lyical music of the second half of the nineteenth century, but the diverse and radical experimentation in European music during this present century has set our many admirable composers of today free from the sentimental Victorian cliché. There are many devotees of the silver and brass wind instruments in our industrial areas and our pop singers play the guitar to accompany themselves, though not always as well as this is done in other countries, but the voice and the harp remain the most cultivated instruments in Wales, and the combination of these two can still be magical. And yet, the voices of Sir Geraint Evans and Tom Jones are probably better known throughout the world than that of Osian Ellis.

Education

I have spoken of the Education Act of 1870 and of the attempt to banish Welsh from the educational system in Wales. During this century it has become the practice for Welsh to be the main medium of instruction in primary schools in an area where Welsh speaking predominates, and English in the English-speaking areas. In 1939, *Urdd Gobaith Cymru* (The Welsh League of Youth) established and maintained the first *Ysgol Gymraeg* (Welsh Language School) at Aberystwyth. It is now under the education authority. The first Welsh-language school primary school within the state education system was started in Llanelli in 1947. Flintshire and Glamorgan rapidly followed suit and from 1949 to 1972 the number of children receiving their primary education mainly in Welsh rose from 81 to 3,300 and continues to grow. Many of these schools are fed from *Ysgolion Meithrin*, Nursery Schools, of which there are today about a hundred, mostly in the English-speaking parts of Wales, all resulting from the setting up of *Mudiad Ysgolion Meithrin Cymraeg*, the Welsh-language Nursery Schools Movement, in 1971. Children from English-speaking homes thus become fluent in Welsh by the time they enter the primary school.

All this led naturally to the demand for secondary education in Welsh and this was met by the establishment of state bilingual schools, where, generally speaking, the arts subjects are taught in Welsh and the scientific subjects mainly in English, so that proficiency in the two languages is maintained. The first school of this kind was Ysgol Glan Clwyd, opened in Rhyl in 1956. There followed other bilingual schools, mostly in the English-speaking areas, at Mold and Wrexham in the North, at Rhydfelen and Ystalyfera in Glamorgan, but also for Welsh-speaking areas at Porthaethwy and Aberystwyth. It is hoped that Carmarthen and Bangor will have their long-delayed Welsh schools before long.

In this restoration of Welsh to our educational system the University of Wales has dragged its feet, dominated as it is by English and anglicised Welsh staff members and unnaturally swollen as it is beyond the requirements of Wales. Bangor and Aberystwyth have been designated as constituent colleges where an increasing amount of instruction may be done through the medium of Welsh but the provision of staff prepared to do this is slow and grudging. The recent talk of devolution has alarmed the foreign majority of our dons into a published plea that the University of Wales should not come under the control of whatever kind of Welsh Assembly may be set up but will remain a British rather than a Welsh university.

There has been some unwillingness on the part of parents to accept bilingual education for their children, conditioned as they have been to regarding the English language as the essential key to good jobs in well-paid professions, but it is gradually being realised that these new bilingual schools are the best schools in Wales at the moment, partly because of the idealism and devotion of the staffs, and that the best English spoken in Wales is often that of Welsh-speakers. The pride of an elderly rural Welshman in his English and his urge to display it has today its counterpart in the refusal of young people to use English at all except out of courtesy or when it is absolutely necessary.

Education in Wales is still far too academic. Welsh parents, especially Welsh-speaking ones, still regard teaching and public administration as the most respectable occupations, with the ministry also still honoured. The economic situation, far worse in Wales than in England, has brought more young men than usual to the Nonconformist training colleges and may be the cause of the mild wave of evangelism which is stirring some of our young people. There is far too little encouraging of boys and girls into technical education, so that there is a dire shortage, among other callings, of estate managers, engineers, doctors, television technicians, to say nothing of carpenters, masons and blacksmiths.

Institutions

1. The National Eisteddfod

The word *eisteddfod* literally means a session or sitting together but it is used chiefly for a competitive meeting of practitioners of literature, music and the arts and crafts. *Eisteddfodau* (the plural form) can last a day, three days or, in the case of the National Eisteddfod, a week. They are organised by chapels, literary societies, committees in eisteddfod-loving towns, organisations like the Welsh youth movement *Urdd Gobaith Cymru* and the Miners' Federation, the administrators of a bequest, as in the Pantyfedwen Eisteddfod of Pontrhydyfendigaid, or, in the case of the National, by the eisteddfod council. They are usually annual events and the National Eisteddfod is peripatetic, held every year in a different town, alternately in North and South Wales. This means that the immense pavilion is erected and taken down and carried from one end of Wales to the other every year, a troublesome and expensive business, but this satisfies our dislike of centralisation and it brings a revitalising cultural effect to every region in turn.

However silly or dignified you may consider the ceremonies and costumes of the *Gorsedd* to be, and however you may deplore or support the principle of competition in the arts, you cannot deny that the National Eisteddfod is a great institution which gathers together an extraordinary number and variety of people, about twenty thousand every year. (*Gorsedd* means 'throne' in English but in the two languages the word usually refers to two very different institutions. *Gorsedd Beirdd Ynys Prydain*, the Throne of the Bards of the Island of Britain, was invented by Iolo Morgannwg early in the nineteenth century to run the affairs of poetry. Members of the *Gorsedd*, led by the Archdruid and other colourful officials, ceremonially open each eisteddfod week and perform the presentation of the main prizes for poetry, the chair and the crown. 'Crown' is another word with different connotations in Welsh and English.) The first known eisteddfod, though not called that at the time, was held at Aberteifi at the behest of the Lord Rhys at Christmas time in 1176, after a proclamation twelve months before that and an invitation to the poets and musicians of the four countries of Britain. The chair offered for the best musician was won by a man from the South, whilst a Gwynedd man took the chair for poetry. This early meeting was a theme for commemoration at the National Eisteddfod at Aberteifi (Cardigan) in August 1976. An important eisteddfod was held at Caerfyrddin about the year 1451, when Dafydd ab Edmwnd succeeded in classifying the twenty-four strict metres of poetry. At Caerwys in 1523 and 1567 eisteddfodau were held to award a silver harp to the best poet and to control the activities of others not so accomplished. In the eighteenth century eisteddfodau were held in taverns and were announced and reported in the almanachs of the day.

If statistics were available of the walks of life of those who today regularly attend the Eisteddfod, international rugby matches, the Royal Welsh Agricultural Show, Welsh pop festivals, fishing competitions and clay-pigeon shooting matches, anyone unfamiliar with Welsh life might be surprised to observe the overlap of interests which would be revealed. I was talking the other day to the manager of a sawmill and timber yard about different kinds of fuel and, in saying how I kept a peat fire in overnight, a traditional method, not my invention, I used the word *dyhuddo* (cover). He showed interest in the word and immediately quoted a line from a Welsh translation of Gray's 'Elegy Written in a Country Churchyard' to exemplify its use. I also discovered that he is interested in field sports and goes annually to the Game Fair. But then, he comes from Ffair Rhos, an upland community in Ceredigion which has produced a large number of poets, many of whom are still writing.

The number and variety of the eisteddfod public explains the perambulation of the great enclosure by actual or prospective members of parliament, preachers wishing to better themselves, authors looking for publishers, people who think they should be on TV, propagandists of strange new or fading old religions, Jilly Cooper and other attractive or unpleasant characters. The Eisteddfod field is the *agora* of Wales, the great meeting-place. There are many who pay for their entrance day after day without ever going into the pavilion to listen to the competitions, which in any case are relayed to the open air, content with catching glimpses of or having a word with famous people (for in Wales almost everyone knows almost everyone), or with visits to the smaller *Babell Lên*, the Literature Pavilion, or the little theatre, or the annually improving Arts and Crafts exhibition. Then there are scores of kiosks which advertise different institutions or views of life, or sell records, books, posters, craft products, milk or ice-cream. No alcoholic drinks are served on the Eisteddfod field.

For foreigners probably the most extraordinary feature of this great gathering is that it is here mainly to honour poets, the winners

223

of the chair and the crown, and that these two ceremonies are the most popular moments of the week. On those occasions when the adjudicators have found no one worthy of one of these prizes and the anxious crowd is baulked of the ceremony and of the excitement of seeing who the pseudonymed poet is, then a gloom falls upon the whole week and, whatever the weather may be like, the Face of the Sun, the Eye of Light, which the Druids invoke in their opening ceremony, suffers a fearful eclipse.

I hope I have made it clear that visitors to the Eisteddfod who don't speak Welsh needn't fear boredom, and for those who wish to follow the proceedings there is an instant translation service they can listen to on freely provided apparatus.

2. The Llangollen International Eisteddfod

This annual event, which takes place in July, is not traditional but a recent foundation which brings together folk dancers, folk singers and choirs from every corner of the earth. For a week the lovely little town is full of lively, colourfully costumed men and women who are prepared to dance and sing on the bridge, in the streets or along the canal bank, as well as in the competitive events of the pavilion. It has made Wales many friends throughout the world.

3. Urdd Gobaith Cymru

This Guild of Welsh Youth, literally, Guild of the Hope of Wales, was founded some fifty years ago by Sir Ifor ap Owen Edwards, forward-looking son of a great father, to give Welsh children the opportunity to enjoy themselves together in their own language. Holiday camps have been established at Llangrannog in south Ceredigion, and at Glanllyn on the shore of Llyn Tegid, near Bala. The Urdd holds its own annual eisteddfod and organises activities throughout the year.

4. Women's Associations

Women's Lib in Wales recognises a difference of interests on the part of men and women and at a lecture or concert or *noson lawen* in a rural chapel vestry the women will often sit on one side of the room, usually the left, and the men on the other. I have always taken the reason to be not one of *harem* and *salamlik* separation but because when the opportunity for conversation arises the matters they talk about are different. Though the Women's Institute movement was founded in Wales earlier in this century, its activities have been almost exclusively in the English language. Ten years ago a movement was started as *Merched y Wawr*, Women of the Dawn, to organise activities similar to those of the Women's Institute but through the medium of Welsh. There was an obvious need for this and new branches are regularly springing up throughout the country. As I write, *Merched y Wawr* have been forced into a reappraisal of their aims and methods. Their founding president has resigned because hymn-singing and prayer have come to figure too prominently in the meetings of the movement, it being taken for granted that every member is a practising Christian. The experience of this movement spotlights something which has to be faced: that although the chapel has been the dominant force in Welsh life for the best part of two centuries, and although religious activity has saved the Welsh language for us, the language no longer depends on religion for its continued existence and many of the young people of Wales are not believers. A movement which incorporates Christian ritual in its practices risks alienating some of the liveliest spirits among our young people. Similarly, it is to be doubted whether compulsory religious instruction in the schools and the beginning of the day with hymns, prayers and pious homilies have the effect of bringing school-children back to the churches and chapels.

5. The Churches

It is, of course, not only in Wales that places of worship are emptier than they were fifty years ago. It's true of the churches of England and of the mosques of Turkey, and I imagine that the central African witch-doctor, if he still exists, doesn't get quite the congregations his predecessors enjoyed. But in Wales the situation is made more extreme by the multiplicity of denominations under the general cover of Nonconformity. During the nineteenth and the early years of this present century, in conditions of full employment, although wages were pitifully low the members of the different sects managed to get enough money together to build their separate places of worship and to fill them. That is the main difference between a Welsh and an English town or village, that in England the church is usually conspicuous and chapels hardly noticeable, while in Wales the chapels, sometimes modestly, sometimes monstrously, are prominent in the squares and main streets and occasionally stand up square and bold in the countryside, unsupported by houses. There is an amazing variety in the architecture of these chapels, from simplified Georgian façades to huge Corinthian-columned frontages and even castellated outlines. The observation of chapel architecture is one of the most interesting occupations on a journey through Wales. But there are today too many of them and the big denominations, more out of a kind of tribal loyalty than adherence to dogma, are reluctant to sink their differences and share buildings.

Here is a rhyme I was told by a man in a station café. It was all the Welsh he could remember:

> *Pedwar o bethau duon*
> *sy'n blino'r plwyfolion,*
> *gwaddod a brain,*
> *ffeiradon a chwain.*

> Four black things
> annoy the parishioners,
> moles and crows,
> parsons and fleas.

But since the Disestablishment of the Church of England in 1920 there have been no tithes to burden countrymen and the ill feeling reflected in the rhyme has disappeared. On the national level the Church in Wales has recently had some notable archbishops, who have spoken and acted wisely in the interests of Wales.

6. Devolutionary Movements

There is no doubt that the majority of Welsh people want some degree of devolution from England, but opinions in this matter range from the call for a completely free Welsh Republic to a modest wish for a kind of cultural autonomy. This variety of outlook, which *Plaid Cymru* is attempting to canalise, is the Government's excuse for delay in establishing a Welsh Assembly. In spite of this, separatist tendencies are already at work. The Welsh T.U.C., however, has not cut itself off from the T.U.C. of Great Britain as has happened in agriculture, where, although the National Union of Farmers is still active in Wales, a separate Farmers' Union of Wales has been formed and is widely supported. And in education a separate Welsh Teachers' Union has been formed, known as U.C.A.C., *Undeb Cenedlaethol Athrawon Cymru*. We have a Welsh Gas Board and Water Board, but for electricity we are split up into the South Wales Electricity Board and Manweb, the Merseyside and North Wales Electricity Board, centred at Chester. And it continues to annoy me that Shrewsbury, of black memories, is my centre for postal coding and that my telephone book gives me all the Shropshire and Here- fordshire numbers but not those of friends and relatives who live only a few miles to the south of my home.

As I put the final touches to the typescript of this book, in the first weeks of 1976, the government's White Paper on Devolution is arousing much discussion in Wales and even some in England. Scot- land would appear to be doing better than Wales, on the ground that there is more demand there for self-government. Reaction to the government's proposals varies from the feeling, on the part of many English people and some Welsh people, that this is a paltry sop to growing nationalism and that the proposed Assembly which is to be merely administrative, not legislative, would be nothing more than another talking shop with no power to do the things the country most needs. Officially, *Plaid Cymru*, the Welsh Liberal Party, the Labour Party and the T.U.C. in Wales, but not the Conservatives, welcome the proposed measure as bringing democratic control closer to the people. The *Plaid Cymru* members of parliament at first gave the White Paper a cautious welcome as a step toward the freedom they desire for Wales, but some weeks later, perhaps in response to wide- spread protest by party members, the party committed itself to flat opposition to the proposals as utterly inadequate. Privately, many supporters of all these parties doubt whether the proposals will ever become law, or whether the Labour Party ever intends that they should.

Sport and Entertainment

The great international sports are largely urban pursuits and interests, for country people do not often take part in organised games, unless they be the rural sports of sheepdog trials or clay-pigeon shooting. I am thinking of competitive sports, not of the field sports of fishing and wild-fowling, to both of which we are much addicted as a nation. I am told that west Wales has a higher number of shotguns per head of the population than any other part of Britain. Wales has very little village cricket and our great rugby teams come from the industrial areas.

I sometimes regret that the old Welsh rural games, such as *cnapan*, *bando* and quoits did not survive the peak period of nineteenth-century Nonconformity, when such frivolities were frowned upon and a boy was not allowed even to whistle a tune in the open air on Sunday. The Irish suffered no such puritanical disapproval of adult games and they have kept their hurling and their Irish football. One might then, like the Irish, have games no other nation played and be spared the passions roused by international competition. I don't think it can be healthy for us to assuage our national frustrations by beating England at rugby. I have already described *cnapan* (page 141). *Bando* was a kind of primitive hockey and great stories are told of the prowess of Margam men at this game on the Margam Sands. Quoits is a fine game for mature and ageing men, the equivalent of the Provençal *boule* but played with bevelled, cast-iron rings or sharpened horse-shoes. Quoits was the only game my father ever played.

I have spoken of eisteddfodau, *nosweithiau llawen* and concerts, pop or choral, the best of the latter being by male voice groups. BBC Wales has popularised new forms of evening entertainment in which travelling panels and groups of prominent entertainers penetrate deep into the country to produce programmes for radio or television and thus provide free entertainment. *Ymryson y Beirdd*, the Contention of the Poets, is much enjoyed, with its various forms of impromptu versifying, one team of poets pitted against another, and it's not surprising, in a country which Michael Drayton said is 'addicted' to poetry, that such competitions should regularly form part of quiz and panel programmes in Welsh.

Drama is popular entertainment in Wales and the acting skill that once went into the pulpits of the chapels now finds an outlet in television drama, in the Welsh National Theatre, which has an English and Welsh company, and in the many dramatic societies. I live roughly half-way between two new, well-designed theatres, those of Felinfach and Aberystwyth in Ceredigion, both of which offer an astonishing range of first-class Welsh and international entertainment. In 1975 the Welsh Arts Council brought Ionesco to visit and talk to our dramatists and drama students, and in 1976, Dürrenmatt.

Welsh people these days 'go for their holidays' to the Costa Brava and Dubrovnik, like their English counterparts, unless they combine their love of sea-food with an interest in fellow Celts and go to Brittany. It wasn't always so. My Glamorgan grandparents went annually to the 'Wells' to take the waters and enjoy the company, my grandmother preferring quiet Llanwrtyd, my grandfather the gayer Llandrindod. I have little experience of today's Welsh holiday resorts, except Aberystwyth, the modest and attractive one near which I live, but I don't suppose they differ much from their English counterparts, except in their background scenery. Porthcawl in the south is quick with the accents of the mining valleys, but Prestatyn, Rhyl, Colwyn Bay and elegant Llandudno are more for Lancashire. Pwllheli has its Butlin's and the rash of white, static caravans along the coast of Cardigan Bay indicates where many Midlanders spend their holidays. Tenby seems difficult to spoil but Abermaw, garbled to Barmouth, I prefer not to think about.

The Land

A prophecy once said of the Britons:

> *Eu hiaith a gadwant,*
> *eu gwlad a gollant*
> *ond gwyllt Walia.*

Their language they will keep,
their land they will lose,
except wild Wales.

But Wales is not so wild as it was and J. R. Jones has told us how we
are losing our land from under our feet. Our best farming land
shrinks as more and more of it disappears under council housing and
speculative estates, caravan parks and motorways. Our less spectacular moorlands are ravaged by tank, artillery and rifle ranges; our
valleys are drowned to provide much more water than we need—
water which we are not so far allowed to sell. Our sky in the rural
areas is torn apart by low-flying jet planes playing their fearful war
games. Our more picturesque parts have been designated National
Parks and we are now realising what this means. A factory bringing
work for the unemployed in Snowdonia would be a small price for
us to pay for the slowing up of depopulation, but no, nothing must
be allowed to besmirch the landscape for the escapist holiday-maker.
Many holiday-makers believe that these National Parks belong to
the nation, their nation, and that the farmers and slate-quarrymen
are there on sufferance. But most of the land in these designated areas
is privately owned and farmed, and the farming and stock-rearing
can be terribly disturbed by the thoughtless and often arrogant behaviour of walkers and motorists. ('How courteous is the Japanese!')
These so-called National Parks are places where people have always
lived and worked, but now they seem to be destined to become play-
grounds for England, just as most of Brittany and Corsica are for
France.

The Forestry Commission has acquired much of our hill-country,
previously grazed by sheep, and planted it with regimented spruce.
Trees are a good crop in damp and steep places but the promised
ancillary industries have not materialised. The landscape has been
gravely altered and made unnatural. The picnic places and nature
walks arranged in the forests are often delightful, but we remember
that they replace the paths of shepherds and their quick dogs and
useful sheep. The result of more walking is uncontrolled erosion of
paths. The paths up Snowdon look like wide, scorched thoroughfares
from Rhyd Ddu and the cliff walks of Pembrokeshire have been worn

to a dangerous condition. Pony-trekking can erode and alter the landscape. Those very bodies which have set out to conserve the beauty of our landscape have, by attracting too many visitors to it, sometimes proved more destructive than any local use of the land could possibly have been.

Another threat to our land is the menace of the second or holiday home. Competition for cottages and small-holdings by people well enough off to do this has forced prices up to an artificial height, so that a young couple wishing to set up house find houses in the rural areas beyond their means and so leave the country for the town or the developed village. On the other hand, one has to remember that some young wives prefer the ready-made or custom-built modernity of a new council house or bungalow to the bother of modernising an old house in the country. In this way rural areas which were once full of people and children have gone silent and dead for most of the year, the land of the small-holdings having been bought or rented by an expanding farmer, the houses full only at holiday time.

We regard with much less repugnance those who escape from the towns beyond the border to live continuously with us and we sympathise with their reasons for doing this. Most of these newcomers are young and they quickly show an interest in the locality they have chosen, often taking lessons in Welsh as soon as classes can be arranged. These newcomers are very rarely Welsh, perhaps because, and this is my daughter's explanation, young Welsh people have not yet become town-sick or disillusioned enough with urban culture to want to get back to the country. I think it is also true that Welsh towns still have much closer links with the countryside than English towns have, so that the impulse to escape from them has not become as strong as in America and England.

Much of our countryside suffers an unnatural seasonal swing from a strange silence to over-crowding, but in either condition there is much beauty left. The few wide, new roads we have now open lovely continuous vistas for the gentle motorist, in contrast to the sudden staggering beauty of views seen at bends in our narrow, tortuous hill-roads. Wales has a loveliness which so far survives pollution and conservation alike.

What Kind of Society?

It has been said that in Wales we have a classless society, but this is to simplify a quite complex situation. There has never been a classless society. Ancient Athens perhaps came nearest, if you forget the slaves who made possible a kind of upper-class equality. Communism has yet to achieve classlessness and our own workers' socialism has its closed shops and rigid 'differentials'. It is probably the smallness and intimacy of Wales and the fading from the scene of the squirearchy which gives this impression of the absence of class distinctions. In England you can still make a fair guess at a man's background from his accent, but this is true in Wales only when English is spoken. Wales has regional accents and idioms and vocabulary, certainly, but in any one region the farm worker, the factory worker, the bank manager and the Nonconformist minister will speak the same Welsh. The manner and vocabulary may vary with the profession and the occasion—the preacher will not use quite the same voice and idiom in the pulpit, at the graveside and in the shop, but from his Welsh you cannot tell whether a man has been to college or whether he's illiterate. The old *Cymraeg gwr bonheddig*, squire's Welsh, was the rarely used Welsh of the landlords, who perhaps deliberately spoke Welsh with an English accent, as Churchill did French. But this has disappeared. The anglicised landowners who remain do not often make any pretence of knowing Welsh.

There is a Welsh middle class which, more especially when it makes English its language, apes the English rotarian, freemasonic, golf club pattern. Women especially of this class affect, with varying degrees of absurdity, what is thought to be an English 'county' accent. I heard a girl from a Welsh background who had been to an English boarding-school pronounce Aberfan as though it were an English word. It seemed to me an insult to that unhappy place.

There are degrees of poverty which almost constitute classes and Welsh novelists from Daniel Owen to Emyr Humphreys have observed and recorded this fact. In the more rigid class system of pre-Norman Wales it was just possible for a man to better himself socially. It's very much easier today, and it is this, coupled with the basic local uniformity of spoken Welsh, that gives us this important feeling of classlessness.

Every nation is unique and we in Wales have evolved in our own way, changed, developed and in some ways declined, partly in response to internal forces, often in reaction to pressures and intervention from outside, over the long millennia of our life in this island and the centuries of our separateness in this land of Wales. Yet, in spite of the antiquity of our traditions, which I have attempted to trace back to Palaeolithic Man, the sequence is unbroken, and I observe in the Welsh youth of today a confidence that this present time is one of renewal rather than of relaxation, of new beginning rather than of ending.

COMMON ELEMENTS
IN WELSH PLACE NAMES

aber river mouth or confluence
afon river
allt hill-side (NorthWales)
      wood or wooded hill-side (South Wales)

bach little (feminine forms: *fach, fechan*)
banc breast, hillock
betws little church or chapel of ease (from English bead-house)
blaen head of a valley, often followed by river name (plural: blaenau)
bod dwelling place
bont bridge (mutated form of *pont*)
bron hill, breast
bryn hill
bwlch gap or pass

caer fort (mutated form: *y gaer*)
capel chapel
carn cairn (mutated form: *y garn*)
carreg stone or rock
castell castle (other form: *cas*)
cefn ridge (as in Cevennes, except for the hard c)
cil corner, recess, retreat (the c is hard, as in *cefn* and *carreg*)
coed trees
cors bog (mutated form: *y gors*)
craig rock (plural: *creigiau*; mutated form: *y graig*)
croes cross (mutated form: *y groes*)
cwm valley, usually narrow, followed by river name

234

dinas   Celtic citadel (in modern Welsh: city)
dôl   meadow
dre   homestead or town (mutated form of *tre* or *tref*)
dyffryn   wide valley

eglwys   church
esgair   ridge

felin   mill (mutated form of *melin*)
ffynnon   well
foel   bare mountain (mutated form of *moel*)

gelli   copse, woodland (mutated form of *celli*)
glan   river bank or shore
glyn   narrow valley, often wooded; glen
gwaun   high wet ground or water meadow
gwyn   white or blessed (mutated form: *wyn*; feminine forms: *gwen*,
   wen)

hafod   upland house for summer grazing
hen   old
heol   road

isaf   lower

llan   enclosure, usually for a church, with name of founding saint
   or later dedication. Look out for mutations after *llan*—Llandudno
   (for St. Tudno), Llangollen (for St. Collen), Llangybi (for St. Cybi).
   Also Caergybi (Holyhead)
llwyn   grove
llyn   lake

maes   meadow
melin   mill
merthyr   place of martyrdom with shrine (cf. Greek *martyrion* and
   English *martyry*)
moel   bare mountain

235

morfa land near the sea, usually marshy
mynydd mountain

nant brook

pant hollow
pen head or top
penrhyn headland
pentre village
plas mansion
pont bridge
porth harbour or entrance
pwll pool or pit

rhiw sharp rise
rhos moorland
rhyd ford

sant saint (other forms: *sain*, *saint*)
sarn raised road or causeway

tal brow
traeth beach
tre homestead or town (other form: *tref*)
tŷ house (plural: *tai*)

uchaf upper (other form: *ucha*)

waun mutated form of *gwaun*

ynys island
yspyty hospital, hospice in old names
ystrad wide valley, vale

(*Note*: *y* or *yr* means 'the' or 'of the'. A table of mutations is useful
in puzzling out place names.)

SELECT BIBLIOGRAPHY

Biography

The Dictionary of Welsh Biography down to 1940, Oxford, 1959

General Prehistory

J. H. Breasted, *The Conquest of Civilization*, London, 1938
Sonia Clark, *The Neolithic Revolution*, British Museum, 1970

The Celts

E. G. Bowen, *Britain and the Western Seaways*, Thames & Hudson, 1972
Nora Chadwick, *The Celts*, Penguin Books, 1970
Proinsias MacCana, *Celtic Mythology*, Hamlyn, 1970
T. G. E. Powell, *The Celts*, Thames & Hudson, 1958
Alwyn and Brinley Rees, *Celtic Heritage*, Thames & Hudson, 1961; (paperback) Merlin Press, 1973
Anne Ross, *Pagan Celtic Britain*, Sphere Books, 1974
Denis de Rougemont, *Passion and Society*, Faber, 1956

Language

Meic Stephens (ed.), *The Welsh Language Today*, Gomer Press, 1973

Literature

H. I. Bell, *The Development of Welsh Poetry*, Oxford, 1936